The Journey at Malloryville Bog

The Journey at Malloryville Bog

Commitment, Teamwork and Tenacity
In Defense of Land and Nature

Robert M. Beck

All photographs are by the author
at Malloryville Bog

www.bobbeckauthor.com
email: rmb24@cornell.edu

ISBN-13: 978-1482049138
ISBN-10: 1482049139
LCCN: 2013903435
BISAC: Nature / Environmental Conservation & Protection

For Gwen
and
The citizen scientists, conservation professionals
and kindred spirits, whose generous participation
made success at Malloryville possible

Acknowledgments

I acknowledge with gratitude the kind people who read and commented on all or part of the manuscript and those who provided helpful suggestions in earlier stages of my writing. I offer my sincere thanks to Arthur L. Bloom, Betsy Darlington, David W. Gross, Jim Howe, Mathew Levine, Heidi S. Lovette, Peter L. Marks, Bard Prentiss, Charles R. Smith and David A. Weinstein. Many of the letters and documents quoted in the book are in the public record within the files of the New York State Department of Environmental Conservation. For use of The Nature Conservancy's Malloryville files, I thank Jim Howe, Executive Director of the Central & Western NY Chapter. And for preparing the Preserve map (at Chapter 13), I thank Mathew Levine, Northern New York Field Representative, The Nature Conservancy.

CONTENTS

Trail entrance at O.D. von Engeln Preserve

PREFACE

M Y WIFE AND I purchased our long-desired "naturalist's dream" home only to be confronted by plans
for a gravel mine and ready-mix concrete plant next
door. Our exhilaration of home ownership, our excitement of
owning our first home, a home among woodlands and pristine
wetlands on land of diverse and wild nature, was chilled with
disappointment, sudden uncertainty and daunting questions of
what to do. Today, twenty-five years later, surrounded by a
peaceful and treasured Nature Conservancy preserve, I write in
the belief that readers elsewhere, perhaps facing similar challenges, may find value in this account of a journey in environmental protection.

Malloryville Bog, an unspoiled wetland complex, lies sheltered in glacier-formed kettles, kames and eskers in the Finger
Lakes Region of New York State. This beautiful and unique
place holds an intimate story of rich natural history, of confrontation with a dire threat, of gaining at length enduring
protection as The Nature Conservancy's 308-acre O.D. von
Engeln Preserve at Malloryville. Here, spanning fifteen years of
challenge, struggle and success, is a personal story, an account
of home and land, of swamps, fens and bog, of gravel-mine
plans and recurring environmental reviews, of conflicting views
of property rights, private gain and the common good, of a

bequest and land deals, and of people, determination and awesome teamwork.

The nature preserve is small in size, but the issues and ideas enveloping us here were large. Inspired by our country's great national parks and preserves protected in perpetuity, and by the far-sighted vision and unprecedented philanthropy that made them possible, could we not also think large, here on our own appropriately smaller scale, here in our own local community? Yet incompatible development next to our land, next to our eskers, kettles and wetlands, if unchecked, would soon spoil an opportunity, rendering our hopes nonviable. We needed to act quickly, though our struggle would prove arduous and long. Powered by an ecological ethic, our case was built on science and logic, and our team in support, called to duty again and again, was magnificent. With perseverance and dedication to a noble cause, my colleagues were inspiring. In the scheme of things, more environmental conflicts have been lost than won. This time, nature prevailed.

At the outset, I found myself trapped, ensnared by unlikely timing and circumstance. My response seemed compelled, failure unthinkable. Our course evolved. The path broadened to encompass a coalition of individuals and organizations, and lengthened to a decade-and-a-half. While success long eluded us, ever remaining just beyond reach, I was yet emboldened, as though advancing shoulder to shoulder with my unwavering colleagues. Events multiplying, taking on ever-larger meaning, the long struggle grew here to become a story of uncommon relevance in the cause of environmental conservation. For those of us involved, it was a challenging adventure, a challenge that, to me, seemed to become a journey in defense of land and nature.

Even as the going was rough and the outcome remained in doubt, as events unfolded and appeared in newspaper accounts, and as I related many times in public talks and woodland walks, people responded with enthusiasm and encouragement. When success at last arrived, with land protected, a nature preserve established and the story complete, I received letters and notes with gratifying and heartwarming comments: "Thank you. Your tale is visionary, instructive, cautionary, and ultimately optimistic. Native son, we salute you! ~ Connie S." And, "Heartfelt thanks for making the world a better place, Bob. Your incredible example will be something for many others to aspire to. ~ Bobby K." And another, "…it still takes at least one dedicated, patient, indefatigable, persevering, idealistic to a fault person to take it over those taxing mountaintops in a blizzard. You surely have what it takes, and we're all fortunate and so grateful to have you in our area. ~ Irene B."

Yet, immodestly having included here these personal thank-you notes, I need to say that never could I accept such praise without replying that it was not me alone, but rather the effort of a dedicated team of many that brought success. Thus, I have written this account motivated with profound gratitude for the commitment and generosity of my colleagues, and with sincere desire and intent to give credit where credit is due, for roles large and small, all important in one way or another, in our cooperative endeavor.

Our journey has been one of personal experiences in the particular location where I chose to live. Still, I am encouraged to believe that this story has relevance beyond protecting one or a few special places, that its examples of direct citizen participation—concerned citizens volunteering time, knowledge and labor, speaking out in environmental reviews, serving on governmental and organizational boards, and giving birth to new projects and organizations (a county-database Inventory of Unique Natural Areas and the Finger Lakes Land Trust here)—could be emblematic of people everywhere striving to conserve the natural world. The larger message is about the possibilities of hope, cooperation and perseverance; the possibilities of wise and good people working together, thinking long-term, dedicated to the urgent cause of defending land and nature, of preserving earth's precious biodiversity. For the future of our planet, it is a message of the possibilities of living and sharing the deep and universal values of the land ethic.

One lady, an author, asked if she could write my adventure

as a children's story. Others asked of me, "Are you writing a book?" Although I found talking easier than writing, I began to think maybe I should give it a try. For fifteen years I had tossed in a box my pocket-sized appointment books with dates and times of meetings, and I stuffed file boxes with thick folders of papers, not knowing if I would ever look at them again. From my accumulated collection, together with The Nature Conservancy's files—kindly made available to me at the office of their Central & Western New York Chapter, in Rochester— I began reconstructing the sequence of events, typing up an annotated timeline, and writing a narrative. This is the outcome. As an environmental case study of sorts, in first person, in my words and the words of many others through their letters and memos, I tell our story.

Preface

Sign at base of Hemlock Ridge, a small esker

1 OPPORTUNITY

Come forth into the Light of Things,
Let Nature be your teacher.
— William Wordsworth

A T DUSK I FINISHED installing the wooden brochure box at the newly constructed kiosk, securing it beneath three descriptive colorful panels under the small cedar-shake roof. As day faded to night I was satisfied, savoring for a moment anticipation of tomorrow's big event, breathing deeply of fresh evening air, feeling the closing darkness, listening to the day's-end staccato call notes of an unseen Wood Thrush.

Next morning early, a task to complete, I hurried down the path from my house to attach a half-dozen temporary, hand-lettered cedar signs to locust posts at junctions along the woodland trails. Morning mist hung motionless among the trees, glowing, magical as in a painting, yet soon to dissipate in the sun's warming rays. Then, after coffee and breakfast, I again walked the trails, traversing new footbridges over small streams and a boardwalk through a swamp, and proceeded up and over the esker to the preserve entrance.

For the tiny rural settlement of Malloryville, in upstate New York's picturesque Finger Lakes Region, the gathering was the largest in memory. Cars overflowed the small gravel parking lot and lined the narrow country road. The morning was bright and warm, mid-summer, the date July 21, 2001. In a grassy meadow next to a rustic split-rail fence, 230 people were assembling under a white tent, a tent complete with catered refreshments and rows of folding chairs, for the opening dedication of The Nature Conservancy's new preserve, the O.D. von Engeln Preserve at Malloryville.

For me, the occasion was sublime, the public culmination of a fifteen-year personal odyssey. A flurry of thoughts swirled in my head that morning—the long chain of events that had begun a decade and a half earlier, the conflict and uncertainty, the twists and turns, the setbacks and advances, and especially the generosity and unwavering commitment of the many good people that would, in time, bring us to that day of celebration. And too, I remembered the particular collision between cheerful and chilling circumstances with which it had begun.

Our journey in defense of land and nature, a story of environmental conservation, begins at that earlier time. I start with events leading to an unforeseen challenge, a challenge that would galvanize my actions and propel our story forward. I had grown up on a farm, lived in the country, attended college in a small city, and moved to a metropolis. There, willingly, I had adapted to urban traffic, crowds, nonstop activity, apartment living and suburbia. But dissatisfied, I felt a deep, insistent desire to live in a setting less disturbed by human endeavor, a desire to live in a home thoroughly immersed in nature. In my blood, seemingly, was a deep need to wake up each morning in a place abundant with nature's diversity, a place close to native plants and animals thriving in natural habitats, a place where, a step from my back door, nature's wildness yet prevailed. Then, through unexpected good fortune, my wife and I were able to purchase a house and rural property—the particular rural property—I had been drawn to for more than three decades.

Events unfolded quickly. When shopping for a home, we described to realtors our ideal. We wanted a smallish, modest house surrounded by natural land of woods, wetlands, a pond or stream, and abundant wildlife. A home next to a publicly owned wild park or forest would be good, but I was more eager to enjoy being a naturalist and a good steward on land of my own, a guardian of land entrusted to my care. I used as my model and would-be first choice a property I knew well, but which was occupied and I thought, for me, forever unavailable. I was thinking of land I had known as a boy, land adjacent to my father and mother's dairy farm. And later, while I was living and working in the metropolis of New York City, this bit of nature had continued to attract me, to stimulate my curiosity, and to renew my boyhood feelings for wildness, seclusion, adventure and mystery. On my mind were thirty-some extraordinary acres of diverse woodlands and wetlands, glacier-formed hills and hollows, streams and a pond, a place locally known as Malloryville Bog.

But our house shopping had turned up nothing that we liked, I was stubborn, and we made no offers. Then I received a phone call. I was out of state, touring the Vermont Castings stove foundry in Randolph, Vermont, when my wife called with an electrifying message. Gwen said, "The Malloryville place is for sale. What shall we do?" Our dream property was suddenly on the market. But another couple had already made a purchase offer, and the owners of seven years had done work on the house and we had no idea what work or how much. Here was a total surprise, a surprise demanding immediate response. Delay would be a once-in-a-lifetime chance, an unequaled opportunity, lost. Did we dare—house unseen—make such a major decision, on the phone, at that very moment...?

We did, and our offer, at the reasonable asking price, was accepted. Upon my return on a late-June day in heavy rain, feeling excitement and trepidation, we drove into the secluded property, slowly, on the long, woodland-sheltered, gracefully-curved gravel driveway, and met Mary McCarty, the lady owner, to be given a tour of the house we were committed to buy, sight unseen. I had known that the small house was originally built fifty years earlier—built by the man from whom my dad had bought our farm—as a simple cabin in the woods, at first without electricity or running water, on high ground above the wetlands. Professor Carl E. Ladd, Dean of nearby Cornell University's College of Agriculture (now, the College of Agriculture and Life Sciences) had constructed the cabin as his retreat for family and personal enjoyment. We were on that day, however, decidedly uncertain about its present condition. Showing us around, Mary carefully and thoroughly explained that over several years they had stripped the walls to the bare frame and installed nearly everything new—wiring, plumbing, insulation, drywall, double-pane windows, cedar siding, roofing. And all was done in a simple style that well suited our tastes. We were exceedingly relieved and pleased. A potentially miserable houseful of headaches, a homebuyers' nightmare, for us, had been averted. Instead, I felt as though we had received a wonderful gift, truly welcome and most pleasant, a gift that was to become our ever-welcome refuge, our permanent home. And so, a memorable phone call from my wife to me in Vermont, bringing news of a home for sale, was to become a bright highlight for me, one of several, that seem now to stand as landmarks along the path of our environmental journey.

Come late August, after the usual wait for a real estate closing, we were ready and excited to move into our first real home-of-our-own. I had, on occasion during the intervening two months, taken the liberty of hiking into the property's woods and wetlands, into the land for whose well-being I was about to assume responsibility. In the acid bog, I had quietly enjoyed seeing the delicate Grass Pink orchids in bloom and insect-trapping Pitcher Plants amid the lush-green mats of *Sphagnum* peat moss. And in the surrounding swamps were green expanses of Cinnamon Fern highlighted with golden-brown fertile fronds and nearby, at the pond, Painted Turtles basking on hummocks and logs, and dragonflies patrolling in morning sunlight. I was eager to acquire title and to revel in property of my own.

Then Gwen overheard a disturbing conversation. At a busy local fruit and vegetable stand one morning in Dryden, a stocky, middle-aged man was boasting of his intentions to become wealthy from undeveloped land he owned next to ours. His plans were in the works for an open-pit gravel mine and concrete plant on the 109-acre parcel upslope from—right next door to—our wetlands. Smaller-scale gravel mining on that property had been discontinued and I thought finished. It was there, in fact, that I had enjoyed watching uncommon colony-nesting Bank Swallows taking advantage of the altered land, gracefully flying to and from their burrows near the tops of those near-vertical gravel-pit sandbanks.

But this time the absentee landowner, an entrepreneurial farmer dabbling in land-development, living twenty miles away, west of Ithaca, was arranging to lease his land to a well-known company that reputedly operated some twenty-five gravel and concrete sites around the state. To me, word of this new plan next to our new home came as a shock, unexpected. Naïve as I may have been—while basking in our good fortune—this circumstance I did not anticipate. Jarring, conflicting visions of noise, dust, truck traffic and degraded wetlands pushed themselves into my head. Anticipation of profound pleasure in our tranquil home in beautiful, diverse, wild nature, was suddenly shaken, unsettled. A new commercial operation at this particular location, next to wetlands, was to my mind grossly inappropriate, unacceptable. Yet, to this property, to this particular, unique place my commitment would not waver, no thoughts of doubt, no thoughts of retreat from our purchase agreement, could enter my mind, our course would not be deterred. On schedule, closing occurred smoothly, and we began settling into our new home. We would thus begin—in September of 1986—our first year at Malloryville Bog, with an unpleasant jolt, an unpredicted burden lying ahead.

Hoping to find support to quickly put a stop to this project, I contacted the Town Supervisor and the Zoning Officer at my local government offices in the Town of Dryden. There, the two men, nearing retirement, knew little of our wetlands, but were aware of the existing, abandoned, gravel pits. They had, in fact, given town approval for the previous mining and were understandably pleased to have had a convenient source of sand and gravel for the town highway department. Was it not in the town's best interest, now, to renew approval for a new, albeit considerably larger, operation? Shouldn't the town cooperate with the landowner's new plans? My answer was clear, "No, it's not a good idea, not again, not there, not next to wetlands." But I realized I was not prepared with effectively strong arguments in opposition. Still, I was thankful to learn that a state-level mining permit would first need to be obtained, a permit required by New York's Mined Land Reclamation Law assuring that "regulated mining operations have an approved mining plan that specifies how mining will take place, and an approved reclamation plan that provided for return to productive use."

I called the regional office of New York State's Dept. of Environmental Conservation (the DEC), whose review and approval are required for mining permits throughout the state. Because of state wetlands protection laws, the DEC surely understands the need to protect wetlands, I thought, and they should be receptive to my concerns. I made an appointment with the man who signs the permits, the Regional Permit Administrator. In his office, I calmly explained my unease with this proposed mine adjacent to sensitive wetlands, my concerns about the removal of higher ground, the likely source of groundwater feeding those wetlands. Further, I explained that the wetland types—fens, rich swamp, acid bog—were scarce in our area and that these were essentially undisturbed and of exceptionally high quality. I asked, "What should I do?" He confirmed his awareness of the project, and of the previous mining, which the DEC had also approved. He said, "The formal application hasn't been submitted yet," and, "the wetland-protection laws aren't relevant because the excavations wouldn't be in the wetlands or within 100 feet." After he explained a few things about DEC procedures and offered to have the applicant contact me—for which I thanked him—I was surprised and taken aback by his next statement. Bluntly, with apparent certainty, he said, "There's no history anywhere of a gravel mine harming a wetland." I hesitated, skeptical, then said, "Really?" He replied, "Yes, that's right, none." His voice was confident, almost cocky, leaving little room for doubt about his intent. I was hoping for encouragement, but he offered none. From his demeanor and words, his message to me seemed evident: I would be foolish to involve myself in this proceeding, the outcome would not be in my favor, I should drop it, go home, and not trouble myself (or the DEC) any further.

I went away from that meeting with the strange feeling that my concerns had been viewed as a bother, an annoyance, and that the man would prefer I not introduce unnecessary obstacles—like more paperwork—that might complicate his job. Perhaps I had been naïve in expecting some understanding, some support from his office, my state's conservation department. Although I had been serious and respectful in his presence, was I yet another of those pesky environmentalists, in his view, like annoying Yellowjackets at a picnic, best dissuaded before becoming troublesome, and quickly shooed away? Trying to avoid cynicism, I was displeased, to say the least, and very disappointed. Help that would be essential, required, seemed to slip away, and I was left with a somber sense of foreboding for the future of our neighborhood, of its wetlands, and of my home.

With that enlightenment, I knew Gwen and I faced an unwelcome fight, a fight we hardly knew how to begin or how to pursue, and we had no way of knowing that resolution of that fight would be more than a decade, almost eleven years, in the future. Nor, through those years, could we breathe easy or casually assume a favorable outcome, much less the truly happy conclusion fifteen years hence.

Thus began my hands-on education, my direct-contact experiences, in land and nature preservation. Even though my new landowner status provided powerful motivation, I nonetheless felt thrust into a frightening unknown. I was unprepared for daunting legal challenges that seemed to loom ahead. How should I proceed, assisted with neither wealth nor political clout, to protect my home and a special piece of nature from a grim external threat?

Rose Pogonia (*Pogonia ophioglossoides*)

2 PLACE

Find your place on the planet.
Dig in, and take responsibility from there.
— Gary Snyder

GROWING UP, MEMORABLE experiences may arrive as eye-opening pleasant surprises. Roaming, as a boy, the seeming wildernesses of Malloryville, the wild places away from the houses, away from the farm buildings and beyond the extensive acres of cultivated fields, I had no concept that to "outsiders" the place might harbor something more special than the explorations I enjoyed.

One early-summer day in my mid-teen years, a kindly man and woman came to our farmhouse and asked me, "Would you be willing to show us the wetlands where wild orchids grow?" They explained that they were visiting nearby Cornell University. I said, "I don't know about orchids, but I'll 1 show you around." We hiked in likely places for a couple of hours, but didn't find the plants they sought. The next day they again stopped by, thanked me once more, and handed me a small book entitled *A Pocket Guide to Wildflowers* in which they had written "To our good guide—Miriam & Victor Block, Montreal, Quebec." They were botanists enjoying the non-destructive pursuit of finding and observing scarce and rare native plants in their wild habitats.

It turned out that the locality was known to botanists to be unusually rich in rare plants, including, as I later learned, sixteen native orchid species, among them, four kinds of the large and beautiful lady's slippers—the pink Moccasin Flower, the large and the small forms of the Yellow Lady's Slipper, and the Showy Lady's Slipper with its dramatic white and pink blossoms.

Beginning in my college years, early on inspired by a gorgeous book—*In Wildness is the Preservation of the World*—filled with Eliot Porter photographs and Thoreau quotes, I wandered for hours in the wilds, armed with field guides, binoculars, camera and tripod, sometimes enduring swarms of mosquitoes in sweltering late-spring humidity or chilled fingers in crisp, dry winter air, encountering and photographing whatever natural subjects I found interesting: a fern fiddlehead about to unfurl, a singing Wood Thrush nearly hidden in spring-fresh green foliage, fall leaves in dramatic color, a brilliant orange fungus, a dragonfly perched on a weed stem, a leaf frozen in ice. Being there, the challenge of capturing pleasing images, taking time for careful framing, experimenting with aperture and shutter to find just the right exposure and depth-of-field, while fully immersed in nature, brought deeply satisfying pleasure. More than for collecting trophies, my camera, like a sportsman's bow and arrow, equally may have been my excuse, my justification, for seeking pleasurable time in the wilds, outside.

Among my subjects, of course, was the amazing variety of woodland and wetland wildflowers. Through the spring and summer seasons of bloom, as I photographed dozens of species—the early-spring, evergreen-leaved Hepaticas, White, Red and Painted Trilliums, Bloodroot, the Canada Lily, the brilliant scarlet Cardinal Flower, the ghostly-white, chlorophyll-lacking Indian Pipe, a relative of the wonderfully aromatic Wintergreen—I was mindful always of minimizing harm to my subjects or of carelessly degrading their habitats. As best I could, I tried to avoid trampling vegetation or leaving footprints in wet ground, or other too obvious evidence of my presence in their lives. Deep in a secluded swamp, the jewel-like blossoms of the small Yellow Lady's Slipper hidden among fronds of Royal Fern and shaded by Eastern Hemlocks, each marvelous, slipper-like flower glowing yellow as though illuminated with an inner light of its own, radiating beauty like an exquisite passage in a Beethoven symphony, provided vivid evidence for me of the value of protecting such wild places.

A black-and-white photograph was labeled "Esker at Malloryville, New York." I was reading a book of geological natural history I had bought at the Cornell University Book Store. Gathered at the top of a long winding ridge, in the photograph opposite page 133, was a group of about twenty-five, probably college students. That esker, a prominent, narrow, curving mile-long hill—curiously rising now above adjacent land—was deposited there, geologists say, long ago as a gravelly riverbed by rushing water once surging inside or under a melting ice-age glacier. Photographed at a spot I recognized, having walked there, the picture, from the early 1900s, was in Cornell Professor O.D. von Engeln's 1961 book, *The Finger Lakes Region: Its Origin and Nature*, a book detailing the unique geologic history of the area. In the book, von Engeln described the esker as:

> ... a notable esker development, perhaps the best example of this phenomenon in the Finger Lakes Region, [and] ...the Malloryville occurrence here described has almost ideal expression.

Oskar D. von Engeln had taught geology at Cornell from 1907 until 1948. Early in the 20th century, he led field trips with his students to the area. At the East Ithaca railroad station near the campus, he and his students would catch a Cortland-bound train and instruct the engineer to let them off, in about twelve miles, at the Malloryville Road crossing, an unscheduled stop at an unpaved country road, conveniently at the very side of the esker. After hiking over and around the varied glacial landforms, students and professor hailed another train, the tracks and trains now long gone, for the afternoon return trip to Ithaca.

I was learning that botanists and geologists both had found worthy subjects for study practically in my back yard. Soon thereafter, I learned that Cornell scientists, from the time of the University's founding in 1865, had visited and written about the site, among many other places not far from Ithaca. My interest piqued, I bought in a local used-book store Karl Wiegand and Arthur Eames' 1926 book, *The Flora of the Cayuga Lake Basin*, and I ordered by mail, from a used and rare bookseller in Chicago, William Russell Dudley's *The Cayuga Flora*, published in 1886. Arriving soon in the mail and in good condition, the 100-year-old book, I was pleased to discover, was an autographed copy, signed by William R. Dudley himself.

The remnants and regrowth of wild nature near my home were surrounded by a working agricultural landscape. I lived among several hundred acres of agricultural fields on the dairy farm owned by my parents, Martin and Lorraine Beck. There, we grew hay, corn, wheat and oats each year as feed for livestock, and cabbage and potatoes as cash crops. My three brothers and I learned early about long hours of work, feeding cattle, chickens and pigs, milking cows, fixing fences, driving tractors and operating machinery, and planting and harvesting crops, sometimes working into the night with the hired farmhands and teenage neighborhood boys to get the last wagonloads of hay into the barn before a rain storm.

Naturally, we didn't always enjoy our duties, getting up early to feed and milk the cows or working in the hot afternoon sun, when we'd rather be playing. Once, I recall, two little boys, younger brother Roger and me, feeling unfairly burdened with work, being suddenly inspired in creative protest, behavior for which we received our comeuppance without delay from our disapproving father—go back out and fix the problem. Brilliantly, we had planted four rows of cabbage seedlings, inverted, leaves down, roots in the air.

At the edges of the working land, the hedgerows and wild

pastures, the woods, swamps, streams and ponds were alive with myriad frogs and dragonflies, salamanders, turtles, chirping crickets, squirrels, singing birds and wildflowers, and tall trees for climbing into the sky. Here, encouraged in my interests, especially by an aunt and an uncle, my father's sister Florence and brother Charles, who loved their nephews and nieces as though their own, I discovered the non-utilitarian values, the amazing diversity and beauty, of wild things living their own private lives in their own wild places. These captured my attention and forever would hold my interest and fascination.

I knew the territory well including a 75-acre wild area of woods, swamp and pastureland, locally called the "punchbowl," where we explored, picnicked, devoured wild blackberries and sour apples, repaired fences and cut our Christmas tree each year. The overgrown stone foundations of a small house and barn were the only reminders of the old farmstead abandoned, like so many others early in the 20th century, on poorer soil in the hilly countryside and less accessible places in the Finger Lakes Region. For seventy years, the previously cultivated fields had been used as daytime pasture for milking cows, and then as summer-long pasture for heifers, and finally lay unused. And now, a slow transformation through ecological succession had begun, from old-field grasses to Goldenrods, to tangles of Blackberries, Red Raspberries and Hawthorns, to become, sometime in the future, a shady mature forest of towering hardwood and evergreen trees, likely a diverse mix of species including Sugar Maple, Red Oak and White Pine.

And west, just across the punchbowl fence from the old, long-ago-drained farm pond—there ice blocks in the dead of winter had been sawed out to be hauled to the icehouse to be buried in insulating sawdust and used year-round to chill ten-gallon steel milk cans filled with milk fresh from the cows—I knew the mysterious Malloryville Bog property, the unspoiled piece of woodlands and wetlands that would eventually become my home and the centerpiece of this story. How a small house came to be built there, next to the punchbowl—the house that Gwen and I later were to buy—and how I came to return, thus form a part of the personal history interwoven in our environmental journey.

With "only fifty dollars to my name," as Dad told it, he had started his studies at Cornell University's College of Agriculture. Like four of his six siblings—who were to become electrical and mechanical engineers, a teacher and a medical doctor—children of first-generation immigrants, my father was determined to get a college education. Although his advisors urged him to delay his studies and come back after working and saving for a year or two, he stayed and earned his way with part-time work—on campus in a Zoology Department histology lab preparing microscope slides and by stoking big coal furnaces in Ithaca's winters, twice a day in the basements of professors' homes. On his own schedule, four years later, he graduated in the class of 1920.

Then, looking for work, Dad was directed to Cornell Professor Carl E. Ladd who owned a farm at Malloryville. Carl Ladd recognized an honest man and hired my father to manage and work the farm, and to live in the stately old sixteen-room farmhouse there, a house reputed to have been an 1800's stagecoach inn, the house in which my three brothers and I were to grow up. Dad's plan had long been to own his own farm. By 1929, through perseverance, hard work and smart management, he achieved his goal and was able to buy the farm from Professor Ladd, his appreciative mentor. Their mutual friendship, built on trust and respect, continued and led to generations of Cornell students—with other Cornell faculty—visiting our farm on class field trips as part of their studies in agriculture and farm management.

Half a dozen years after Dad bought the farm, Carl Ladd, by then Dean Ladd, requested from him a return of a favorite piece of land from the punchbowl on which he wanted to build a retreat, a woodland cabin above the wetlands. Dad agreed, requesting no payment. A survey map was prepared, a deed was drawn up, and title for sixteen acres was transferred in 1935. And so, the house that was to become mine a half century later, was built on land that belonged twice to Cornell's Dean Ladd and once to my father.

Although I chose to leave the farm, I could never lose my affection for the open, undeveloped spaces of farm fields and wild edges, or my high regard for the sustainable use of land in agriculture. For these early experiences, working and playing as a boy living in the country, I am enormously grateful.

I had moved, after my college years at Cornell, to a big-city metropolitan area. I was living in and near New York City. But increasingly I longed to own a home, to live and work in a more natural, less human-dominated environment. I wanted a home surrounded by land and nature, a goal out of reach for me where I was. Across the street from my southern-Westchester apartment, I was saddened as I watched the last woods in the neighborhood, where my dog and I walked and ran, become yet another housing development. As did Edwin Way Teale in his wonderful memoir, *A Naturalist Buys an Old Farm*, I felt a need for solitude, space and nature.

A fellowship from the New York Zoological Society had brought me from Ithaca in upstate New York to the Bronx Zoo, for a year, smack in the middle of The Bronx. Then I accepted a faculty position at Sarah Lawrence College, the excellent, small liberal arts college in southern Westchester County, just north of the big city. There, in a tiny five-member science department, I derived enormous pleasure teaching and sharing exciting ideas in science—in biology, animal behavior, natural history—challenging students in small groups and in-dependent studies to think in new ways, while always trying to remain open, in exchange, to learning something new from them. Some, I happily recall, signed up year after year for more of my classes.

It may have been a hint, a nudge, to me of the need for change from the rush of city life when my dog Rufous (named for his reddish-brown color), my otherwise well-mannered companion in hiking, canoeing and camping, accompanying me in the college Administration Building—to my astonishment and dismay—lifted his leg and left his territorial signature on the chair-draped sport coat of the gentleman standing nearby, the Dean of Faculty.

While I knew that many of Earth's strongest environmental advocates choose to live in the city, and I was thankful for my experiences there, my thoughts were drawing me away. Nature, where I was living, was subdued, dominated, or worse, totally trashed, by the human presence. Without traveling a distance, I could not escape the presence, the work or waste, the pressure, of my own species within a few feet in every direction. Not that city and suburban life for me was intolerable—it certainly wasn't—yet I felt an incessant inner need for the wildness of nature near at hand, every day, for a place untrammeled, where nonhuman life and natural processes prevailed, unspoiled, where the eyes and ears were not reminded every moment of our own unchecked domination.

In January, I wrote a short letter of resignation to the President of the College, completed the academic year and, knowing I would miss my students, resolved to return to my native habitat in upstate New York.

I returned to the rural countryside of the Finger Lakes Region, a place of green hills, clear streams, blue lakes and beautiful skies, a land of villages and small cities with colleges and bountiful culture, a place that was always welcoming and home to me. Then, a house with a parcel of land, "a naturalist's dream," as described in the realtor's tiny newspaper ad, became unexpectedly available. It was a place of unspoiled beauty and exquisitely rich natural diversity. We moved in. And so, a curious coincidence in timing had brought us simultaneously face-to-face, across Malloryville Bog, with our gravel-mine adversaries.

Place

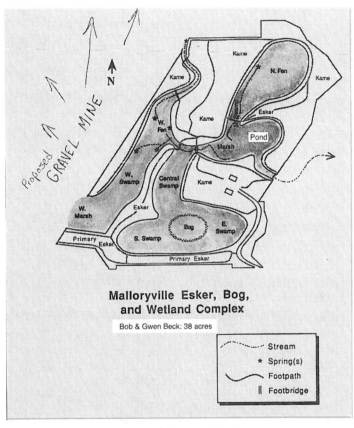

My small map, 1986

3 DIVERSITY

Those who contemplate the beauty of the earth
find reserves of strength
that will endure as long as life lasts.
— Rachel Carson

I UNFOLDED FROM my shirt pocket, a letter-size one-page map I had drawn from my excursions, my early, agreeable explorations of every nook and cranny of our new 38-acre property. Creased, increasingly tattered, the map showed, shaded in blue, the water of wetlands, streams and pond, like an asymmetric blue amoeba with pseudopodia extending in five directions; higher ground outlined, separating and surrounding the wetland arms; extensive trails lined in, looping and interconnected; features identified and named—Malloryville Esker, Hemlock Ridge, Hardwoods Kame, House Kame, West Marsh, Bog, North Fen, West Fen, Springs, Central, South, North and West Swamps, and Pond—in all, a richness and variety hard to appreciate, even being there, exceptional diversity packed into a single, not that large, parcel of land. In enlisting support for our case against gravel-mine plans, I had begun leading walks for individuals and small groups, walks on footpaths through the woods, climbing over the kames and eskers, negotiating essential crossings of small streams on an existing wooden footbridge and, in spots, on natural bridges of tree roots or balancing on a fortuitously-located fallen tree trunk, and venturing, in dripping boots or wet sneakers, carefully into the wetlands.

As a naturalist and teacher, I knew that first-hand experience of the place would be the best motivator for speaking out in its defense. Words and pictures were good, but could not provide the emotional equivalent of actually being in such a remarkable environment. While freely admitting my strong personal bias for this small piece of nature, I wanted to share some of what I knew and some of my feelings as my guests and I walked and talked on leisurely field trips.

Walking, you begin to experience the shape of the land, manageable-sized hills and valleys created by a long-ago melting glacier. You soon realize that the land surface is unusually complex, yet here you see no ice-sculpted rock of mountain terrain, nor any of the exposed bedrock of our Finger Lakes Region's spectacular rock-walled gorges as in many of our state parks—places like Watkins Glen, Taughannock Falls, Enfield Glen, Buttermilk Falls and Fillmore Glen, or the Fall Creek and Cascadilla Creek gorges bordering the Cornell University campus, or lesser-known treasures like Lick Brook, Coy Glen, Carpenter's Falls and Great Gully. Sculpting of those memorable gorges and waterfalls continues today, as it has for 10,000–12,000 years, by the power of flowing, freezing and thawing water in creeks descending glacially over-steepened slopes, the Finger Lakes' valley sides, since the retreat from our area of the most recent ice-age glacier.

Rather, at Malloryville, in a very different setting, you are surrounded by many rounded hills of varying shapes and sizes, composed through and through of gravel, sand and water-tumbled, rounded rocks, all of which were deposited there by glacial meltwater still in the presence of the receding glacier, hills now mostly tree covered, grown to upland woods rich with spring flowers and fall colors. And today, as you walk through the complex, interconnected, wooded low areas between the hills, you pass near year-round flowing marl springs, streams, swamps, fens, an acid bog and a pond. The woods and wetland communities, having developed within the glacier-formed landscape through the millennia since the glacier's retreat, present to us a unique and wonderfully enchanting place.

On a walk, you feel as if you have been transported further north to the wilds of the Adirondack Mountains or Canada. The woodland terrain and short sight distances lend a sense of remoteness and mystery, and make it easy, initially, to feel momentarily lost. You sense you will discover something new around each corner, and you are not disappointed. You enjoy the sounds and sights of wildlife, the wildflowers, the smells of the forest. You can explore for hours and not tire for variety. And the near-pristine wildness, the diversity of habitats and species, and the ever-changing seasons, are sufficient to sustain your interest for many return visits.

Among the eskers, kames and kettles—geologists call the hilly terrain "kame and kettle" topography—I try imagining the glacier here 12,000 years ago at the end of the Pleistocene, the last Ice Age, thousands of years before the first human civilization, but hundreds of millions of years after the lives of sea creatures fossilized in exposed rocks elsewhere in the region. A glacier, a continental ice sheet as much as a mile thick, had flowed slowly south out of Canada picking up, along the way, quantities of rocks, gravel and sand that became thoroughly mixed in the ice. Now melting, as the climate has warmed, I imagine the glacier's southern edge, now at this latitude. The ice may continue flowing from the north, but it is melting back at the edge as fast as it moves forward—it is stagnated. Large volumes of meltwater are running off the ice sheet.

Today, from a woodland trail at the edge of a swamp, we turn to look up at the tree-covered side of Malloryville Esker, rising from next to us upward in a steep slope to its rounded ridge top high above us, and I attempt to imagine its creation. Meltwater streams and rivers are rushing in glacial crevasses and forming tunnels in or under the ice, melting out rocks, gravel and sand, and depositing rocky, gravelly streambeds under the moving water. I envision a streambed lining the bottom and sides of a tunnel insulating the glacial ice from the running water, restraining downward and sideways melting, and forcing upward melting in the ice as the deposited bed gets ever thicker. I imagine the rushing water depositing a bed of varying thickness along its length and, confined and under pressure in its glacial tunnel, flowing even uphill at times before emerging finally into daylight from the melting wall of Pleistocene ice. Then, in years, decades or maybe centuries as the glacial ice eventually melts away, the raised gravel streambed settles to the solid ground below, leaving a long snaking ridge, an esker, rising above the surrounding land. Today, these "inverted riverbeds" of northern latitudes, worldwide, vary from quite short in length to miles long, and their narrow tops sometimes make for fine hiking trails or even roadways.

The Malloryville Esker, described in Dr. von Engeln's 1961 book, is the largest of several here. It's more than a mile long, paralleling Fall Creek and the old railroad bed to the east, and our small road to the south, and it rises as high as sixty feet above adjacent wetlands and creeks. As a boy, long before I knew about eskers, I crawled under bushes, my first binoculars in hand to discover a singing male Rufous-sided (Eastern) Towhee, and repaired pasture fence in the woods on that curious punchbowl ridge. On one dark summer night with my father and brothers, after herding escaped heifers back into their pasture, I remember watching close-up with our flashlights a seemingly unafraid mother Opossum, our only native marsupial mammal, with her litter of babies clinging to her naked, prehensile tail curled on her back. On a less pleasant occasion, Dad and I found the desiccated body of an adult Great Horned Owl attached spread-winged to a barbed-wire fence, probably placed there by an unenlightened neighbor with a gun.

In my mind, I visualize a stream cutting through an esker. Glacial meltwater, having dammed up behind a newly formed

esker ridge, forming a pond or small lake, would quickly over-
flow at a low point, erode a channel through, and drain most
of the water, leaving only pools in the low spots. Such natural
breaches, breaks in the esker, are evident today in the Malloryville Esker where streams, in two places, flow through and
empty into adjacent Fall Creek—Cayuga Lake's longest tribu-
tary—on its way to Ithaca where it passes through the Cornell
campus, then over Ithaca Falls and into the longest of the elev-
en Finger Lakes.

Kames, rounded or irregular hills, add to the complex land
surface here. As we walk, our woodland trail follows the curves
between a swamp on our left and the base of a forest-covered
hill, a kame on our right. In my imagination I attempt to see
the wall of the stagnated, melting glacier, water cascading from
it. The flowing meltwater is creating hills as it deposits mounds
of gravel, sand and rocks off the front or sides of the ice, or
sometimes in depressions on the ice surface and sometimes
against adjacent higher ground, leaving kames and kame terrac-
es of varying shapes and sizes once the ice sheet has retreated
further north. Unlike glacial moraines, where gravel and rocks
were pushed, as if by a giant bulldozer, into their shapes by the
front and sides of the advancing glacier, our kames and eskers
were created by moving water flowing from the crumbling,
retreating glacier. And today, much of those upland kames and
eskers around us are covered with mixed woodlands of Red
and Sugar Maples, Black Cherry, White Ash, Red Oak, White
Pine and more, where spring wildflowers grow in profusion
and autumn colors can be spectacular.

My youngest brother, Rick, and I, our ages about 7 and 12,
on a hot August day, noticed smoke at the top of the punchbowl's tallest kame from our farmhouse a quarter mile away.
We ran to investigate and discovered a fire in the old pasture's
dry grass and brush, already having blackened a half acre or so,
quickly spreading in all directions from someone's abandoned
campfire. Madly stamping our feet and pounding with sticks
for what seemed like hours, we managed to extinguish the
flames and hobble home, soot-covered with tender, reddened

feet and cracked soles on our shoes. A couple of months later we were surprised to receive in the mail business envelopes containing personalized printed checks for $2.50 each from the U.S. government for our firefighting services. Although I never learned for sure, I suspect that it was our good neighbor, Charles Baldwin—former New York State Commissioner of Agriculture—living down the road next to the esker, who notified someone of our adventure. We cashed the government checks then, but I regret that mine is not framed on my wall, today.

On convenient footpaths, we walk among diverse wetlands—marsh, mineral-rich swamps, mineral-poor swamps, fens, and acid bog—all having developed in the glacial kettles and other low areas between the eskers and kames, the gravel deposits having altered and blocked the more direct streamflow routes downslope towards Fall Creek. We realize that the wetlands became what they are today because of the shape of the land. Together, intimately related, the landforms and wetlands are a legacy of the glacier, the last of the Pleistocene ice age. Here, the five wetland types, each in an area small in size, but each high in unspoiled quality, are, for their diversity, intriguingly located in close proximity to one another. In contrast to visiting a large expanse elsewhere of a single kind of wetland, here we can experience wetland diversity, all within minutes. And because of their pristine condition, the wetlands harbor numerous locally scarce and rare plant species, many of which are common only much further north.

I asked F. Robert Wesley to accompany me and share with me his knowledge, especially of the plants and natural communities occurring here. Robert, as a field botanist with an amazingly intimate, detailed knowledge of the diversity and identification of plant species and of their ecological communities, has been an invaluable "natural resource" for all those in our area who need his expertise. Whether for interested landowners, project developers or organizations needing plant surveys, or for college and university faculty and students doing biological research, Robert's detailed knowledge has helped fill a vital need in our area. Because he was already deeply familiar with the wetlands and woodlands here—as he was with most of the special wild areas in central New York State—Robert's time with me enabled my knowledge to take a quantum leap in understanding wetland plant species, the variety of wetland community types tucked into our small area, and the special, uncommon conditions that enable them to exist here.

The mineral-poor swamps and acid bog, unlike the groundwater-fed rich swamps and fens, receive their water primarily from direct precipitation of rain and snow and runoff from the immediately surrounding land surface. Swamps—defined as wetlands with trees—often are bordered at the edge by a wetter area, as we notice next to our path, an area wetter than the interior, a muddy moat or "lagg," seeming to provide protection from trespassers. The poor swamp, around which our loop trail passes, is dominated by Eastern Hemlock, Red Maple and Yellow Birch trees and in places we view a lush understory "forest" of three-foot high Cinnamon Ferns on hummocks, and groups of wildflowers like *Clintonia*, sometimes known as Blue-bead Lily, and Water Arum, also called Wild Calla.

We pause at a wet vernal pool corner of the swamp, a place which comes alive once a year as winter ice gives way to spring melt with the "clack-clack-clack," duck-like mating calls of the bronze-colored, black-masked Wood Frogs. They have made their way, along with the quiet, but no-less wondrous, eight-inch adult Spotted and Jefferson Salamanders, from the warming woods to the opening water. For a brief week or two, frog-mating activity continues as jelly-covered eggs are laid. With an early start and in a hurry before the ephemeral pool dries up in the summer as vernal pools do—thereby providing fish-free safety—the frog's eggs must hatch, the tadpoles grow, develop legs and lose tails, transforming into tiny froglings which disperse quickly into the woodland leaf litter of the adjacent eskers and kames. There the young and adults will remain, eating and growing in summer and fall, and enduring in winter even bitter cold, hidden, some frozen nearly solid—as with Spring Peepers too—waiting in suspended animation for life's return in next year's spring thaw.

We leave dry ground, crossing the muddy lagg stepping and hopping, carefully, from tree root to tree root, and make our way to the interior of the poor swamp towards an opening clear of trees, towards the acid bog. Inside an encircling ring of Highbush Blueberry and Black Chokeberry shrubs, we find a deep carpet of luxurious-green *Sphagnum* peat moss and Cotton Grass sedges covering the surface of the bog. Here the *Sphagnum* generates acidity in the water, water which is already lacking in both minerals and nutrients, thus creating a hostile environment for most plant species, but in which unique bog plants thrive. Growing in and above the thick, sponge-like cushion of moss, we observe the evergreen leaves of heaths, Leatherleaf and Bog Rosemary and the tiny mouse-like leaves of Small Cranberry, and all around us we see the rosette leaf clusters of insectivorous Pitcher Plants, each water-containing, vase-shaped leaf adapted to trap and drown unsuspecting insect prey to supplement the plant's diet with dissolved nutrients. Here in 1995, Jessamy Rango, a Cornell graduate student studying several species of insects whose immature stages, interestingly, are adapted to live, and are found only, in the water of pitcher plant leaves, feeding on the remains of other species trapped and drowned there, chose to wear swimmer's boogie boards on her feet in order to protect the bog surface on her many repeated visits. And should we return to the bog in late June or early July, we might see the last maroon petal fall from the flower of a Pitcher Plant, and enjoy dozens of Grass Pink, *Calopogon* orchids, their beautiful, delicate pink flowers on grass-like stems in full bloom on the *Sphagnum* mat. Here, in the snow and frozen cold of winter, a Short-tailed Weasel, in camouflage white but for its black-tipped tail, was visible for an instant before disappearing under the snow-covered bushes, and, on a warmer occasion, a raptor, perhaps a Red-tailed Hawk, frightened by my approach, flew from its dinner, a plump, cleanly-plucked, headless body of a Ruffed Grouse, in all appearance, like a small chicken ready for roasting in the oven.

Standing in this unique bog environment, I contemplate its history. I think of the hidden gravel bottom, a glacial kettle, far below where I stand on the spongy mat of the bog's surface. A kettle, a circular, bowl-shaped depression in the land, begins its formation when a block of ice, sometimes huge, is separated from the front of a receding glacier and becomes surrounded or buried in thick sand and gravel deposited by meltwater. Later, when the ice block eventually melts and gravel settles, a depression in the land, a kettle, is formed, some a few hundred feet across, sometimes more than a mile, and while commonly under 30 feet deep, some kettles have a depth up to 200 feet. Although some may remain filled with water as ponds or small lakes, others may, over thousands of years, become transformed into fen, bog or swamp wetlands as open water becomes overgrown with a mat of vegetation and the depression slowly fills with layer upon layer of peat, partially decayed vegetation. And, as we were to learn a few years later from the studies here of Syracuse University Professor Donald Siegel and his hydrogeology students, 33 vertical feet, representing thousands of years of sediments and peat layers, lie under us in the glacial kettle at Malloryville's acid bog, its kettle pond long since fully overgrown and filled in.

At the end of the ice age, Mastodons sometimes became mired in wetlands, a male perhaps seeking refuge from a stronger rival, dying in a bog, unable to escape, becoming buried and preserved in layers of peat. Often I have wondered, though we shall never know, what preserved animals may lie beneath the wetland surfaces here, perhaps the remains of extinct mammals such as the Saber-toothed Cat or a mastodon, like the full-skeleton, magnificent specimen now on display at the Museum of the Earth in Ithaca, or even, possibly, mummified or skeletal human remains as have been found in northern Europe and in central Florida.

Leaving the bog, we continue through the mineral-poor swamp, crossing a lagg on the opposite side to regain solid ground. There, a dry and convenient path, next to a kame, follows the curving edge of the swamp to a wooden foot-bridge, our crossing, over a stream exiting the swamp and flowing into a sheltered, woodland-surrounded, shallow pond that we see on our right. Flowing year-round, the stream's water arises from multiple springs in the nearby swamps and fens, and, because of its mineral richness, small snails, clams, amphipods and many aquatic insects thrive there. A small earthen dam, built decades earlier by a former owner, had cre-ated the pond by flooding, unfortunately, a small fen or bog adjacent to the meandering stream. Though that alteration was unwise and certainly would not be done again, the pond's ani-mal life of Wood Ducks and Mallards, Great Blue Herons, Belted Kingfishers, turtles, frogs, Red-spotted Newts, min-nows, dragonflies and more, adds much to the site's diversity and interest. When needed, my brother Roger volunteered to repair the small dam, although, perhaps sometime in the fu-ture, that may be removed enabling the eventual return of a wetland bordering the stream.

Over the bridge and continuing on the path, we find that we must cross a stream again. Here, previously, many others and I, including my father and my ninety-year-old Aunt Flor-ence, had balanced across a fallen tree, until I placed a long, single plank across a narrower spot, an easier crossing which we use on our walk today. Little did I know then, that some years in the future, we would be crossing these same streams and swamps, in several places, on attractive, substantial foot-bridges and boardwalks providing needed protection for the streams and wetlands, in a new Nature Conservancy preserve.

Then we arrive at the edge of a mineral-rich swamp, named West Swamp on my folded map. Fens and rich hem-lock-hardwood swamps, two of the wetland community types here, are considered scarce or rare in New York State because, as Robert Wesley emphasized to me, both are dependent upon a supply of mineral-rich, but nutrient-poor, alkaline groundwa-ter emerging in springs within or near the wetlands. The water, originally falling as rain or snow on higher ground, acquires alkalinity, dissolved calcium and other minerals by slowly percolating through the thick deposits of sand, gravel and rocks, the kames and eskers, left behind by the melting glacier. These kames and eskers, adjacent to the wetlands, are composed entirely of the valuable material desired for mining. It was this land that was to be hauled away.

Scientists Robert Wesley, and later, Barbara Bedford, a wetlands ecologist at Cornell, and Syracuse University's Donald Siegel, after thoroughly exploring the wetlands and their upland surroundings, concluded that mining and removal of the nearby higher ground could have the serious effect of altering the direction, the flow rate and the chemistry of the groundwater feeding the wetlands, thus endangering the survival of the many ecologically sensitive, scarce and rare plants living there. Together, they felt that such a risk was unacceptable, given the rarity, diversity and nearly pristine quality of our wetlands.

On our walk, we see several springs giving rise to small streams at the base of slopes near the edge of the wooded rich swamp. And fens nearby, more open and absent the swamps' tall trees, also dependent on a constant supply of seeping mineral-laden water, are especially fragile and easily degraded or destroyed. Their rare plants, such as Globeflower, may be extirpated, as they often have been, by trampling, filling, draining, flooding or pollution. Yet, outside of the tropics, fens harbor more plant species than any other natural community. Here, Barbara Bedford, Robert Wesley, Carol Reschke of the New York Natural Heritage Program and Nancy Slack of Union College, in a Natural Heritage Program study of New York State fens, counted, in one small 5-by-20 meter plot (about 16-by-65 feet), a remarkable 103 plant species.

Next to the trail near the juncture of two streams and the north end of Hemlock Ridge, the small esker separating the mineral-rich West Swamp and the mineral-poor Central Swamp, we notice holes in the trunk of a tall White Pine, a Pileated Woodpecker's precision-formed oval-shaped excavations and a pile of fresh, white wood chips beneath, and further off in the woods, we hear its loud "kik-kik-kik" calls. Here, I recalled photographing a fuzzy, fledgling Screech Owl, newly emerged from its nearby Yellow Birch nest cavity, perched on a twig of a fallen branch close to the ground and squinting into a bright shaft of late-afternoon sunlight. And that evening, passing by on a walk in near-darkness I saw no fledglings and, meaning no harm, I was greeted, nonetheless, by both parents flying close overhead with excited alarm calls and loud beak clicks.

We continue our walk up the woodland, park-like path that follows the top of the small esker, looking down on the swamps on either side. Farther off, among hardwoods upslope on a kame, we hear the enthralling, always beautiful, flute-like song of a Hermit Thrush. And nearby, in shadow on the forest floor mat of Hemlock and White Pine needles, we admire a broad, flat-topped *Amanita* mushroom and a splendid group of Painted Trilliums in delicate white and crimson full bloom. On the slopes to the sides of our path we notice several shallow depressions in the ground, each with an adjacent earthen mound, "pit-and-mound" micro-topography, evidence of uprooted, fallen trees, long-since decayed and recycled on the forest floor. Then, at our feet in the middle of the trail we observe, close-up, the scat of a Coyote, droppings larger than that of the more common Red Fox and Gray Fox, filled with the fur of its prey, and probably deposited there the night before.

We pass near a marsh dense with Marsh Marigold's golden flowers, later in the summer to showcase tall Joe-Pye Weed's pinkish-purple flower heads, a wetland fed by water probably more rich in nutrients than the close-by swamps, fens and bog. And a bit later, a Ruffed Grouse flushes, in a loud whir of wings from the brushy undergrowth, as we climb over the esker on our return to the road. As we conclude our walk, we feel a deeper appreciation of Malloryville's natural history, of the intimate interconnections between an ancient glacier, curious landforms, varied wetlands and the rich biodiversity of plants, animals and other life forms at home there, thriving in their own natural communities.

Base of Hemlock Ridge

4 QUESTIONS

A man is rich in proportion to the number of things
he can afford to let alone.
— Henry David Thoreau

NEARLY SIX YEARS before Gwen and I moved to our new home, a significant public hearing had been held by the Dryden Town Board. The date was November 11, 1980. The transcribed minutes reveal arguments for and against a Special Permit application for gravel mining at Malloryville.

The absentee landowner, Alfred Eddy, had applied for a new permit for the same site after five years of disuse. The landowner-applicant's attorney presented their case, and the surveyor hired to prepare the required mining and reclamation plans, made it known to the assembled group that everything would be done properly and there would be no problems. He said, not only is the Town's Special Permit required, but also "...you have to get a permit from DEC. The term of the [state] permit is 3 years, and has to be renewed every 3 years. There has to be an annual report which has to have an update of what was done last year and what reclamations were undertaken that year." And he said, "There is a requirement for a security bond to be posted [it was set later by the Town at $5,000]."

Then several concerned neighbors, homeowners and residents living on well-kept properties close to the site—Lyman Armentrout, Irving Trusky, William White, Richard Zelinsky—spoke strongly in opposition. They asked serious questions about heavy truck traffic, safety, road maintenance and potholes, property values, and neighborhood quality. Mr. Zelinsky, resident, at the time, in the house that was to become mine, spoke in defense of the wetlands. He said:

> We have the Malloryville Bog which has certain ecological features... The bog tends to be a fragile ecosystem in its own and it is not hard to change its character by changing the amount of water that runs off [the gravel area]. There are at least 2 main draws that run from Mr. Eddy's property right into the bog, which during high water periods they become a stream. Anything that goes on up above, on the slopes of the banks, will wash right down into the bog. We are trying to maintain this as a natural area. We don't have any plans for bulldozing or lumbering or anything else. We like the idea of the bog and a lot of other people also do, because of its uniqueness...

A voting Town Board member responded by saying:

> I admire any person that will try and take some of these private enterprises. We need more in this county like [the gravel mine applicant] and we have a roomful of people who want to turn him down... The gravel bed [gravel mine] was there before and didn't do any harm then, and it won't do any harm again. These people want to kill this gravel bed, but if the gravel has to be gotten 20 miles away they don't realize that with this plant it will pay in the end. This gravel bed was there when the people moved into the area and they knew that.

Zelinsky replied:

> I have no intention of trampling on Mr. Eddy's private enterprise rights, all I ask is that he doesn't trample on mine. I think natural resources are important, I think just as important as making a dollar. The bog was there before the gravel pit and what I care about is that the gravel pit doesn't do anything to the bog. If I can have the guarantee that Mr. Eddy is accountable for what he does, he can make as much profit as he wants...

The public hearing was closed and a decision was tabled until the next meeting. A month later, after a careful presentation of legalities by Town Attorney, Mahlon Perkins, confirming that the plans met local and state requirements, Resolution #162 was voted upon and approved by the Town Board—apparently without dissent—and the Special Permit was granted. New York State mining and reclamation permits were issued shortly thereafter. Neither the quality-of-neighborhood concerns of residents, nor the close presence of the wetlands and the potential disturbance of groundwater feeding them had sufficient weight to compete with the economic interests of Mr. Eddy.

Now, six years had passed, and again the gravel pits were inactive, abandoned. I had just moved in on the opposite side of the wetlands and, like neighbors before, I also had known of the previous mining. In the wind now was a new plan, this time by a much larger corporate entity, which, to some, was good economic news. In my view, enough was enough; they were looking at the wrong place and needed to be stopped. Knowing what I knew of the wetlands, I wasn't willing to contemplate an inevitable, disappointing repeat performance, another, bigger, loss for Malloryville.

Initially, I needed to ponder some questions. This was a threat I was compelled to fight. Thoughts of concession or loss seemed abhorrent. I knew I could not risk having my responses either ignored or laughed at, derided as naive, ignorant, shrill or belligerent. Good questions deserve thoughtful answers. I needed to do my homework and to stay calm. My thoughts began to go as follows:

"Are our wetlands and glacier-formed hills—eskers and kames—really worth the hassle?" From what I knew to that point, the wetland complex together with the large esker were significant in the Finger Lakes Region as excellent examples of scarce or rare natural features, high in quality and harboring exceptionally rich biodiversity. I believed they deserved protection, and that the risks from an adjacent gravel mine were unacceptable. I was feeling a responsibility for ensuring the well-being of an environmental treasure—one remarkable in diversity, not large or grand in scale, yet, to my mind, a treasure nonetheless. But I was perplexed, angered, that my state-level environmental conservation department—at least a central person in a critical office there—seemed singularly unhelpful. My local government officials, perhaps, could be excused for not appreciating the significance, the uniqueness, of the area as they had no training in ecology, botany or geology, and they did not yet employ an environmental planner or have a conservation board to deal with the issue. But the state-level conservation specialists ought to have the knowledge or easy access to it, and I had thought that it was their job to be helpful to concerned citizens like myself, to be helpful in conserving the natural environment. Yet, I was not encouraged.

When confronted with cold reality, the possibility, the probability, of this mining application sailing smoothly ahead, gaining rapid, easy approval, signed permits issued, and trucks starting to roll, I found I could not simply acquiesce and do nothing. I could not take the comfortable, easy route as had been suggested. I found I needed to take action. Uncomfortably at first, I was becoming an activist. But, from the first, I was determined that knowledge, good science, diplomacy, persuasion, and hopefully the law, be our tools. More radical protest, at least at that stage, I believed would turn people away and be counter-productive. Still, this was new territory for me. I had no previous experience with the environmental review process, impact statements, legal procedures. I was scrambling for help.

"Aren't you just being a selfish neighbor with a 'Not In My Back Yard' (NIMBY) reaction?" In opposing a neighbor's plans, I do not deny that I felt a selfish, albeit normal, NIMBY urge to protect my home and my property. Supporters of development often tend to unfairly categorize and diminish neighborhood opposition as selfishly motivated. But noisy rock-crushing machinery, dust and a stream of heavy concrete and dump trucks in my neighborhood seemed to me reason enough to oppose this plan. Still, my intuition was telling me that those reasons would not prove sufficient to stop it. In the neighborhood we already had the ongoing operation of farm tractors, trucks and machinery, as well as the powerfully rich aroma of cow manure spread on the fields. The close proximity of my relatives' large dairy farm, my own local farm upbringing, and the fact that complaints about normal farm operations by newly arrived, citified neighbors were not well thought of, complicated my feelings and my response. I was opposed to gravel trucks next door, but not to agriculture. While I didn't expect overt support from my farming relatives, neither did I wish to make them my enemies.

I believed, nevertheless, that my concern for the health of a very special natural environment was entirely valid. This particular natural environment required additional consideration beyond the more commonly raised, sometimes fully justified, NIMBY neighborhood objections. My training was, after all, in science, in biology, and I did have knowledge of the environment. But I was also defending my own home, and I was sensitive to a potential problem. I could easily be perceived and accused of misusing science, of distorting facts for my personal, perhaps selfish, reasons, thereby compromising my credibility and weakening our case. I was determined to avoid that pitfall, determined to build our defense using good science while maintaining my integrity. That was important to me. I had chosen my home, in fact, for its remarkable natural features, and my focus was on defending the wetlands, biodiversity and eskers for their own sake, for their unimpaired survival beyond my time here.

"Don't you care that more gravel, sand and concrete are needed for construction and economic development here in central New York State?" Yes, of course, I was aware and agreed that local sources of gravel, sand and concrete are essential to much human activity, including some of my own, like maintaining my long driveway, but I felt strongly that the proposed location was inappropriate. An alternate, less sensitive, location could well be entirely acceptable.

"Don't an owner's property rights entitle him to economic gain from the land in the way, whatever way, he chooses?" I was keenly aware of strong opinions concerning rights of property owners. But, I believed firmly, contrary to some outspoken rural landowners, including some of my neighbors, that certain restrictions on the use of private property, in rural as well as urban areas, are entirely reasonable. Federal and state environmental laws and local property-use regulations, viewed by some as erosion of essential freedoms and inalienable rights, when fairly administered, are essential, I knew, in a human-populated world. Arguments that environmental regulations are unconstitutional "takings" under the Fifth Amendment—that government, i.e. taxpayers, should be required to compensate for an owner's costs and claimed loss of property value for disallowed development projects—are illogical and have not been upheld in the courts.

A revolution in environmental awareness had produced monumental advances in law. The United States' Clean Water Act of 1948 and 1972, the Wilderness Act of 1964, the Clean Air Act of 1970, the Endangered Species Act of 1973 and, in New York, our state's Freshwater Wetlands Act of 1975, for example, as well as local zoning ordinances that help direct development in ways that are compatible with the land and our human communities, are in fact keeping the earth, today, a better place. And as human population density increases and technology magnifies our power, our laws and our government officials, more than ever, must give increased consideration to the plight of the nonhuman environment, to the natural lands, air and water, the plants, animals and their habitats that cannot directly speak for themselves. Otherwise, our shortsightedness inevitably leaves the earth and the lives of our descendants ever more impoverished.

Earth's need for our understanding of the land ethic, Aldo Leopold's seminal idea, remains urgent, perhaps more so every day. Like life itself, powerful ideas, memes, evolve and propagate. Ideas have power. Knowing that fundamental truths, environmental truths misunderstood and resented in one generation, will endure and gain widespread acceptance in the next, gives me courage and reason for hope.

I was comfortable with these answers to my first questions. In the locality where I lived, some, I realized, would see my views as overly idealistic, even radical, but I was confident I could, as needed, be quietly diplomatic in public, as likely would be more useful and productive. I was, however, quickly learning that my convictions, my personal answers were inadequate. I sensed that they and I alone, against economic interests and powerful opposition, possessed insufficient weight to sway sometimes uninformed, stubborn or biased government decision-makers. I lacked the critical weight of persuasive facts, arguments and authority that would be necessary to win our case.

"So, how can I, a citizen and neighbor, have my opposition heard and taken seriously in the permit-granting process? What is the legal procedure for providing information and influencing decision-makers before a land-use permit is granted?" I met with the Tompkins County Planning Department's staff coordinator for our county volunteer Environmental Management Council (the EMC). In her office in Ithaca, Barbara Eckstrom said, "You need to understand seeker..." I said, "What's that?" She responded, "Well it's actually SEQR or SEQRA, the State Environmental Quality Review Act, but pronounced 'seeker.'" New York's law was pretty new then, definitely new to me and to many others. Based on the National Environmental Policy Act (NEPA) of 1970 for federal agencies, I learned that SEQR was New York State's law enacted in 1975, spelling out in detail the procedure to be followed by state agencies and local governments to ensure that environmental concerns are addressed prior to approval of applications for development. In fifteen or more states and in the District of Columbia and Puerto Rico, similar "mini-NEPAs" are now in place, the California Environmental Quality Act (CEQA), having been the first.

Barbara then handed me a helpful packet of information and introduced me to SEQR's precisely defined step-by-step process, to its alphabet soup of Environmental Assessment Forms, (EAFs—long and short versions) and draft Environmental Impact Statements (dEISs), and to the critical role of the Lead Agency in the Determination of Significance, a decision leading to either a Negative Declaration (NegDec) if the proposed action will not have a significant impact on the environment, or a Positive Declaration (PosDec) if the proposed action may have a significant adverse impact, thus requiring the preparation of a dEIS. NegDec and PosDec, then, are New York State's SEQR equivalents to NEPA's Finding of No Significant Impact (FONSI) and Notice of Intent—to prepare an impact statement (NOI).

I was thankful for the law, for the existence of a careful, thorough review process, a powerful legal environmental safeguard, the means by which citizens provide input to government decision makers. SEQR then became central in our long battle to protect Malloryville Bog. Achieving a PosDec was to become a first major goal and a milestone. But to succeed, I needed to find help, quickly.

Questions

Spring-fed stream

5 COALITION

Optimism is the faith that leads to achievement;
nothing can be done without hope.
— Helen Keller

OUR FIRST AUTUMN in our new home, a month here,
Gwen and I were just settling in, still unpacking boxes, arranging furniture, stacking firewood to feed our
wood stove in the coming cold season, beginning our first year
at Malloryville Bog.

Year 1: 1986/87

Later, as I began to think of our accumulating years here, I
reckoned them as running from September to September—we
had moved in on September 1st—and I began to number them
as such.

I was in heaven, now on land of my own, freely hiking and
exploring, discovering hidden places and unknown details,
following White-tailed Deer trails and defining new ones,
trimming brush where needed, naming features, and drawing
and labeling my new map. Red maples around the wetlands
had turned blazing scarlet. But uncertainty cast its shadow. I
didn't know how soon a gravel application would appear, yet I
felt urgency in preparing a response, urgency to be ready with

an effective defense.

What to do? In my mind, our new property deserved protection as a wild natural area, a treasure to be preserved. As owners, Gwen and I planned to provide that protection, as good environmental stewards, as we and our guests enjoyed the property. Yet, the unexpected, unnerving problem we faced was external to our land and outside our direct control. An obvious solution could have been to simply purchase the next-door property, just buy it, to own and control it. That, unfortunately, was not an available option for us. The owner was boasting of plans to make a bundle of money from gravel, far more than ordinary land values in our area, and we were without resources with which to make any offer.

Initially, contact with my local government, the Town of Dryden, produced only discouragement. The elected Town Board and part-time staff did not welcome my problem and the town had neither an environmental planner nor a conservation advisory board with whom to consult. Six years earlier, in the previous mining permit hearing, the contentious issue was perceived property rights, disagreement about a property owner's right to use land for profit versus neighboring owners' rights to protect homes, neighborhood and the natural environment. Then, the profit motive won the day. The same issue was again in play.

I knew that cooperation with a conservation-minded organization could help. There was no local land trust at the time, which otherwise could have been a good first contact. The Finger Lakes Land Trust did not yet exist, and would not for several years. The Nature Conservancy, however, as a land trust with a national scope and a presence in every state, was a possibility. And perhaps Cornell Plantations, with their off-campus Natural Areas, the University's prized nature preserves around the county, could help.

Yet, no arrangement of my land with an environmental organization would, in itself, have stopped the mining threat, a danger from outside my property. And for any land protection organization, consideration of a property's defensibility is critical. If a threat is unresolved, a property may be considered indefensible, a lost cause, and therefore unattractive to any organization, an unwise drain on limited resources of time and money, better to direct efforts elsewhere. Was our cause sufficiently worthy? Was Malloryville defensible? While our threat remained, or if the adjacent gravel operation commenced, would the site be deemed an unwise investment, all-but-lost? Would it be possible, with such uncertainties, to attract support, a firm and lasting commitment, quickly, from a credible environmental organization? I didn't know, but I had to try.

Our first priority was clear. We needed to prevent the approval of mining permits and not allow mining to start. Stopping it later would surely be even harder. I needed to search for support, to find people who would understand the threat, who would be willing to speak out in defense of the place, and who might bring their expertise to the cause. And we needed to prepare quickly. The need was urgent. I began by talking with, and listening to, anyone I thought might be receptive and helpful in some way. I racked my brain, made phone calls, arranged meetings, wrote letters. Some contacts were dead ends. But I was pleased, enormously, as one promising lead led to another and we began to build a coalition of organizations and a team of individuals, many of whom would continue working together in sustained effort, in what would become, as it turned out, a very long haul.

Years earlier I had met Dr. John Kingsbury, Cornell University professor of botany, author of the book, *Poisonous Plants of the United States and Canada*, a founder of the Shoals Marine Laboratory on Appledore Island—six miles off the coast at the Maine/New Hampshire border—and now the acting director of Cornell Plantations. [Then, when I was a student, he had recommended I not apply for the very first summer class at Shoales because, the previous summer, I had already completed an invertebrate zoology course at the Marine Biological Laboratory at Woods Hole on Cape Cod. But his objection opened another opportunity for me. Instead, with National

Science Foundation support of the program, I was fortunate in being able to study tropical biology for a summer with the Organization for Tropical Studies in Costa Rica.] Meanwhile, I had long enjoyed and admired Cornell Plantation's wild Natural Areas—McLean and Ringwood Preserves, Eames Bog, Coy Glen—each a protected gem of nature, and I believed Malloryville's diversity and quality were equal to the best of those. I met Professor Kingsbury at his office. He was friendly and welcoming and asked, "How is your father, Martin?" I should have known he knew Dad through gifts to the Cornell Arboretum from Dad's "Class of 1920." And he asked about our bog, which I was pleased to learn he also knew personally. He said, "Plantations isn't in a position to consider purchasing any new properties, and there's no way we can directly intervene. But, our Natural Areas Committee should be able to help." His interest was genuine, and he put me in touch with the staff and faculty of their Natural Areas program—Heather Robertson, Natural Areas Coordinator, F. Robert Wesley, field botanist, who we met in a previous chapter, and Dr. Peter Marks, professor of ecology in Cornell's Department of Ecology and Evolutionary Biology. Cornell Plantations was joining our effort and was to become a long-term member of our informal team.

Dr. Kingsbury, I was surprised and happy to learn, was also an active member of The Nature Conservancy's New York State board of trustees. He said, "You must present your situation to the trustees of The Conservancy's Central New York Chapter," and he arranged a contact with board member Scott Sutcliff of Ithaca. With Scott's help, I met with the Central New York board at their next meeting, conveniently held that time in Ithaca, and talked to receptive individuals about our wetlands, the esker and the problematic gravel plans. At that initial meeting, among about fifteen like-minded environmentalists, another enduring link was established. Thanks to Professor Kingsbury's help, not one, but two organizations were becoming the first of our team, the core of our new Malloryville coalition. And after the board meeting, Harriet Marsi of Binghamton, chair of their Nominating Committee and a long-time Nature Conservancy supporter, graciously asked, "Would you consider accepting a nomination to join our board." Very pleasantly surprised, I thought for a moment, and cautiously said, "Yes, I would." I started attending meetings, and at the next general-membership Annual Meeting was elected to the board.

Support of neighbors, community members, and friends further away was important. I tried to talk with members of every household within a half mile—about fifty homes. At first I found that few were aware of the gravel plans, but most wanted to learn more. Their questions, as well as mine, pertained to heavy truck traffic on our small, winding rural roads; dust and noise from rock crushing and other machinery; potential spills and pollution; and decline in residential property values. Initially, concern for the wetlands was not their priority, but many good neighbors were willing to listen and learn. Not surprisingly, however, some were simply indifferent, unwilling to get involved, and a few believed me to be out of line in opposing another's desire to profit from his land. Around me, I heard or sensed some pretty strong feelings, suggesting that I should mind my own business and not trample on other people's rights. But our team grew to include many dedicated neighbors and friends, whose letters, attendance and comments at repeated public meetings, over the ensuing years, became strong components of our defense.

Because of the Malloryville Esker, which Professor von Engeln so admired, and our other complex kame and kettle topography sheltering the wetlands, I wanted a professional geologist on our team. I contacted Professor Arthur Bloom, a senior member of Cornell's Geology Department. He knew the esker and surrounding glacier-formed land, and kindly agreed to write a letter when needed.

Tree leaves fell, migratory songbirds had flown south to their subtropical and tropical wintering grounds, autumn had passed and the woods and wetlands were now quiet, snow-covered and deep in winter. Frogs in our pond, the Leopard Frogs, Pickerel Frogs and Green Frogs, and the Painted Turtles were under water, buried in mud at the bottom, life systems slowed to nearly a stop for five or six months, inactive, shut down each year, for almost half the duration of their lives. But Skunk Cabbage flowers, mottled-purple spathe and spadix, were generating heat and melting small circular caverns in the snow, and the Great Horned Owl parents, I was sure, were about to brood shivering hatchlings in their nest. I had continued exploring, learning and, at every opportunity on hikes, introducing others to the beauty and complexity of the place.

February 24, 1987. Yesterday at home, I received a phone call from Doug Hicks, Vice President of Corporate Development for B.R. DeWitt, Inc., the company preparing its application for the gravel mine and ready-mix concrete plant. He offered to meet me at 12:30 on the land, at the old gravel pits. He was professional and cordial at our meeting in his pickup truck, and confident of his skill in public relations. We talked. From the DEC, he had learned that I was a neighboring homeowner with concerns about the adjacent wetlands. His intent was to allay my fears, to preemptively pacify me, a potentially troublesome neighbor. My intent was to listen and ask questions, to learn all I could about his plans, while avoiding any hostility that might make him angry or defensive and less open. My need to learn from him, right then, as nothing yet was on paper, was more important than arguing. He assured me, "We'll be good neighbors," that my wetlands, downslope, were, "...not a concern," and that B.R. DeWitt's excavations, removing 1.7 million tons, 40-50 vertical feet, and eventually dredging out gravel well below groundwater level, would leave a large pond, after 15 or so years, which would be "great for neighborhood fishing and swimming." Choosing not to reveal the depth of my displeasure, I politely expressed my opposition to his plans at this location and asked for a copy of their formal application when submitted. He agreed to mail me a copy.

Things were kicking into a higher gear. Earlier, at 11:45 that morning, I had called Henry Slater who was taking over as the new Zoning & Building Code Enforcement Officer at the Dryden Town Hall. He was, in fact, becoming the Town Hall's first full-time employee. We talked and he was refreshingly supportive. Henry knew the situation and would be meeting Doug Hicks that afternoon at 2:00 to discuss Dryden's Special Permit requirements. Then, at 3:00 I drove to New York's Region 7 DEC office in Cortland, eleven miles from home, where I met with Ray Nolan, Wetlands Specialist, to request an extension, a correction, of the wetland boundary map, that should have shown the wetland extending, in two places, from my property into the gravel parcel. New York freshwater wetlands law provides protection for wetlands 12.4 acres (five hectares) or larger and a hundred-foot buffer. My state-designated wetland (#GR-12) deserved accurate mapping and full protection. At DEC also, I was introduced to Patrick Snyder, Associate Environmental Analyst, whose role in SEQR, the environmental review process, would soon become prominent. And two days later I learned from Dryden's Henry Slater that Doug Hicks at B.R. DeWitt planned to submit their application "within a month."

Robert Wesley, field botanist extraordinaire, earlier had been hired by the New York State Natural Heritage Program to survey Central New York's best sites for scarce and rare plant species and ecological community types. The Natural Heritage Programs had been established by The Nature Conservancy across the country and were jointly administered by the Conservancy and each state government's conservation department. Robert's survey at Malloryville had confirmed the presence of rare and scarce species and communities and I wanted to be sure that that information was part of the files at DEC. Wendy O'Neil, at The Conservancy's state office in Albany and Carol Reschke, Community Ecologist at the Natural Heritage Program state office, kindly had the sensitive, confidential information, identifying the precise locations of threatened or endangered species, sent to Brad Griffin, Regional Supervisor of Natural Resources at DEC. At the same time, Wendy was also arranging to have my property formally recognized with The Nature Conservancy's New York Natural Areas Registry Program.

I had had a very positive meeting with Brad Griffin in his DEC office in Cortland, and he quickly took charge in coordinating information among agency personnel. On March 12, 1987, in a DEC memo to staff, Brad wrote:

> I will consolidate all of the enclosed information and data sheets with you so that all staff and parties-in-interest can refer to it in total. Also, I will ask you to make it part of the application(s) record files as they may arise.

I was pleased, in part, because I had received no reply, in over five months, to a letter I had written, and addressed by name, to the Regional Mined Land Supervisor in DEC's Division of Mineral Resources. My feeling was growing that personnel dealing with mining had little concern for wetlands or other things biological. Brad was interested, however, and he included those indifferent parties in his memo, and that, apparently, prompted a polite and helpful phone call to me from Joe Moskiewicz, the Regional Mined Land Supervisor from his Syracuse office.

And in anticipation of B.R. DeWitt's application, I wrote letters to the State Director of The Nature Conservancy, requesting his help, and to the Dryden Town Board and Town Supervisor.

As word of our situation was spreading, I was invited to attend a monthly meeting, in Ithaca, of my county's EMC, our volunteer Environmental Management Council, as authorized by New York State Conservation Law, and similar to many municipal advisory boards around the country, a body which reported to and presented resolutions on environmental issues to our elected Tompkins County Board of Legislators. I briefly presented the threat that faced our wetlands. Although the timing of the mining application remained uncertain, council members listened with interest and I answered some questions.

I was encouraged and said, "I need your suggestions and support."

Some weeks later, April 27, 1987, Susan Pearce-Kelling, then chairperson of the EMC's Plant and Animal Life committee, wrote a letter to my wife and me:

> Dear Bob and Gwen: I am writing to let you know where we are in the process of looking at the gravel and cement operation's effect on the Malloryville Bog. As you are probably aware, at the time I write this letter, no application has yet been submitted to the Dryden Town Board by the DeWitt Co. After a discussion in the March EMC meeting and the April Executive meeting, it was decided that no resolution should come from the Council until an application has been submitted.
>
> This does not mean that there is not a great deal of concern for the preservation of this ecologically sensitive area. Many people on the Council are interested in keeping informed on the topic so that if and when action can be taken we are prepared to do so. It appears that the Town is aware of the SEQRA (State Environmental Quality Review Act). By following the process of SEQRA there will be ample time to discuss and hopefully better resolve the threat that a gravel and cement operation might have on the bog. Your effort in bringing the problem to the EMC's attention is greatly appreciated!
>
> Along these lines, many of us were wondering if either of you are interested in becoming a member of Council. Neither the Town nor the Village of Dryden is currently represented on the EMC. It seems an efficient way to remedy this would be to speak to the Town Supervisor or the Board and indicate your willingness to become a member.
>
> Thank you for your active concern about this

unique natural area and please continue to keep us informed if there are any pertinent developments. I hope to see you on Council soon.

Respectfully, Susan Pearce-Kelling

I had, in fact, quietly sat in on that March meeting as a guest, and was disappointed when more cautious, more pro-business members, persuaded others to wait to see B.R. DeWitt's application. I was hoping for a strong, proactive statement directed to the County, the Town and the DEC, and I was concerned that the Council might not be able to respond quickly enough in the SEQR process when really needed. And, when that time did arrive, my intuition, on that very point, would be proven correct: time, in fact, was insufficient for review in committee and a resolution by the full EMC.

But, Susan's committee, it turned out, was beginning to develop a detailed inventory of our county's unique natural areas. I was motivated and wanted to be a part of that effort in protecting special wild places, including my own. I said, "Yes, I am interested..." and agreed to join the EMC. But, because of what I perceived as possible disagreement or conflict with the Dryden Supervisor and Town Board concerning the anticipated mining application, I didn't request appointment as the Town's representative. Rather, I became an at-large member of the EMC, representing all of Tompkins County, in what was to become, for me, a long-term commitment to the Unique Natural Areas project.

March 27, 1987. A letter, proactive, excellent and welcome, from Cornell Plantations to the Dryden Town Board, signed by Prof. Peter Marks, Heather Robertson and F. Robert Wesley, precisely stated our scientific case:

> Dear Town Board Members: We are writing to you about the Malloryville Bog area (Tompkins County tax number 24-1-20.2) which is owned by Robert and Gwen Beck. We have learned from Robert Beck that a proposal to extract gravel from an adjacent parcel of land is due to come

before the Town Board within the next few weeks. The various wetlands of the Malloryville Bog area have special scientific and educational value for the local region and we are concerned that they would be adversely affected by the proposal.

Botanical and geological interest in the Malloryville Bog goes back at least 100 years. The first published flora of the local area (Dudley, W. R. 1886. The Cayuga Flora. Andrus and Church, Ithaca) both lists the site in question on the map of local areas of special botanical interest and mentions the Malloryville Bog as one of only four local Sphagnum swamps and peat bogs worth visiting in 1886 (page xvi of Dudley's book). The second (and last) published local flora (Wiegand, K.M., and A.J. Eames. 1926. The Flora of the Cayuga Lake Basin, New York. Cornell University Agricultural Experiment Station Memoir 92) also specifically mentions the Malloryville Bog as an area of special interest (page 463 of Wiegand and Eames' book). It harbors a very rich flora, including rare and uncommon species such as globe-flower (*Trollius laxus*), which is endangered in New York State [threatened with endangerment], showy lady's slipper orchid (*Cypripedium reginae*), white bog orchid (*Platanthera dilatata*), pitcher plant (*Sarracenia purpurea*), and rose pogonia (*Pogonia ophioglossoides*).

More recent botanical excursions confirm that today the wetlands of Malloryville have even greater significance. During the last hundred years other equivalent areas of special interest in the region have been damaged or destroyed, making the remaining sites all the more important. Malloryville remains in perfect condition. In addition to the peat bog mentioned by Dudley, Malloryville contains a number of small open seepage marshes or springs that are particularly important because they are the habitat for the rare globeflower. These marshes are very vulnerable to changes in water supply from surrounding land because their continued existence largely depends on upwelling of cold, limey groundwater flowing out of the gravel deposits.

Because of the potential damage that gravel extraction could do to the vital water supply of Malloryville's wetlands, we ask you to consider carefully the consequences of the current proposal. We believe that damage to the Malloryville wetlands would represent a significant scientific and educational loss. Thank you for your consideration.

Sincerely, P.L. Marks, H. Robertson, F.R. Wesley

We were gaining support. A coalition was coming into being, not with any kind of formal agreements, but loosely, informally among individuals and organizations—neighbors, friends, Cornell Plantations, The Nature Conservancy, the New York Natural Heritage Program, my county's Environmental Management Council, and potentially, encouragingly, my Town Hall and the state Department of Environmental Conservation—all responding to an environmental threat and seeking ways to aid a worthy cause.

Expecting an application to appear any day, weeks turned to months—April, May, June—with no word from B.R. DeWitt. A delightful, exciting first spring in our new home had arrived and passed. I had followed the emergence and blooming of woodland spring flowers—Hepaticas, Spring Beauty, Trilliums—the frogs and turtles returning to life, deciduous trees and shrubs greening with new leaves, the songbirds returning, males establishing and maintaining their territories, filling the fields, woods and wetlands with the music of their songs.

I listened to a male Wood Thrush sing his exquisite three-parted flute-like songs, each male distinct from other males, individual in his repertoire, unique in his preferred combinations of fixed phrases, and never singing the same song twice in a row. A male's complex vocal phrases, many of which are composed of two overlapping notes or overlapping fast trills simultaneously differing in pitch and timing, like internal duets, are produced by the two sides of the bird's voice box, its syrinx. And I was thinking of individual birds returning after their winter migratory absence, remarkably, to their identical territory of previous years.

With fondness, I recalled a Wood Thrush that I had referred to as Male 16 in Sapsucker Woods at Cornell's Laboratory of Ornithology. As a student, I had recorded several singing males on their territories for four successive springs, Male 16 among them each year. Two weeks into the season in the fifth year, he had not returned and two unfamiliar singing males had divided his territory. In mid-May, about 6:00 a.m., with parabola and tape recorder, I was recording his familiar old rival males on neighboring territories when I heard Male 16's distinct song phrases. I thought to myself, "He's back! And he's aggressive!" I witnessed and recorded intense song duels between him and the new males occupying his space, and physical contact as the birds flew against one another and tumbled to the ground. Within two hours, he had pushed his competitors out and he had reclaimed his familiar territory. I wondered but could never know why he had arrived late that season, and I marveled again at how any bird or other animal could migrate hundreds or thousands of miles and return again and again, without printed maps or electronic devices, each to a particular tiny place on Planet Earth they knew as home. And today, I always enjoy a new reminder that, as with our family, friends and animal companions, wild animals too are unique as individuals.

July 8, 1987. Letter from Patrick Snyder, DEC:

Dear Mr. Beck: We have received an application

for a mining permit for the site adjacent to your property... I know you are very interested in this situation and I would like to invite you to our office to review the materials that have been submitted.

Sincerely, Patrick M. Snyder

July 9. Letter from Henry Slater, Town of Dryden, to my wife and me:

Please be informed that I have received an application from B.R. DeWitt for a "Special Permit" to operate a Ready Mixed Concrete Plant... Mr. Patrick Snyder of the D.E.C. Fisher Ave. Cortland, New York will be doing the Environmental Assessment and has declared the D.E.C. as the lead agency. The Dryden Town Public Hearing is scheduled for Tuesday, August 11th... 7:00 P.M. You and all other residents in the area of the proposed site will receive written notice beforehand...

Sincerely, Henry M. Slater

Patrick Snyder and Henry Slater had conferred. Dryden had declined the SEQR Lead Agency role, probably because of the deepening scientific issues that were becoming apparent. Still, Dryden had scheduled a public hearing for further input for its own deliberation. DEC would take the lead in reviewing the Environmental Assessment Form (long version), the mining and reclamation plan, public comments, and in determining significance (NegDec or PosDec). Based on past disappointing encounters with both the town and the state, my feelings about Lead Agency status were mixed. Yet, on the whole, I was pleased with the decision, that New York State would take the lead. But in the lengthening years ahead, on occasion, I would come to have serious doubts about the wisdom of that decision, though I believe, at about that time, the DEC began assuming SEQR lead agency status on all mining applications in

New York.

At his DEC office, Pat Snyder welcomed me, "Here are the file folders. You can sit and read at this table and make whatever copies you want." I did, and began preparing to contact members of our team for their review and response. B.R. DeWitt had prepared the EAF and the Application Form, and had hired Dunn Geoscience Corp., a consulting firm in Albany, to prepare their "Mined Land Use Plan," a 22-page document dated June 18, 1987, very professional in appearance.

And I read a letter from Alfred Eddy, the absentee next-door landowner, addressed to Al Coburn, DEC's Regional Permit Administrator, stating the he was discontinuing the spreading of septage, pumpings from residential septic tanks, on his land, saying, "This is being done in a effort to facilitate the issuance of a Mined Land Reclamation permit on this property." But this additional unpleasant topic, septage disposal on my neighbor's land, was an issue with which I was already dealing, a challenge to which we shall return in another chapter.

I was about to gain a deeper insight into just how the environmental review process, SEQR, works in a real-life situation. I was anxious to see how B.R. DeWitt and their consultant had dealt with environmental concerns including the adjacent wetlands, certainly known to Vice President Doug Hicks since our meeting at the gravel site four-and-a-half months earlier. Would they be upfront and honest with the facts, or would they ignore or distort inconvenient details?

Here is the gist of their application, a very brief compilation, a summary of their statements, their words placed in quotes:

> "To excavate and process sand & gravel, and to manufacture ready-mix concrete," "1/2 mile from Malloryville, nearest population center Groton," near "some scattered residences," for "15 years," ultimately using "74" acres, leaving a water surface at completion of "15 acres," removing "3 million tons" of gravel, using water at a

rate of "6,000 gals/day max," with vehicle trips on the road at "2.8 average" per hour. As to whether noise will exceed local ambient levels, the question was unanswered. They indicated that there are "no" unique or unusual land forms on the site, that "the project should have no effect on the local groundwater system," and, as to whether there are any lakes, ponds, or wetlands within or contiguous to the project area, they cavalierly stated, "none, the overall drainage direction is to the southeast, into Fall Creek."

And here are some of my comments and corrections to their misstatements: The site is actually adjacent to the settlement of Malloryville, 1/4 mile, not 1/2 mile, from its center and, though the site is on the USGS Groton quad topographic map, the hamlet of McLean, and villages of Freeville and Dryden are all closer than is the village of Groton, showing a complete lack of appreciation for the local communities; there are more than a few scattered residences nearby, actually about 50 within a 1/2 mile, with one adjacent to the project entrance and others very close; a new 15 acre pond, where none existed, seems more like a small lake to me, and there is no mention of how deep below groundwater they would have dredged; a heavy truck about every 20 minutes on average, and many more at peak times, on our narrow, quiet road is a huge, unacceptable increase; noise, clearly, would far exceed current quiet ambient levels; there is no mention of the prominent Malloryville Esker crossing the site; the statement that "the project should have no effect on the local groundwater system" is unsubstantiated and grossly misleading; and of the presence of any wetlands, they say "none, the overall drainage direction is to the southeast, into Fall Creek;" implausibly, there is no mention at all of the downslope, contiguous wetlands directly between the gravel site and Fall Creek.

If no one was watching or checking for errors, unintentional or deliberate, Doug Hicks, B.R. DeWitt and Dunn Geoscience could easily get away with this sloppy application, as they apparently thought they would. Fortunately, SEQR allows for citizen and scientific input, and we were there, watching, very closely. It would prove easy, in this case, to counter some of their statements. On the other hand, they weren't planning to excavate within the wetlands, just up to a hundred or so feet away from them. State and federal wetlands laws don't say "no" to that. We had to argue hydrology, and that was less clear, a much bigger challenge.

Hydrology, the study of earth's water, especially its underground location and movement would be a central issue of contention here, the groundwater relations between the area of the gravel mine and the wetlands. Through a referral from Lyle Raymond, a fellow member in the county EMC, Mark Walker, a professional hydrologist with Cornell's Water Resources Institute and the Center for Environmental Research, agreed, on short notice, to visit the wetlands and gravel site with me, to read the application, and write up his comments to be forwarded to the DEC and Dryden. Mark's comments, July 27, 1987, stated, in part :

> The loss of uphill slopes, which likely act as a slow conduit for infiltrating waters, could affect groundwater flow and direction and, accordingly, the volume of flow to the springs and seeps contributing to the wetlands... In order to verify this, further studies should be undertaken to assess the effects of gravel mining on water quantity and groundwater flow...

Mark then suggested the form of specific hydrologic studies and concluded:

> I would recommend that the granting of a mining permit be questioned because of reasonable doubts about overall effects on the quantity of water available to sustain the wetlands.

Meanwhile, in defense of the area's unique geology, Prof. Arthur Bloom, the Cornell geologist with whom I had talked earlier wrote a letter to DEC on August 14, 1987:

Dear Mr. Snyder: ...For probably 90 years, geology classes from Cornell have visited and studied the Malloryville esker, the sinuous ridge of gravel... [It is a] unique landform, representing a special set of late glacial conditions when water flowed through a tunnel under the melting ice sheet and filled the tunnel with gravel. These unusual gravel ridges are described in almost every geologic textbook. They are common in Scandinavia and formerly in New England states, but most of them have been mined for the generally well-washed gravel in them.

I hope that the educational and scientific value of the Malloryville esker will be considered as a reason for preserving it from removal or burial by the proposed gravel mining operation. More generally, the esker is part of a unique area of at least several hundred acres in and around Malloryville that includes an interesting assemblage of glacial landforms such as kames, kettles, bogs, and deranged stream channels. The whole region is worthy of preservation in its current state as a unique example of the work of the last ice age.

Sincerely, Arthur L. Bloom

And Thomas Grasso, a Consulting Geologist from Rochester, wrote to DEC, concluding with:

Of all the glacial features that typify New York geology, eskers are by far the rarest and therefore their preservation is of paramount importance. This is especially true for the esker at Malloryville as it is a classic, textbook, example.

Cornell Plantations' eloquent letter, by Peter Marks, Heather Robertson and Robert Wesley, is forwarded to the DEC files.

Dorothy McIlroy, dedicated and highly-respected amateur ornithologist, and long-term associate of the Cornell Lab of Ornithology, walked with me and then wrote to Pat Snyder:

> Dear Mr. Snyder: ...In the 1950s I visited Malloryville bog with a nature study group led by Dr. Eames, retired head of the Botany Department at Cornell University. He took us there to show us one of the finest examples of wetlands resulting from the retreat of the ice sheet. The bog with its pitcher plants, Calopogon and other special plants and the marsh with purple fringed orchids were most interesting, as he explained how fragile this habitat is, being dependent on the local drainage system, much of the water coming from springs associated with the adjacent esker.
>
> I recently visited Malloryville bog and found it to still be much the same—deep sphagnum, Calopogon, pitcher plants... To further mine huge amounts of gravel from this formation would certainly be tragic for the wetlands. The short-term profits from gravel pit and cement plant, and the few jobs associated with the operation are meager compared to saving this important and very interesting left-over from the end of the Ice Age. There are not too many examples of this type of habitat as fine as this one.
>
> I hope you will refuse a permit for this operation. Whether even a much scaled-down version could be compatible with saving the wetland area is questionable.
>
> Sincerely yours, Dorothy W. McIlroy

Neighbors also wrote letters in defense of our neighborhood. Alice and Allen Green started their letter this way:

This letter is to register our strong opposition to the creation of a cement plant and excavation facility... Our families have been property owners nearby this site for thirteen years. We chose to build our homes and raise our families here largely because of the beauty, quiet and privacy of the area...

A letter, by Robert Crouch, appeared in the Cortland Standard and Ithaca Journal newspapers:

On May 10... I witnessed one of the most beautiful slide presentations I've seen, presented by Robert Beck... The presentation covered wetlands and bogs ...in the sequence of seasons and flowers and birds of those seasons. Bob explained that the Malloryville Bog may be in danger... People in the audience showed concern and asked if there was any way they could help... Let's stand behind him and write... [send letters to the Town and DEC].
Robert Crouch

July 28, 1987. On a brief vacation with Gwen at her parents' home at Green Lake in Wisconsin, we pound out, on my old Smith Corona portable typewriter, our detailed three-page letter to Pat Snyder. We point out and correct the excessive and gross inaccuracies and omissions in B.R. DeWitt's EAF and Mined Land Use Plan, while stating the value of the wetlands and the esker, and include copies of Prof. von Engeln's description and esker photograph from his 1961 book, and mail the envelope off. And we send a copy to Henry Slater in Dryden. Now we must await Patrick Snyder's determination of significance, fingers crossed, PosDec on our minds.

August 7, 1987, SEQR Positive Declaration; PosDec(1):

The NYS Dept. of Environmental Conservation as

lead agency, has determined that the proposed action... may have a significant effect on the environment and that a Draft Environmental Impact Statement will be prepared.... Reasons Supporting This Determination: There is a likelihood that this project, as presently proposed, will lead to a change in air quality, ground and surface water quality and quantity, traffic, and noise levels; a substantial increase in potential for erosion; impacts on a significant habitat area; substantial adverse effects on rare plants; the impairment of the existing character of the community; and the creation of a material demand for other actions (following reclamation) that would result in several of the above consequences.

Patrick M. Snyder

We are thrilled, relieved and encouraged. We had won the first round. Patrick Snyder did the right thing, and the DEC's Regional Permit Administrator, with whom, in his office, I had had my earlier discouraging, angering, encounter, had not intervened in Patrick's decision.

In the quick 30 days or so between DEC's receipt of the application and their Positive Declaration, my county EMC was unable to draft a resolution in committee and vote on it in a general meeting in time to submit it, as I had anticipated would be the case, as part of the environmental review. Happily, however, the current outcome was in our favor. Yet, if we had been caught unaware, with no preparation, no organization, and only a month's notice to respond (SEQR specifies only 20 days), the result, I fear, may well have been quite different: a Negative Declaration, with no SEQR requirement or provision for public input or further review at that point, mining permits promptly issued, and gravel and concrete-mixer trucks rumbling from our neighborhood. Had that occurred, any challenge to overturn DEC decisions and permits would have been outside of the SEQR process and would have required us to file an Article 78 proceeding through the New York State Supreme Court, a potentially expensive civil lawsuit, probably much harder to win against an already approved project, a prospect I wasn't prepared to think about.

Alone, I couldn't have achieved what we did. Nearly a year had passed since I first learned of the gravel plans, nearly a year since I started searching for support, and began recruiting and building our coalition, a group whose collective input, now, had become a force to be reckoned with. My hope was that our powerful, coordinated response would discourage B.R. DeWitt from preparing an impact statement, that they would look for their gravel elsewhere, and that landowner Alfred Eddy would not persist with plans unwelcome in our neighborhood. But time, as we would learn, would bring unwelcome new confrontations, each requiring renewed input, each demanding our response, each heading the wrong way if unopposed.

The scheduled Town of Dryden public hearing wasn't necessary and didn't happen, and we waited for the applicant's next move.

August 28, 1987. The Ithaca Journal, headline newspaper account:

> DeWitt Cement Co. Plans Plant in Dryden. The $1 million gravel mining project could be operational by the spring. [DEC's Patrick Snyder was reported as saying:] "The next step is for the company to submit a draft environmental impact statement," [and Doug Hicks, B.R. DeWitt's vice president said:] "...the company would like to have the paperwork complete in time to begin mining on the 110-acre plot in the spring."

Nearing summer's end in our home, in a woodland clearing on a kame, Gwen and I, with continued uncertainty in the air, were about to begin our second year at Malloryville Bog.

Coalition

Yellow Birch (*Betula alleghaniensis*) in winter

6 TRUST

Let us leave a splendid legacy for our children...
let us turn to them and say, this you inherit: guard it well,
for it is far more precious than money... and once destroyed,
nature's beauty cannot be repurchased at any price.
— Ansel Adams

CCESS TO OUR new home was through a long, tree-
sheltered gravel driveway, gracefully curved and gently
sloped. Yet the driveway, in fact, belonged to the adjacent punchbowl farm property. Use of the driveway was guar-
anteed through a legally binding right-of-way written into our
deed, but I wanted to own, to hold title to, the driveway as
well. I was starting to learn, then, about the intricacies of property transactions and the occasional foibles of lawyers.

The owner of the punchbowl and driveway was my older
brother, Ron (with his wife Carol), who had been in partner-
ship with and acquired the farm from our dad. He generously
agreed to the property transfer, and I arranged for a survey to
separate the driveway parcel from the old pastureland. Then,
through our local bank, Gwen and I obtained a mortgage for
our house, land and driveway. At the closing, the bank's attorney, pompous and impatient with my desire to scan quickly
through his written description of our properties, insisted eve-

rything was just fine and rushed us to apply our signatures. At home, reading the details, I was fascinated to find that the mortgage we had obtained applied to the driveway only, not to the house or land. In his rush, he had gotten it quite wrong. In good faith, however, I took it to the bank's vice president, Bob Porteus, who cleared it up and, acknowledging with humor the lawyer's shortcomings, thanked us kindly in a letter. Instead, I suppose we could have defaulted on the driveway mortgage, kept the house with 36 acres, our wetlands and all, and owing nothing, lived here debt free. Well, tempting as that may have been, we didn't do it.

Exploring our property lines, scrambling up hill and down, through dense thickets and windfall-tree-root tangled swamps, I was enjoying my search for long-overgrown surveyor's stakes and rusted pipes, and clues from ancient, abandoned fence lines. As a new rural landowner, I discovered the challenges of trying to follow irregular and unlikely property lines. We were newly in possession of a truly wonderful property, but a property contained within a complicated, irregular boundary, a boundary line of multiple corners, odd angles, and long and short segments, some with ambiguous, ill-documented histories.

I frequented the offices of the county clerk and tax assessor searching for and copying deeds and maps, and found myself immersed in legal documents of land transactions and maps of tax parcels of mine and my neighbors, and fat abstracts-of-title with dozens of property descriptions, names and dates, recording the histories of ownership. Outside, on the land, I was puzzling over deed descriptions such as the southwest corner of Revolutionary War "Lot No. 8" and "nine feet north of an elm tree 24 inches in diameter..." and measures like "27 chains and 2 links east..." on deeds written generations before the modern electronic precision of GPS units and orbiting satellites far above the earth.

I found that often the old property lines did not follow the natural contours of the land or respect the boundaries of ecological communities. In two small places on my newly acquired land, parcels of two neighbors projected into mine in ways that I wished could be changed. One extended to my side of the top of the large esker near my driveway, and the other cut out a triangular wedge, entirely over the esker and into my South Swamp, right into the vernal pool, Wood Frog breeding site. A third piece belonging to me and extending adjacent to a neighbor's driveway was unimportant to me, and I would be happy to give it up. I was thinking long term, knowing that with future neighbors may come unhelpful ideas about use of the land. I wanted to assure as much protection as possible for the esker and wetlands, even while also defending against a gravel mine.

Familiar with the deed descriptions and survey maps, and trying to be creative, I played with property lines on paper and developed a plan: lines could be redrawn, whereby several fragments of acres would be exchanged between parcels. In the fall, I approached those two neighbors sharing our irregular property lines, both friendly, with a proposal that could benefit each of us at little cost. By swapping four odd-shaped fragments of our parcels among the three of us, each of our properties could be enhanced and rounded out in pleasing ways. To the first neighbor, I proposed to contribute a piece of my land, the piece I didn't need, that would greatly benefit the driveway end of their property if they, in exchange, would be willing to give up two smaller pieces: the first, to me, the triangle wedge cutting into the esker and swamp, and the second to the other neighbor, a piece jutting into that neighbor's property. To the second neighbor, I proposed that they accept the piece from the first neighbor, thereby gaining a neater, straighter property line, if they would be willing, in turn, to give to me their piece extending slightly over the top of the esker by my driveway.

The plan needed each of us to say, "Yes," and would fall apart if any one of us said, "No thanks." Both neighbors liked my idea and, together, we agreed to proceed. As a result, my neighbors were happy, and I was able to safeguard the swamp and my stretch of the esker, little knowing then, in 1988, that those land swaps would be important to the integrity of a new nature preserve, still years in the future. And, without transfer of dollars between neighbors, only the surveyors and attorneys received monetary compensation from our amicable land deal.

Gerry Smith, Land Steward of the Central New York Chapter of The Nature Conservancy, was the sole employee of the chapter at the time I joined the Conservancy's board in 1987. An ardent and outspoken conservationist, he worked half-time out of his home office for the Conservancy and half-time, as an expert birder, for the Onondaga Audubon Society of Syracuse where he tallied the impressive, concentrated migration of hawks at Derby Hill Bird Observatory on the southern shore of Lake Ontario. Within the national scope of The Nature Conservancy, New York State is unique in having several chapters, at the time seven dividing up the state, in addition to a statewide NY chapter office. Historically, multiple chapters were established because New York is the state in which the organization was founded, in 1951, with Mianus River Gorge as its first preserve, an hour's drive north of New York City. Our Central New York Chapter was large, encompassing 19 counties in a broad swath from the St. Lawrence River and Lake Ontario in the north to the Pennsylvania border in the south, was supported by nearly 4,000 chapter members, and was very active, protecting twenty preserves with more projects always in the works.

Officially, the Conservancy's "…Boards of Trustees advise chapters on strategic issues, assist in setting goals and, importantly, subject the chapter's work to additional critical thinking." Yet, at our Central New York Chapter, with a paid staff of just one very dedicated person, board members, in fact, together with Gerry, did all of the work of both staff and board. The work was exciting and challenging, and we were intimately involved in every aspect of our chapter's activities.

With my congenial board-member colleagues, heavy with scientists from Cornell, Ithaca College, SUNY Cortland, SUNY College of Environmental Science and Forestry in Syracuse (SUNY-ESF) and more, as well as nonacademic conservationists, all volunteers, we mutually shared and reinforced our dedication to conserving nature. In board meetings, on site visits with the Project Review Committee and on many happy outings in the field monitoring and posting preserve boundaries with Gerry Smith and my fellow members of the Stewardship Committee, I felt privileged to be working with a remarkably successful organization, professional and scientifically based, with the clearly-stated mission: "to preserve the plants, animals and natural communities that represent the diversity of life on earth by protecting the lands and waters they need to survive." And early on, on a Chapter field trip, Robert Wesley and I introduced an enthusiastic small group of board members and supporters to Malloryville's diversity and wonders as well as to its looming challenge. I was seeking their understanding that the site was worthy of our defense and their support, that the unresolved threat, while off-putting and scary, did not, and should not, render the place a lost cause.

Then, a year or so after I joined the Conservancy board, growth and reorganization would bring important changes. An Executive Director was hired to oversee the operation of both our Chapter and the Western New York Chapter, to operate from a new Conservancy office in Rochester. Wayne Klockner became our first full-time employee, with more employees to follow, and, not long after, the two chapters officially merged, becoming the new Central & Western New York Chapter, covering half of the entire state. And almost immediately, Wayne would become a key player in our efforts next to my home.

In January of 1976, Craig Tufts, then a graduate student at Cornell, completed his Master of Science thesis, titled, "A Preliminary Inventory of Some Unique Natural Areas in Tomkins County, New York." With guidance and inspiration from Cornell Professors Richard Fischer, Larry Hamilton, Peter Marks and Robert Clausen, nearly a century of publications of Cornell naturalist scientists, field help from Robert Wesley, and the full cooperation of a young Tompkins County Environmental

Management Council, Craig selected, inventoried, and wrote up data summaries for 84 sites, concluding with a review of strategies for natural areas conservation in the County, recommending establishment of a "county-wide conservancy group," like a local land trust, "to monitor, acquire, preserve, and coordinate use of the natural areas." And he wrote:

> This thesis is dedicated to the hope that 100 years from now, both the spirits of the great naturalists of Cornell's past, and the children of today's children's children may still find the beauty, knowledge, and satisfaction that I have experienced among the Tompkins County woodlands, glens, swamps, and meadows in this year 1975.

I made a copy of Craig's dissertation to learn more details of the area, including Malloryville Bog of which he wrote (tersely):

> Of four acid bogs in county, this one most diverse, least disturbed. Known for almost 100 years to local botanists. Geology classes visit esker. Suggested by many people.

And I enjoyed many outings exploring the diversity of nearby familiar and unfamiliar wild places. Appreciating Craig's desire to find ways to protect such places, I was excited to learn of the EMC's plan to work towards a major update and expansion of his Inventory, and to make official the County's designation of Unique Natural Areas (UNAs). In 1987, I was eager to join in that effort.

Botanist Robert Wesley and Nancy Ostman of Cornell Plantations, through the County Planning Department, had been hired to work closely with our EMC's Unique Natural Areas Committee to select sites and to do on-the-ground surveys of known and candidate sites to inventory their natural features. Environmental qualities our committee chose to use as criteria for UNA designation included these categories:

1. Important natural communities (state-designated wetlands, old forests, scarce or rare community types, diverse plant and animal populations, wilderness character)
2. Quality of example (best representatives of natural communities or resources in the county)
3. Rare or scarce plants or animals (identified at the global, state, or local level)
4. Geological importance (unique formation or paleontological site)
5. Cultural significance (outstanding scenic beauty, historic or archeological significance, recreational values)

And within the report for each UNA, data would be organized under these headings:

- Map of the UNA
- Site Name and Code
- Location (municipality, latitude and longitude, USGS topographic quad and tax parcels)
- Site and Vegetation Descriptions (general characteristics)
- Reasons for Selection (Why is this a UNA?)
- Special Land-use Information (land-use or legal designations, water resources information)
- Conservation Information (adjacent land use, sensitivity of site to visitors, evidence of disturbance, management)
- Physical characteristics of the Site (slope, elevation, soil types, geological features)
- Biological Characteristics of the Site (ecological communities, plant and animal species present)

For each site we needed to request permission from private landowners for Robert and Nancy to enter their land. But, to do that, first we had to determine the names and addresses of the owners, often multiple owners of each area, using USGS topographic maps together with tedious study of tax maps at the County Assessment Office. With areas and identified owners divided up among our few committee members, we then called owners to arrange meetings with them, usually at their homes, to explain the purpose of our project, to share what we thought was special about their land, to make clear to them that UNA designation does not open private land for public entry, that it's not a regulatory designation, and does not provide legal protection for an area, and, finally, to ask for their okay for Robert and Nancy to walk their land. For that, we needed their signature on a County permission letter, a letter that also freed the owner from any liability.

At kitchen tables and dairy-farm milk houses and stables, I talked with many rural landowners, most of whom were agreeable and interested in knowing more about the property they owned. Some, however, were concerned that any confirmation of scarce or rare species would unfairly restrict future use of their land, and a few took our meeting as an opportunity to vent nonstop, sometimes for an hour, their anger and frustrations with regulations, taxes and government in general. Yet, by listening with patience and nodding in agreement where I could, I was able to obtain the willing cooperation and signed permission letter from each landowner that I met.

Of course, our goal was to record as much as we could about as many as possible of Tompkins County's best remaining natural areas. Our hope was to encourage owners to appreciate and be good stewards of the natural portions of their land. But further, as worded in the Tompkins County UNA brochure, to be produced later, the inventory ought to, "...help people make informed choices about development in or near these areas." And for municipal boards, "The UNA inventory is another piece of information that should be included in responsible land-use decision making," and "The report is also tailored to help people prepare State Environmental Quality Review (SEQR) forms," like the Environmental Assessment Form (EAF), either the short or long version, required at the start of each project review.

After three years filled with dozens of committee meetings, countless hours of work, and the facilities and help of the County Planning Department we assembled thick loose-leaf binders, each nearly 800-printed pages, containing reports on 180 UNAs. Those binders would be distributed, in 1990, one each to area libraries, to the DEC and to our municipal governments, with a committee member presenting and introducing the Inventory to governing boards in each of the County's nine towns, six incorporated villages and the City of Ithaca. We hoped to persuade decision-makers to refer always to the UNA Inventory as standard practice in every environmental review.

Then, a decade later, after more site surveys by Robert and Nancy and lots more committee work we completed a significant update, in 2000, greatly helped with the excellent support of Katie Borgella, staff member of the County Planning Department. Katie, earlier had been instrumental in recruiting the Planning Commissioner's support for our continuing fight, in writing a letter to the DEC as we were defending against a third gravel mine application. In our updated UNA Inventory, this time we introduced two major improvements: incorporation of UNA boundaries into the County's GIS mapping system, and all data were entered into a relational computer database, making site data much more easily updated, searchable and retrievable.

Much earlier we had promised to notify each landowner of the results of the survey on their land, yet that, over my objection, had not been done, as some County personnel were concerned about a possible negative response. But the EMC Education Committee did just that, and they set up a telephone hotline to receive responses. Then, in the fall of 2000, having recently relinquished my EMC seat after thirteen years on Council, I received a letter from EMC members Steve Nicholson and Susan Brock:

> Dear Bob, We wanted to update you as well as thank you personally for helping... at our Unique Natural Area letter stuffing party on July 18,

2000. The Unique Natural Areas landowner notification process has been an unqualified success.

With much appreciated help, we sent out 2600 letters, to approximately 8% of the households in Tompkins County. The responses have been gratifying. So far, the UNA notification has stimulated offers by several landowners who have considered donating a total of over one hundred acres to the Finger Lakes Land Trust or to the Cornell Plantations for permanent conservation. Nearly all the calls we received on the hotline were positive, and the majority of UNA landowners seemed thrilled to learn that they own part of one of the special natural places in our county...

The Unique Natural Areas 2000 Project, including the landowner notification mailing, has been entered in the New York State Association of Environmental Management Council's Project of the Year contest. We will keep you posted.

Sincerely, Stephen C. Nicholson, Chair, Education Committee; Susan H. Brock, Chair, Tompkins County EMC

The Unique Natural Areas 2000 Project was honored, that fall, with the top award as the statewide Project of the Year, earning first prize just as our first edition, the 1990 Unique Natural Areas Inventory, had in the same contest, ten years earlier.

One memorable evening in autumn of 1988 after a monthly EMC meeting in Ithaca, an energetic, confident young man named Andy Zepp, a guest at that meeting, introduced himself to me and explained that he was contacting people who might be interested in starting a local land trust. After working for The Nature Conservancy in Connecticut, Andy was back in Ithaca, two years after completing his undergraduate studies at

Cornell, to pursue a masters degree in Cornell's Department of Natural Resources, with creation of a land trust as his thesis. We had no local land trust and the notion to actually start one was new to us, but it sounded like a great idea. I said, "Count me in."

Local land trusts, at the time, were beginning to be welcomed in a wave of establishment across the country. Like The Nature Conservancy as the model, the granddaddy, national-scale land trust, local land trusts, in their noble goal of protecting land and nature, were working effectively with landowners, local governments, government agencies and businesses in facilitating diverse property transactions and making land-saving deals important to local communities, frequently on a scale smaller but more numerous than would be possible for a national organization. Through legally binding arrangements with a land trust, landowners, caring deeply about the natural qualities of their land and realizing that future owners may feel otherwise, are able to achieve land protection in perpetuity. Confidence and trust among the participants, clearly, are major ingredients in land trust success.

After our first meeting, on November 21, 1988, the group of thirty-some narrowed itself down to become the eighteen enthusiastic founding board members of a new phenomenon in our area, and we got right to work. We had to decide how big a territory we hoped to cover—a county, a lake's watershed, a region of the state—and what to call ourselves. With lively debate, we bravely chose to think large and settled on our name as the Finger Lakes Land Trust.

With Andy's superb guidance, we wrote a charter and by-laws and applied for New York State incorporation and federal 501(c)(3) charitable organization, non-profit tax status. We elected officers and chose as our first president, plant physiologist A. Carl Leopold, son of environmental pioneer Aldo Leopold. As an all-volunteer organization, we chose a logo, set up membership levels, designed and wrote brochures, created a letterhead, wrote press releases for the news media, met with other organizations and local government agencies, and started a quarterly newsletter. We began recruiting members, started setting priorities and criteria for projects, and met with landowners to talk about conservation and to suggest that we work together to protect their lands.

But, we had a lot to learn about the array of methods land trusts use in achieving their aims and meeting the desires of landowners. We devoured publications of the Land Trust Alliance, the national umbrella organization, including their *Conservation Easement Handbook* and their professional magazine, *Exchange*, both full of ideas and examples. We learned about the mechanics of land transactions and the tax consequences for landowners of donations and bargain sales of land to the Land Trust. With a clear agreement with the donor, some properties would be maintained as nature preserves and others, as tradelands, could be sold to raise money for other projects.

And we learned about the conservation easement as a major tool in land preservation wherein the landowner would maintain title, and could sell the land in the future, but certain development rights, individually determined for each property, would be transferred in a legally-binding deed to the Land Trust, either as a donation or a sale. By the Land Trust's agreement not to exercise those development rights, and to monitor the land into the future, the conservation values of the land would be preserved, while the current and future owners could continue using the land as agreed.

For landowners who cared deeply about their properties and who wanted to maintain title and the right to future transfer of ownership, the conservation easement provided an ideal arrangement. A little over a year after our first meeting, Betsy Darlington, one of our most devoted and hard-working founding board members, and her husband Dick, donated our first conservation easement protecting the natural features while allowing continued use of agricultural fields on their 225-acre country property south of Ithaca. Soon after, two other environmental advocates and Land Trust supporters, Katy Payne and Nancy Gabriel, donated conservation easements on their two properties near Ithaca.

In about 2 1/2 years we felt ready to hire a staff person, an executive director. As my gainful employment was in transition, I gave serious consideration to offering my application to my fellow board members. Having worked intensively with the group since the beginning, I felt reasonably qualified for the position. In deciding to proceed, I presented my qualifications, including my training in field biology, teaching experience, computer knowledge, board membership with The Nature Conservancy, my work with the County EMC's Unique Natural Areas Inventory, and my recent experience with land transactions at home. And also, I felt I had excellent rapport with the variety of people the Land Trust deals with, including potential benefactors and suburban and rural landowners, and I already knew a sizable number of those people. And having grown up on a leading Tompkins County dairy farm, I understood working landowners' perspectives and I felt they could relate to me.

I was hired, and instantly became the employee of my former board-member colleagues, perhaps, as it turned out, not the most desirable situation. But, as a labor of love with a fledgling organization on a shoestring budget, I then, for nearly two years, experienced working as the Finger Lakes Land Trust's first Executive Director, from my home, without an office, on minimal salary, and without paid benefits. We were on a mission together, but as a professional organization we were still just beginning.

Our first nature preserves were acquired quickly. We accepted donations of three small parcels of land, each with valuable natural features, from three generous owners, and agreed to keep all as nature preserves. With our volunteer attorney we were learning more about land transactions, and we held public gatherings to celebrate our successes.

Then a dear person and strong supporter of our work, who wished to remain anonymous, donated to us a 67-acre forested property on Mt. Pleasant, east of Ithaca, to keep or to protect and sell as we chose, as a tradeland. We decided to sell the land after dividing it into two portions and placing conservation easements on each, allowing up to two houses on one, and no buildings on the other. A neighbor had expressed interest in the smaller portion next to his home. My task was to market the larger property and negotiate the sales. Our first attempt, working with a realtor who was unhelpful and wanted his full commission, was unsuccessful after several months. Next, Alton Reed, a realtor and supporter of our work, freely donated his efforts in finding our buyer. I then met to negotiate price with our new potential buyer and separately with the neighbor. Reporting back to the board, I was pleased to communicate that my meetings were congenial and that we had obtained signed agreements for our full asking price on each parcel. The money raised from land donated by our anonymous and generous benefactor was the first truly significant addition to our small bank account.

In the beginning, Andy Zepp had worked with the Land Trust for about nine months before completing his graduate work and accepting employment, again with The Nature Conservancy, this time with Executive Director Wayne Klockner at the still new Central & Western New York Chapter office in Rochester. When Wayne had asked for my recommendation, as a Conservancy board member, I had expressed enthusiastic support for Andy's hiring. There, at his new Conservancy job as Director of Land Protection, Andy's work, together with Wayne's, as we shall see, would be important in Malloryville's future.

But only a few months into our new Finger Lakes Land Trust organization, before I had been hired as Executive Director, Andy had asked me to join him for a restaurant luncheon with the owner of land that we all enthusiastically agreed was a top priority, Andy's and my first choice, for protection. Close to and in view from the southern Route 13, Cayuga Inlet valley, entrance to Ithaca, the land is 127 acres of undeveloped hillside forest, steep at the bottom, more gentle near a small road at the top, including a segment of the Finger Lakes Trail and a pristine, secluded rock-walled gorge containing shear cliffs and waterfalls, one, a 140-foot drop in a spectacular amphitheater. The gorge and creek are known as Lick Brook and the owners were Moss Sweedler, a professor of mathematics at Cornell, and his wife Kristin.

As I had met and talked with Moss several years earlier, I was aware of his hopes for his property at that time. He loved the land, but was candid in expressing his desire to sell it for a handsome profit enabling him to "get enough for it to change our lifestyle" and maybe retire to a nice place, "like Hawaii." Later, as I will soon explain, I came to know Moss quite well, and he, since, has agreed to forgive me for sharing details of our times together as I describe a significant and memorable land transaction.

On July 26, 1989, Andy and I met with Moss and had a pleasant conversation over lunch at a quality, small restaurant called Danny's Place. We talked about our new land trust, and Moss listened while Andy presented our interest in finding a way to achieve permanent protection for his wonderful wild land and gorge so close to Ithaca. And Andy asked Moss if he would consider working with the Land Trust towards that goal. As usual, Moss was direct in his answer: He thanked us, but made it clear that our ideas were "not in my plan." We parted with the agreement that if he should reconsider and wish to talk with the Land Trust at any time, we would be happy to meet with him. He gave no encouragement that he would.

Two years passed. I was newly employed as Executive Director when Moss contacted us with an offer. Interesting and quirky, as he was known to be, Moss proposed an unlikely deal. He and Kristin wanted a secluded pond, close to Ithaca, for swimming and outings for themselves and their friends. Moss said if we could find and purchase a pond for him, that he liked and approved, the Land Trust could have Lick Brook. But, he stipulated that the pond must be very close to town, very private, and that it not be west, through Ithaca's infamous tangled intersections then known as the "Octopus," an aggravating hold-up at rush hour.

We were elated with Moss' renewed contact. But this was

definitely offbeat, and it would prove to be a most unusual undertaking for a land trust. It certainly would be easier for us if Moss, on his own, first found his pond, and we then arranged to buy it for him, but he wanted us to do all the work. Meanwhile, some board members suspected he was playing a game with us, pulling our leg, and that he would not follow through. But clearly, we wanted Lick Brook, and I didn't want, in any way, to dissuade Moss. It was a tenuous situation and, on this one, he was calling the shots.

Among my many other tasks as employee, I then took on the job of locating ponds for Moss' inspection. Studying maps and photographs, driving the roads, and talking with our board members, realtors, landowners and many others, I visited ponds that might be suitable and potentially available for purchase. I ruled out many and arranged for Moss and me to visit each of those that I thought surely he would love.

Saturdays were usually the days Moss was available. Whenever I had another pond, weather permitting, I called him and set a time to meet at his downtown Ithaca house. There, his two very large, very friendly dogs, Boo and Tigger, would greet me, their new friend, with excited anticipation, ready for a happy romp and swim in yet another pond. We all piled into Moss' minivan and each time, before starting, he reset his dashboard odometer to zero and started his stopwatch. When we arrived at our pond, following my directions, Moss immediately read his stopwatch and odometer and, each time, without fail, I learned that it was too far, that the miles, time or usually both, by a mile or a minute or two, exceeded his criteria. Nevertheless, we invariably had a pleasant walk around a beautiful pond, ones that I would have loved to own myself, while Moss threw sticks for his joyously happy, bounding and swimming dogs to retrieve.

Our outings were always enjoyable, I was having fun, and Moss and I were getting along just fine. But, a lot of time was going by. The warm seasons of two years had nearly passed, I had lost count of the number of ponds visited, and we still hadn't found the right one. The board members were becoming more impatient with me, their only employee, and I felt their pressure. Was this becoming a waste of precious Land Trust time that might better be focused on our overflowing plate of many other projects and activities? It wasn't that I was slacking on doing all those other things. I was, in fact, working overtime on multiple fronts. But relations were becoming strained. And each time I deposited my paycheck, I was acutely aware that I was draining money from our uncomfortably small bank account, dollars donated in part by my former colleagues, board members with whom I had previously been a volunteer, all of us working together without pay. From some, I sensed resentment. The transition was problematic. But I needed to remind myself, and should have reminded others, that it was I who had given up other work opportunities, other income, for this job, and I had bills and a mortgage to pay. My home and land was not a freebie.

Relations between a few board members and myself were becoming difficult and stressful. What could have been helpful and used for guidance, at the time, was the not yet available, soon to be published, *Land Trust Standards and Practices*, by the Land Trust Alliance, which would contain exceedingly helpful guidelines for proper professional roles and interactions of board and staff members in a successful organization. In our young land trust, with an inexperienced board and a first executive director, our roles were thoroughly tangled. And my new responsibilities as employee came devoid of clearly defined delegation of authority from the board to me.

My concerns about some issues were deemed, by key board members, as bothersome unnecessary details without need of clarification, even though they were vitally important to me and to the nature of my job. Questions remained unanswered. I knew something of organizational structure and the importance of clear understandings, but, to some, I was seen as out of step, or my questions, self-serving. The meaning of my job as Executive Director differed among board members, and I realized, of course, that I had been naive in accepting employment without a more clearly defined job description. Responsibility without authority was becoming unhealthy for me and for our organization. Although the situation was unsettling, unfair and misunderstood, we were still, in fact, all working together for a greater cause, and I was not a whiner, generally choosing not to complain. But we were clearly ill at ease and tensions were mounting.

Meanwhile, Moss was not in a rush to select a pond. But I knew him, and I thought any pressure from the board or me would kill the deal. I knew that, in a flash, the marvelous Lick Brook property could be lost to development. My intuition told me this can still work. While there was a chance, I was not giving up. The prize was not just ordinary, it was a gem of nature deserving protection and preservation for its own sake as well as for the enjoyment of all who appreciate undeveloped wildness. It was, after all, Ithaca's treasured Lick Brook.

Then our pro-bono legal counselor, Judy Rossiter, gave me a lead to a farm pond owned by a client of one of her colleagues. It seemed unlikely. It was west through the Octopus, a bit too distant, and, though among trees, was adjacent to a new housing development. Neither direction, nor distance, nor locale fit Moss' criteria. I checked it out nevertheless, thought it nice, but improbable, a long shot, and showed it to Moss. As usual, when we pulled up at the site, his odometer and stopwatch said "too far." I hadn't expected otherwise. We walked around the pond, talked, and played with Boo and Tigger. It was a pleasant day, warm and clear, and we were enjoying our outing. Then, as we approached the van, about to leave, Moss said, "I like it!" My heart leaped! Wow! In almost two years, this was a first! He said he wanted to show it to Kristin. He did, and in short order, with her approval, he told me, "Yes, this is it."

The pond was part of a farm from which the parcels in the nearby housing development had been sold. When I talked with the owner, he agreed to sell the pond, which would need subdivision approval, but made it clear that he would have no further contact with the Town of Ithaca government with whom he had angrily fought in earlier deals. I then became his agent, a new experience for me, in navigating through the subdivision process, and I found the Town entirely helpful, even enthusiastic, considering the pond's connection with protecting Lick Brook. And as part of the pond deal, I hired and worked with a surveyor to map the new property line Moss and I had marked out, ensuring adequate acreage and a comfortable buffer for his and Kristin's needs, obtained a market-value appraisal, and negotiated the price with the owner.

To simplify the property transactions, the Land Trust then bought the Lick Brook tract from Moss and Kristin as a bargain sale at one-third of its appraised market value, the exchanged dollars equaling the full price of the pond. They, then, purchased their new pond directly from the farmer. Thus, the Sweedlers had made a generous charitable donation to the Land Trust of two-thirds of Lick Brook's value and could claim the appropriate tax benefits.

The board, Moss and I were happy with the conclusion to a very long, but ultimately successful undertaking. In his willingness to reconsider his options, in his words, "to do something worthwhile with the property," Moss and Kristin had made possible the permanent protection of a wonderful and unspoiled jewel of New York's Finger Lakes Region, the "Sweedler Preserve at Lick Brook." Patience and perseverance had paid off for the Land Trust's biggest success to date.

But as the Lick Brook deal was nearing its conclusion, the growing pains and tensions of our young organization remaining unresolved, I had quietly, without rancor, resigned as Executive Director. On October 20, 1992, in our story's Year 7, while confronting a third gravel mine application, I wrote a memo confirming my spoken announcement:

> Please excuse my brevity, here, in explaining my decision, but understand that I have put a great deal of thought into it. Suffice it to say that frustrations due both to the nature of the job and to its impact on my personal life and family have prompted my decision. My support for the mission of the organization is undiminished.... Both

the Land Trust and I need a change at this point. It is my hope that the Board will take this as a welcome opportunity to discuss, analyze and come together on important decisions about future directions and growth of the Land Trust, including the future role of staff in the organization. Bob

I was proud to have helped create, from the beginning, an altruistic environmental organization on an honorable, truly worthwhile mission. With bittersweet emotions, I was leaving the Finger Lakes Land Trust, but felt satisfied with my work.

Several months later, I received from Moss Sweedler a copy of a letter, dated April 24, 1993, he had just sent to the Land Trust Board:

Dear Board Members: Over the years I've been involved in a number of land deals and have learned by experience the qualities necessary for a potential transaction to reach a happy conclusion. The transfer of my Lick Brook property to the Land Trust was a complex transaction, involving diverse personalities and stretching over a long period of time. I'd like to record Bob Beck's key role in making it happen.

The search for a suitable pond, and subsequent negotiation required many skills, unusually many to find in one person. Over the long haul I've seen and been impressed by Bob's ability to work with a wide range of people; commitment to the goals of the Finger Lakes Land Trust; gentle and generous manner with people; firmness when required; general negotiating skills; patience; sense of humor; stamina and tact.

Given all the twists and turns which occurred, it is a minor miracle we were able to reach the sought after goal. I believe that miracle is named Bob Beck. As an indication of Kris and

my appreciation for Bob's role, we refer to our
new pond as Beck Pond.
    Sincerely, Moss

Reading Moss' wonderfully kind words helped to lift my
spirits, to fortify my strength and to renew my resolve in dealing with the simultaneous, ongoing challenges we continued to
face and couldn't ignore, in defending our diverse wetlands and
my home. And some years later, when he was ready to retire
from Cornell, Moss phoned me to say that he was about to sell
his pond before moving away. He wanted assurance that it was
okay with me. I assured him it was.

Cinnamon Fern (*Osmunda cinnamomea*)

7 RERUN

Individual commitment to a group effort
—that is what makes a team work, a company work,
a society work, a civilization work.

— Vince Lombardi

RUCK TRACKS IN the grassy vegetation approached the top of a steep slope leading down to an arm of the wetland. There, two tank-truck loads of septage—pumpings from rural residential septic tanks—had been dumped over the bank, and tons of the waste had flowed down the slope. That was before we had moved into our new home. It was a sunny day in August, 1986, twelve days before closing. I had been walking on the neighboring property, near the old gravel pits, when I noticed the wheel tracks and followed them to the edge of the slope. I was aware of use of that property, with county approval, for disposal of septage, though I certainly wasn't pleased with the operation that close to home. But dumping over a bank into a wetland was illegal and not okay. I was, in fact, disgusted and angry. Illegal dumping into a wetland couldn't be allowed to continue. I was determined that it be dealt with and stopped immediately.

I called the office of our Tompkins County Environmental Health Division and talked with Carl Burgess, Public Health

Sanitarian, who agreed to inspect the site. He did, and talked with the truck driver who worked pumping septic tanks and transporting truckloads, in a 1500-gallon tank truck, for the permitted operator, Paolangeli Contractor, Inc. of Ithaca. The driver, not surprisingly, denied knowledge of any illegal dumping.

The new Ithaca Area Wastewater Treatment Plant, the sewer plant under construction, was not yet accepting waste from residential septic tanks (tanks not hooked up to a municipal sewer system, and which may benefit by being pumped, perhaps once every few years) and the County needed places to dispose of that septage. Alfred Eddy made his land available, and Francis Paolangeli acquired a permit from Tompkins County (the DEC had delegated authority to the County for septage disposal) with strict requirements on precisely where and how to dispose of the waste. The rules were to spread the material in thin layers, like farm manure, on a specific few designated acres where it would quickly decompose, or to store it temporarily in a dug lagoon only when snow and frozen ground or heavy rain prevented spreading, and to pump the lagoon empty and spread the septage as soon as weather permitted. The septage was not to stay in the unlined lagoon, nor was the lagoon to be filled higher than two feet from the top, because leaching of the concentrated material into the ground would risk contamination of groundwater.

While outright illegal dumping, as into a wetland, did not recur, more often than not when I checked over the next six months, I found the lagoon full, or only inches from the top, and frequently overflowing the earthen dike on the lower side, in violation of permit rules, the same conditions which neighbors before me also had reported many times with little or no effect. But early on, the alarming prospect of a gravel mine and concrete plant on the same land had demanded most of my attention, and my energies were focused more on defeating that project before it got started, gathering support in our first fall and winter in expectation of an application for a mining permit.

Still, when I learned that Paolangeli Contractor's Tompkins County septage permit was up for renewal in March, I wrote to John Andersson, Director of Environmental Health, Carl Burgess' boss, expressing my concerns about potential groundwater pollution and the proximity of sensitive wetlands downslope from the lagoon and spreading field. I requested, at minimum, the lagoon be emptied and that spreading not continue on the area closest to my wetlands. On March 10, 1987, nevertheless, the County Board of Health, apparently thankful for available land and a willing septage hauler, voted to renew the permit.

Then, on June 26, 1987, dated the same day as B.R. DeWitt's mining application, landowner Alfred Eddy wrote his letter to Al Coburn at DEC, stating that he was discontinuing septage disposal. He said:

> Dear Sir: Please be advised by copy of this letter, that I wish to discontinue my permit to discharge septage in the lagoon located on my property at W. Malloryville Road, Dryden, NY.... It should also be noted that any residual material will be cleaned up and disposed of in a sewage disposal facility.... This is being done in an effort to facilitate the issuance of a Mined Land Reclamation permit on this property [a New York State mining permit].
>   Very truly yours, Alfred Eddy

But despite Mr. Eddy's definitive statement, septage disposal continued as usual throughout that summer, fall and winter, the lagoon frequently remaining illegally full and overflowing.

Year 2: 1987-88

Meanwhile, I was angry that neither the DEC nor the County were enforcing their own rules about temporary use of the lagoon. As a member, now, of the County Environmental Management Council, I presented the continuing problem to the group a year after the Board of Health had renewed the permit despite my objection. On March 15, 1988, the EMC voted on and passed a resolution strongly urging closure of the septage lagoon and spreading operation, and Herb Engman, EMC Chair, wrote a powerful cover letter directed to the Board of Health, with copies to the County Board of Legislators and to Brad Griffin at DEC, stating in his concluding paragraph:

> In evaluating the potential for damage from septage at this particular site, the especially narrow environmental tolerances of rare and uncommon plants must be considered. A species may be rare primarily because it survives only in a specific, narrow range of environmental conditions. Relatively small alterations of chemical conditions, including changes in pH, and addition of pollutants or nutrients can easily drive sensitive species to extinction. Such may well be the case at Malloryville Bog.
>
> Herbert Engman, Chairman

And together with the EMC resolution and his letter, Herb sent copies of Craig Tuft's descriptions of two of our Unique Natural Areas: "Malloryville Bogs, Marl Springs" and "North End Malloryville esker/Kames/Kettles/Swamp"

Happily this time, with strong urging from the EMC, the Board of Health chose not to renew the permit, but rather to issue a variance, to allow only emptying and closing the lagoon, by June 30.

I had reviewed the record of complaints, site inspections and citations at the County Environmental Health office. I made notes and counted 23 formal notices in five years, from Carl Burgess or John Andersson, and two from Kevin Hanifin, Solid Waste Management Specialist at the DEC, to Paolangeli Contractor for failure to empty the lagoon and for allowing it to remain filled and overflowing. The citations repeatedly threatened action, saying:

> You must discontinue use of the lagoon until it is cleaned and this department notified. The septage material must be landspread on approved areas.... If the material is not removed, action will be taken. This could include revocation of your permit to use the site and/or a fine...

Still, as far as I could determine, no actual enforcement was carried out or any fines levied. The violations simply continued as usual. On June 14, I met in person with the full Board of Health to reinforce our concern and to suggest again that final spreading of the lagoon contents be on the portion of the permitted area farthest from the wetlands. The Board agreed, and approved a variance to clear the lagoon and spread the contents, with no additional material brought in, with a further extension until July 30 to complete the closure.

Yet even then, nothing happened through July, August and into September. Non-compliance seemed forever to be the rule. I was both annoyed and exasperated, and wanting this to be completed and done I pressed for action by calling Kevin Hanifin at his DEC office in Syracuse: On September 19, 1988, he wrote to Paolangeli saying:

> Dear Mr. Paolangeli: This office has received information that work which was to be completed by July 30... has not even been started. This work must be completed within fifteen days from the receipt of this letter.... Failure to complete the work by the end of the time period may result in tickets being issued, and administrative action being taken....
>
> Very truly yours, Kevin B. Hanifin

It was then that the dike on the lower side of the lagoon was dug open, septage allowed to ooze out, and the remaining material covered with dirt and smoothed over. And that was it, septage was not spread as ordered, and neither the county nor the state issued any further citations. Two years and a month had passed since I first reported the illegal dumping into the wetland.

Year 3: 1988/89

B.R. DeWitt Company, apparently, was looking for gravel elsewhere. A year since Doug Hicks' quote in the Ithaca Journal, saying they would be mining by spring, the company hadn't prepared an impact statement. Time passed, and we didn't hear from them again. Gradually, I was beginning to feel a bit more comfortable that our team effort was paying off. Septage disposal had stopped, and it appeared we had turned away plans for a gravel mine and concrete plant. Perhaps, now, my neighboring landowner would be thinking of less intrusive uses of his land. And into my third year in our new home, I was becoming deeply engaged with the EMC's Unique Natural Areas Inventory project for the county, with The Nature Conservancy's Central New York Chapter board and its Stewardship Committee, and that November, we met, with Andy Zepp, for our very first organizational meeting in starting the new Finger Lakes Land Trust.

January 3, 1989. The Town of Dryden and the DEC received the first portion of paperwork for an application for a 20-year gravel mine from Francis Paolangeli, of Paolangeli Contractor, who had arranged to lease the land from Alfred Eddy, as had B.R. DeWitt two years earlier. Paolangeli was claiming that his application was for a renewal of Eddy's old mining permit and that all was in compliance with the Town's land-use plans and laws. Henry Slater, Zoning and Code Enforcement Officer of Dryden, responded in writing, forcefully, to Paolangeli saying Eddy's old permit was non-transferable and that a zoning change, enacted the previous year, would now require first obtaining a zoning variance.

January 13, 1989. Henry wrote:

> It has come to the attention of this office that you have applied to D.E.C. for a mining permit at

the former Alfred C. Eddy Gravel Pit Site on Malloryville Road in the Town of Dryden. At this time I would like to take this opportunity to inform you of the situation as I see it.

Since you are applying for this permit, I must inform you that, at this time in order for you to operate this pit, the only way you could would be by variance. There are several reasons why this would be the situation and are detailed below.

The previous permit was issued to Alfred C. Eddy. There were several conditions, which were attached to that permit. Among those, was item 10 which states that the permit is nontransferable. Secondly, this area of the town has undergone a zoning change. Previously this area was zoned R.C. which permitted this type of use. Since May 8th, 1988 it is zoned R.B.-1 which does not permit this use. I also believe that your D.E.C. Application is invalid. Item 24 of that application asks if a local [mining] permit is required. Since you have not applied, nor could you apply under current zoning, you may have a problem in obtaining this permit as well.

If you would desire to pursue this further, you may obtain a variance application from this office...

Sincerely, Henry M. Slater

And Henry sent copies to Eddy, to Jim Schug, Dryden's new Town Supervisor, to Mahlon Perkins, Town Attorney, and to DEC's Ray Nolan. At the same time, Al Coburn at DEC wrote that a new application, not a renewal, was required by the state since the old permit had expired several years earlier. I was pleased with the quick responses from Dryden and the DEC.

Well, now we knew that Mr. Eddy wasn't giving in, and that the same Mr. Paolangeli of septage noncompliance was now pursuing gravel, attempting shortcuts with inaccurate statements, apparently trying to deceive the DEC in his application. Mildly comforting to me, though, was the possibility that the applicant might trip himself up with his loose handling of facts. But Patrick Snyder had left the DEC to pursue a law degree, and Ray Nolan, now Sr. Environmental Analyst, would be in charge of the SEQR review. Earlier, in the B.R. DeWitt review, Ray, without explanation, had failed to show up for an appointment with me to walk the wetland edges for marking an expansion, a correction, of the DEC-mapped wetland boundary adjacent to the gravel property. I was disappointed to learn of Patrick's departure and was unsure of what to expect from Ray Nolan. But our Malloryville coalition, our team, suddenly had more work to do. We were about to participate in opposition to a second mining proposal, in a second round of SEQR proceedings.

Our Nature Conservancy chapter board hired Wayne Klockner as our first Executive Director, and he was setting up office in Rochester. Wayne and I had discussed past events here, and I urged him, right away, to visit the site. In a letter on January 13, 1989, I reviewed the situation and told him that a new mining application, the second in two years, was in the works. I ended my letter with these two paragraphs:

> My wife and I thoroughly enjoy owning and living at Malloryville Bog, and we remain steadfast in our determination to protect this gem of a natural area with its bog, swamps, fens, globeflowers and 16 or so species of orchids. We are concerned about continuing threats from the upslope neighboring property and realize at least a portion of that property is essential as a buffer in ensuring the long-term integrity of the wetland. Prompt action is desirable, but at the present time, we are unable to acquire it ourselves.
>
> We encourage you to pursue the idea of eventually creating a TNC [Conservancy] preserve of several hundred acres to include Malloryville Bog and the other nearby woodlands, swamps and

fens of this highly diverse and fascinating kame, kettle and esker landscape. While we choose not to sell or donate our property in the near future, we would like to explore other possibilities with you, if this is of interest to TNC...

Sincerely yours, Robert M. Beck

I had put in writing, cautiously, for the first time, my acknowledgement that true protection of the wetlands, necessitating, as it did, somehow gaining considerable control over the gravel property, which I could not do alone, would likely entail my letting go of some or all of my prized rights of land ownership, for me cherished, still fresh and exhilarating. That thought, of letting go, did not come easily to me.

February 24, 1989, 9:00 a.m. Wayne Klockner met me at my house where we talked in detail and then toured the property, around the wetlands, on the eskers, in the uplands, and on the adjacent gravel parcel. He had accepted his new job position after working for the Conservancy in Maryland, and was well qualified to evaluate a property for its natural features. I wanted to be sure that he fully understood the value and uniqueness of the land, that he would view it as worthy of a vigorous defense, that its richness in biodiversity was equal to the Conservancy's demanding scientific criteria, and that he could personally take a stand for its protection. I wanted him on our team. But I also was aware and concerned that directives from the national office to state chapters were beginning to shift the Conservancy's focus away from smaller sites, towards larger, landscape size, "megasite" protection projects, and Malloryville, I knew, would not measure up, size-wise, to megasite criteria.

Robert Flumerfelt worked for Francis Paolangeli preparing his mining application and site maps, and pieces of the puzzle began appearing at Ray Nolan's DEC office. Like Pat Snyder before him, Ray allowed me to review accumulating paperwork in the application's file folders, and to keep on top of things. I made regular visits to the DEC building on Fisher Avenue in

Cortland. Dated March 2, 1989, the SEQR Environmental Assessment Form appeared with questions mostly answered and blanks filled in by the applicant in its four-page PART 1—PROJECT INFORMATION section. And a letter of the same date, from Flumerfelt to Al Coburn stated that, "…According to the records of the owner of the quarry, Alfred C. Eddy, at least 1,000 tons of gravel were removed from the gravel pit each year…" since the permit had expired four years earlier. That was simply untrue, a story concocted, records fabricated, if any records existed at all. I knew the pits had been inactive for at least four years, and probably more. Apparently, Paolangeli and Eddy were still trying to establish that this application should be a renewal rather than a new one, even though they had been told otherwise, and were attempting to grandfather the operation in order to bypass Dryden's new zoning ordinance, possibly to get the DEC, as Lead Agency, to disregard or override Dryden's objections. Paolangeli and Eddy were hopeful the state would be cooperative, knowing their poor odds of being granted a variance in Dryden, against strong opposition.

In fact, New York State law pertaining to mineral extraction, natural gas and oil wells, and gravel mines as overseen by the DEC's Division of Mineral Resources, prohibits local governments from enacting or enforcing laws written specifically to regulate mineral extraction. New York's Mined Land Reclamation Law (ECL Article 23, Title 27), as enacted in 1975, was written precisely to supersede and preempt local regulation of mining operations.

But did state law apply with force to a local zoning ordinance that prohibits mining, among other actions in a zone, but that allows an applicant to apply for and possibly obtain a variance? Without a required local zoning variance, but with a state mining permit in hand, would the state say, "It's okay, go ahead." Whether the state would supersede Dryden's new protective zoning would remain perplexingly unclear to me. Yet, at about that time, that very question would be tested in court cases in other New York localities, the results of which would lead to clarifying amendments in 1991 to New York's law.

Meanwhile, Ray Nolan at DEC knew of Dryden's objections, but he wasn't requiring Paolangeli to get a variance first, nor apparently did SEQR require that. What was certain, in this confrontation, was that New York State's DEC, as the SEQR lead agency, was in charge of the environmental review and would determine its outcome. The state, not the Town of Dryden, would make the Determination of Significance, PosDec or NegDec. And we needed to be ready, again, to provide our input on a moment's notice.

On April 11, 1989, Flumerfelt provided to DEC updated site maps showing Ray Nolan's revised wetland boundaries, as I had requested during the B.R. DeWitt review two years earlier. But apparently, the application was still incomplete. Then, three weeks later, on May 3, Ray Nolan wrote to Paolangeli, sending a copy to Joe Moskiewicz, Regional Mined Land Supervisor, saying:

> After reviewing all of the material submitted in support of the... application I have determined that there is yet one outstanding issue to be resolved. The protected wetland adjacent to your proposed activity is considered highly sensitive to any changes in existing drainage patterns. None of the information provided addresses the possible consequences to the wetland by the mining of adjacent areas.
>
> In this situation it appears that a draft Environmental Impact Statement (dEIS) should be required. Such a document, would, when properly prepared, identify all potential negative impacts resulting from the proposed activity and then provide alternatives that would allow those impacts to be avoided or mitigated.
>
> In an effort to avoid requiring the preparation of a dEIS I am asking you to consider preparing a complete hydrological study of the area so that any negative effects on the wetland from the proposed

mining activities can be identified.

I am suspending further processing of your application until I hear your thoughts in this matter.

Very truly yours, Raymond J. Nolan

This time, things were becoming more complicated. Knowing our concerns about potential changes in hydrology, Ray was requesting more information, a hydrological study, from Paolangeli and Flumerfelt, and was stopping the SEQR clock, temporarily putting the SEQR process on hold. But surprisingly, only days later, on May 8, 1989 (Ray's letter was dated May 3) Paolangeli's completed mining application, prepared by Mr. Flumerfelt, arrived at the DEC office and included a brief four-page narrative titled Malloryville Quarry. And attached was a report, 1 1/2 text pages and a drawing, from Forrest Earl, consultant and Manager of Environmental Services at Empire Soils Investigations, Inc., who had walked the site on May 4 with Paolangeli, Flumerfelt and Alfred Eddy. The plan was to excavate 68 acres, over twenty years (no concrete plant this time) while preventing surface runoff to the wetlands. Summarizing Forrest Earl's recommendation, apparently, their "hydrological study," Flumerfelt wrote:

> ...a sedimentation/infiltration basin will be developed to keep any surface water runoff at least 100 feet from the wetland boundary. Excavation of gravel will then proceed starting in the central part of the site and working towards the sides such that the pit faces will form a natural barrier keeping all surface drainage internal with no surface runoff to the marsh.

Of course, I thought, as a first step, prevention of surface runoff and siltation of the wetlands would be an essential requirement in any mining operation, but the consequences of altering groundwater hydrology by removal of quantities of gravel, the risk to groundwater-fed sensitive fens and rich hemlock-hardwoods swamps, was left unaddressed.

Ray then suggested to Paolangeli and Flumerfelt that they invite me to meet them at Paolangeli's business office in Ithaca to see their mining plans and maps, and then for us to meet together at Ray's office at DEC. I accepted the invitation, having doubts about the value of such a meeting, and somewhat uneasy about meeting, face to face in his office, Mr. Paolangeli, owner of his noncompliant septage disposal operation, shut down with my heavy involvement just over seven months earlier. On May 12, 1989, at 1:00 in Ithaca, Mr. Flumerfelt laid out his gravel-pit contour maps for my inspection, and the three of us had a polite but cautious conversation, carefully avoiding any mention of septage. Then separately, we drove to Cortland where we met with Ray at 3:00.

Ray was under pressure from Paolangeli, and probably from his superiors at DEC, and I didn't know whether he was hopeful that I would be conciliatory and willing to consider some agreement enabling him to issue a Negative Declaration, allowing the mining to go forward, or if he wanted my objection as ammunition to avoid a NegDec, at least for a time while SEQR proceedings were suspended. My suspicion is he wished to hear compromise from me. The alternative, a PosDec, requiring an impact statement, would mean a great deal more time and work for him and for the applicant, but a NegDec, with my acquiescence, would be the easy thing, simple. Ray asked me, "Well Bob, what do you think?" Needless to say, I wasn't willing to make a deal. I said, "The proposal only addresses surface runoff, not groundwater hydrology," and I restated my concerns for the wetlands, which hadn't changed. The problem unresolved, we went our separate ways.

PosDec or NegDec, we didn't know which Ray Nolan would choose in his review of Paolangeli's application. But as with Pat Snyder's review, two years earlier, it was time, again, for us to provide written comments, this time for Ray's consideration. I was fearful that Ray could easily and very quickly choose NegDec, just a short step from approval of mining. And I was frustrated that our hard work, our many, many letters and strong arguments against the DeWitt application, for the same land, next to the same wetlands, seemed locked away, closed files at DEC, certainly known to Ray, but apparently unavailable for review and consideration in the present SEQR proceeding. What he already knew, alone, sensitive wetlands, scientists' concerns, strong neighborhood and Town of Dryden opposition, plus Paolangeli's paltry non-hydrological, "hydrology study," should easily have been enough, in my opinion, to justify a Positive Declaration and a draft Environmental Impact Statement (dEIS), but that seemed not forthcoming. Keeping in contact with our supporters, our unofficial, informal team, still evolving, still growing, I alerted them, once again, to the need for our letters, our arguments, our vigorous defense of a special natural environment, its wetlands, its esker, and its neighborhood, providing persuasive leverage to help Ray make the right decision against strong pressure from the gravel-mining proponents.

So, within our first three years at Malloryville, we started writing and sending our letters opposing a second mining application, requiring another round of critical comments directed to the DEC, the second rally of our team in support. Another letter from Gwen and me, dated May 30, 1989, spelled out many of our criticisms of Paolangeli's proposal, from his misleading statements about Dryden's zoning and permit requirements, requiring first a zoning variance and then a special permit, his and Eddy's contention that the application was for a renewal, not a new permit, inaccuracies in their maps showing no residences, when in fact three houses are adjacent to the project site boundary, their incorrect statements about the proximity of wetlands, saying only that there is, "...a marsh area approx. 2,500' south of site center," when their own Mining Plan Map shows the wetland, in places, to be little more than 100 feet from the excavation with the wetland edge and gravel pit running nearly parallel to each other for approximately 1300 feet, and we restated the risk posed by alterations in hydrology to our mineral-rich groundwater-dependent wetlands. And we countered their assertion that no unique or unusual landforms are present by again arguing for the educational and cultural value of the Malloryville Esker, while attaching to our letter its photograph and three pages of text copied from von Engeln's book.

Professor Peter Marks, Robert Wesley and Nancy Ostman, the new Natural Areas Coordinator of Cornell Plantations, sent their revised letter, again eloquently defending the historic and scientific value of the wetland complex.

Betsy Darlington, a board-member colleague of mine with the new Finger Lakes Land Trust, wrote:

> Dear Mr. Nolan: I would like to express my strong opposition to the granting of a permit to mine gravel near the Malloryville Bog. Because the bog is fed by water from the gravel area, the bog could be irreparably damaged by the hydrological disturbances that the mining would cause.
>
> The Malloryville Bog is a significant and valuable resource, named—with good reason—as a unique natural area by the Tompkins County EMC, and recognized by The Nature Conservancy's Registry program. We simply must not allow the greed of a few destroy this resource forever. It is unfortunate that they care more about a fast buck than the preservation of a valuable and delicate ecosystem for future generations. But luckily, we have the DEC to protect us from such degradation of our state's resources.
>
> Thank you for any help you can give!
>
> Sincerely, Betsy Darlington

My neighbors, Scott Sheavly and Marcia Eames-Sheavly, their house, one of the nearest to the proposed mine, wrote on June 15, 1989:

> Dear Mr. Nolan, ...We recently moved into our new home... on West Malloryville Road. We are

expecting our first child in a few months and we chose this location because of its lovely setting, its peaceful environment, and the pleasant residential setting which it provides. This area seems like the ideal spot to raise a family. Needless to say, we are angered and disillusioned at the possibility of the reopening of this gravel pit near our home.

First of all, recent zoning law changes prohibit the gravel mining operation. Secondly, in a residential area, we believe a complete environmental impact study should be undertaken to fully understand the effects on the local neighborhood. Such a study would need to address the impact of heavy road traffic, excessive noise and large machinery. Clearly, this would harm the quality of the human habitat and have detrimental effects on the unique ecosystem in the area surrounding the proposed mine.

As homeowners and taxpayers, we strongly feel we deserve the right to have our concerns addressed in a complete and thorough manner. With the same certainty that Mr. Paolangeli has the right to pursue profit from this gravel pit, we too share the right to protect our [home and neighborhood], both economic and cultural.

Respectfully, Scott Sheavly, Marcia Eames-Sheavly

In a powerful letter to Ray, my friend, Ron Schassburger, defended with passion the site's unique wetlands and glacial topography, and wrote in his closing paragraph:

...I would ask you to let me know how such threats to this area can be dealt with on a long-term basis, in particular by your office. Those of us who are concerned with the area's integrity would hope that every time a new threat arises we don't need to begin from scratch, each time, the process of letter writing campaigns, citing proof of the fragility and value of the area, and extolling the virtues of maintaining natural diversity in a world which is being increasingly despoiled for the sake of short-term economic profits...

Respectfully yours, Ronald M. Schassburger

When I called Cornell geology Professor Arthur Bloom to request a new letter, his knowledge of the esker and geology being important, he expressed to me his annoyance at having to write again, a feeling that I too shared, and seeming to be annoyed with me for asking, said that he didn't like being involved in "a neighborhood squabble." That phone conversation prompted me to express some of my thoughts about my involvement and what we were up to, in a letter to him.

On June 11, 1989, I wrote::

Dear Dr. Bloom: Please permit me a few comments concerning our telephone conversation yesterday.

1) Once again, I thank you for your letters to the DEC.

2) My involvement with environmental issues extends well beyond Malloryville. My training in biology at Cornell provided an excellent and broad background, and currently, I am a trustee of The Nature Conservancy (Central New York Chapter/19 counties), a director of the Finger Lakes Land Trust, and a member of the Tompkins County Environmental Management Council.

3) The Malloryville esker and Bog area ranks among the very top sites in this part of the state in terms of geological and biological distinctiveness, diversity, rare elements, and unspoiled quality.

4) Yes, I have a special interest in the... site: my wife and I own 38 acres here; it is our home,

and we plan to stay. My interest here is long-standing (40+ years) and will continue. I intend to do whatever I can to ensure its preservation and to deter activities that would degrade its quality.

5) To stop a proposed gravel mine before a permit is issued (as we did two years ago with B.R. DeWitt and as we are trying to do now) makes a whole lot more sense than does waiting (as you suggested yesterday) to fight a court battle at a later date (at far greater cost in delays, time and money).

6) As you know, input from the general public and from respected professionals (in writing and at hearings) is what it takes to preserve our remaining unique natural areas. The current situation... is decidedly not "a neighborhood squabble," and fully deserves professional input.

Sincerely, Robert M. Beck

I was hopeful my letter wouldn't be found too impertinent, as I wanted Prof. Bloom's support. He did write to Ray Nolan:

Dear Mr. Nolan: ...In response to similar information two years ago, I wrote a letter dated August 14, 1987, a copy of which is attached. I have no reason to change any opinions of the geologic uniqueness of the area that I expressed in that letter, and I ask that this letter, with the attached copy, be made part of the record of the current environmental review.

I regret that the procedures of the New York State Department of Environmental Conservation require me and other taxpayers to rewrite letters such as this for each new review, when you have an existing file on the site. I believe our interests are not well served by your current department procedures.   Sincerely, A.L. Bloom

Again, wanting input from a professional hydrologist, I recontacted Mark Walker at Cornell's Water Resources Institute. In response to Paolangeli's application, he addressed to me this report, dated June 14, 1989:

> Concerns about gravel mining adjacent to wetlands:
>
> Please accept the following observations about the proposal to mine gravel on lands adjacent to the wetlands. I submit these not as statements of fact, but rather as legitimate questions that should be answered about the possible effects of mining on the groundwater flow regime that maintains the wetland. If, as you say, the plant species in the wetland cannot tolerate changes in either the chemical quality or the quantity of recharge water, then the following topics should be considered before a mining permit is issued for this property.
>
> 1). At what depth is the water table found and how much does this fluctuate throughout the year? My previous concerns about mining below the water table were based on the possibility that evaporation and drainage would change the flow patterns through the area and affect both the chemical quality and the quantity of water flowing into the wetland. The new request for a permit suggests that mining would not take place below the water table, but I see no evidence that the elevation of the water table has been identified. Proper identification of the water table would include more than a single measurement at one point. It would require the installation of piezometers that could be used to relate the water table to discharge points in the wetland. These piezometers would be linked with a survey and water levels in each would be recorded periodically to assess the degree of fluctuation

associated with annual periods of recharge. The information from this assessment would be used to establish a maximum permissible mined depth and perhaps a desirable safety zone, below which mining should not take place.

2). What is the character of the gravel formations? Are there clay lenses or layers that divert recharge horizontally towards the wetland? If so, can gravel mining avoid such small but potentially important features?

3). What is the recharge area for the wetland? Does the proposed gravel mine comprise a significant portion of this area? I would suggest that it may be useful to do a simple topographic identification of the potential recharge area for the wetland to put the proposed mining operation in perspective. This might involve a process similar to that used to delineate watersheds for surface water bodies. The proposed mining would disrupt some portion of the recharge area for the wetland, but the proportions and relative effects have not been addressed thoroughly.

In proposing the above, I am not suggesting that the proposed gravel mining is likely to either have or not have an effect on the adjacent wetland. I am, however, suggesting that the likely effects of mining on the wetland could be most thoroughly assessed by identifying the boundaries of the wetland's recharge area and the internal dynamics of groundwater flow (both in space and time) within those boundaries.

Mark Walker

I provided Mark's excellent recommendations to Ray Nolan to be added to the Paolangeli files. That was the kind of hydrological study, I thought, an applicant ought to be required to undertake, after a PosDec, as part of an impact statement, not the cursory walk-over report that was in the application, nor some token substitute providing an excuse for a NegDec, as Ray seems to have suggested when he wrote, "In an effort to avoid requiring the preparation of a dEIS..." But, curiously, it seemed to me, plenty of information was already available to Ray, already in the files, from the Town, the neighborhood, the wetlands, to easily justify a PosDec and a dEIS, and even denial of the permit.

Next, Ray scheduled a meeting to be held at DEC on June 20, 1989. to be a discussion, not a hearing, among interested parties to explore the issue of hydrology and the wetlands. In attendance from the DEC, in addition to Ray, would be Frank Trent, geologist, and Al Coburn, the Regional Permit Administrator. And applicant Paolangeli, consultant Forrest Earl, and landowner Alfred Eddy would be there. This was serious and important, not to be messed up; the outcome would be consequential. I was determined to prevent a NegDec, and we needed strong scientific representation from our side. Ray was accustomed to seeing me at his office and had read our comments, but now he needed to see our support first-hand, real people, scientists, in person. Botanist, Robert Wesley had introduced me to Dr. Barbara Bedford, a superb Cornell wetlands ecologist who would become one of Malloryville Bog's strongest advocates. Barbara, in turn, introduced me to Syracuse University Professor Donald Siegel, a highly regarded hydrogeologist, who would become a vital and major force on our team. Both would soon take on long-term interests in the diverse wetlands and, with their students, would undertake research projects here. Together, Robert Wesley, Barbara and Don agreed to participate in Ray's meeting.

Jules Burgevin, a sociologist at Ithaca College and a member of the EMC with me, expressed interest in attending and suggested that he invite his long-term friend, environmental attorney Ted Lavery, from Skaneateles, to attend also. And, my friend Ron Schassburger agreed to be there. Then, I wanted Wayne Klockner to be there representing The Nature Conservancy, to help bolster the seriousness of our intent, especially in the eyes of Ray Nolan, and perhaps Alfred Eddy, demonstrating the Conservancy's awareness and concern, even if, in the delicate, potentially confrontational, situation, he said nothing. When I called, Wayne was reluctant to attend and initially declined, but I, feeling urgency and arguing with vehemence, gained his consent.

During my visits to the DEC office in Cortland, where, with Ray's approval, I reviewed the files and made whatever copies I needed, Ray frequently wanted me to accompany him during his long smoke breaks, where we talked extensively on the porch outside the front entrance. In his job, Ray was between a rock and a hard place. I imagine he felt pressure from his boss or bosses, who may, in turn, have felt pressure from Albany, the state capital, where economic development often took precedence over environmental protection. And I'm sure Paolangeli and Eddy pressured him. From our side, he was reading our letters, and knew our position. Yet, I believe Ray enjoyed my visits and our talks, and I think he came to respect my determined approach to a difficult problem. He knew my hopes for finding permanent protection for the site, and he knew the area was highly ranked by the New York Natural Heritage Program and The Nature Conservancy, but we didn't discuss anything about Conservancy involvement. We talked, avoiding argument, but I couldn't shake the feeling that he might simply follow the path of least resistance and, of course, he didn't or couldn't tell me what his next move would be.

June 20, 1989, 10:00 a.m. At Ray's meeting, Forrest Earl presented his argument that Paolangeli's gravel mine would do no harm to the wetland. Barbara Bedford and Robert Wesley argued eloquently for protection of the wetlands and their unusually diverse plant life, pointing out the special, uncommon conditions required by fens and rich hemlock-hardwood swamps, both being fragile and scarce natural communities, dependent upon their supply of mineral-laden groundwater from adjacent land. Don Siegel pointed out, with clarity, the weaknesses of Forrest Earl's position, and explained the hydrological issues that needed to be considered and questions that ought to be answered. Answers to those questions of hydrology, of course, were not available. We didn't know with absolute certainty, couldn't say for sure, that mining, in fact, would be harmful.

I wasn't asking any scientist to make absolute statements we couldn't defend; rather, just to state the possibility, perhaps the probability, of harm being done. To some in the room, the lack of definitive answers seemed to lead to the suggestion that gravel mining should proceed anyway, not to worry, there won't be any problems, it'll be okay. Or even that the site could serve as a useful scientific experiment in finding answers: The effects of gravel removal and alteration of hydrology on sensitive wetland plant communities, could be determined by observing changes, alterations, degradation, slow or rapid, in the fens and swamps over time. Such an experiment, documenting irreversible damage, sanctioned by the DEC in support of private gain, is not what I had in mind, offering Malloryville Bog as an experiment, placing at risk, then watching, as a unique, diverse, beautiful natural area, sadly, goes the way of so many others before. Rather, with Robert, Barbara, Don and our other good friends, we would argue: When in doubt, err on the side of caution, respectfully, and avoid placing a natural treasure at risk.

For the most part, on the topic of hydrology, I was pleased with the meeting, with the content and depth of discussion, and with Ray's attentiveness. And I was happy that Wayne Klockner had been there for the Conservancy.

That evening, Ron Schassburger and I talked about an issue that had not been discussed, Eddy and Paolangeli's previous misuse of the land, the same people that were now asking for the state's trust in obeying mining regulations. A day later, June 21, 1989, Ron wrote the following:

> Dear Mr. Nolan: I want to thank you for allowing me to attend and participate in the meeting held yesterday to discuss the potential impacts of the Eddy/Paolangeli mining operation on the Malloryville wetland complex. However, in talking with others after the meeting it became clear to me that certain information regarding past land-use

practices—at the same site in question—by both Mr. Eddy and Mr. Paolangeli were relevant to and should have been brought to the forefront of discussion.

I believe a number of us at that meeting were left with the impression, fostered by both Mr. Eddy and Mr. Paolangeli, that the former is a poor farmer just trying to earn a living on his land and that the latter is an environmentally concerned contractor. I believe Mr. Paolangeli impressed all of us with his willingness to compromise, minimizing environmental disturbance, and even participate in studies (albeit to his personal profit and likely disturbance of the... wetland) designed to prevent further environmental degradation as a result of future commercial activities. What I heard subsequent to that meeting from Mr. Beck has altered my perception considerably, and even angered me. Following is a list of specifics:

1) Mr. Eddy—an absentee landowner, as his... property was purchased for investment and never was his farm or residence—has a tarnished reputation with the Town of Dryden. He has taken gravel illegally from the... site after his permit expired, he never paid the agreed upon bond, and the town attorney has determined that his... permit was invalid from the day it was signed.

2) Mr. Eddy stated in a letter to the DEC... that he was discontinuing his septage (septic tank pumpings) dumping operation... The dumping, however, continued without letup.

3) Mr. Paolangeli, contractor and permit holder for the septage dumping..., was in nearly continuous violation... of Tompkins County Department of Health and DEC permit conditions (the septage lagoon—600 feet from the wetland—was nearly always full and often overflowing).

Furthermore, he ignored numerous notices of violation and orders to close the operation from both the Department of Health and the DEC.

4) Mr. Paolangeli, when ordered by the Department of Health and the DEC... to empty the lagoon, spread the material and then close out the... operation, instead cut through the dike with a backhoe, allowed some of the material to drain out, let it partially dry in the summer heat, and then buried it all with a bulldozer.

These assertions can be verified in numerous resolutions and correspondences from the Town of Dryden, the Tompkins County Environmental Management Council, the Tompkins County Department of Health, and your own New York State Department of Environmental Conservation. It troubled me that this information was not brought to light at yesterday's meeting; however, I understand the limited scope of that meeting, as well as Mr. Beck's own desire to stay in the background and avoid any contentious confrontations. Nevertheless, I find the above contemptuous violations of law highly relevant to your present obligation in deciding on a positive or negative declaration with regard to the granting of the mining permit in question. Hence, the urgency of this letter, which I am copying to Mr. Beck, along with a request to him to supply you with copies of the above resolutions and correspondences.

In closing, I would urge you to use extreme caution in responding to any statements and offers made by Mr. Eddy and Mr. Paolangeli. I find it nothing less than duplicitous in the impression they gave at yesterday's meeting that their business relationship is a most recent one— following the aborted permit effort with DeWitt Cement. Their past record of activities at Malloryville clearly indicates a lack of environmental concern and blatant disregard for compliance with permit conditions. Are these the kind of people with whom the DEC and concerned environmentalists can work with closely, work out compromises and ensure the integrity of our environmental resources for future generations?

Sincerely, Ronald M. Schassburger

Although Ray already had some of that information in his files, I agreed with Ron that he should be updated on the full story, and I provided copies of the multiple documents that substantiated Eddy and Paolangeli's past behavior.

Two days later, on June 23, 1989, Jules Burgevin wrote an appreciative letter to Ray. In it he said:

Dear Ray... The manner in which you conducted this conversation was certainly commendable. In fact it was one of the most reasonable group conversations I've been to in many months...

I am not a geologist. I am a sociologist... I took 2 1/2 pages of notes on what Mr. Forrest Earl said. My sense is, in reading these notes, that he did not answer the question: How will the proposed mining affect the water table in and around [Malloryville Bog]? His statements in this conversation were based, as he said, on "assumptions." He concluded that, "We cannot guarantee that the mining would not affect the water table in the bog." Since the many various unique parts of this natural area depend on water for their life one cannot make major mining decisions in such a fragile area based on assumptions. Before one does any disruptions to unique areas one has to be able to prove, beyond a reasonable doubt, with specific tests, research, studies and guarantees, that what is proposed will not in any way disrupt or destroy, these natural areas of the environment. It sounds as if we need a good deal more data before one can make any clear judgment in this matter...

There's a new principle emerging among some very significant environmentalists and economists. This principle is based on a new way of seeing, assessing, determining what to do where questions of the environment are raised. In simple terms it is based on the idea that considerations of the environment take precedent over considerations based on human economic desires and needs. The needs of businesses, development, progress, become secondary to the needs of the environment. A new way of thinking as a species. A new way of seeing beyond the human. Seeing the human is one of many species. No longer seeing the humans as a special species with environmental privileges which take precedence over other species, and the earth's bio-systems.

SEQR says that we look at the effects on the geology of the area. Then we look at it in terms of what it will do to humans. My sense is that this whole concept has to be enlarged and revamped. That is, we look at a proposed development, changes, in terms of what these will do to the air, the land, the water, all life species, in an area. And we look at these changes with a geological base but we expand or enlarge this. There are many more factors and variables to look at in an environmental perspective. That is why this "conversation"... was so special and significant. All "conversations" and "hearings" having to do with any environmental changes, should really listen to such a diverse, unique, individualized group of beings who speak for the plants, the water, the air, the insects, the birds, the land, the animals, the trees, the children, the pollution, the waste, the recycling, the streams, rivers, the past, the food, the future...

All new developments of any type, any place

in New York State must be required to make an in-depth environmental study and statement, with "conversations," and "hearings." Too much of life is being worn away, destroyed, permanently polluted... The Department of Environmental Conservation (DEC) must be strongly weighed to the side of preserving the environment. Otherwise it moves into the mode of becoming the (DED)—the Department of Environmental Destruction. That is why, in my judgment, this application for mining and many, many, similar applications for changing this fragile environment we live in, and on, should be turned down.

Most sincerely, Jules D. Burgevin

And attorney, Ted Lavery, on June 23, 1989, wrote:

Dear Mr. Nolan: I represent Jules Burgevin, Ph.D., and was present at the conference held on the Malloryville mining application.

The report given by Forrest Earl on behalf of the applicant was based on assumptions and estimates, rather than physical measurements. The experts who commented clearly raised the need for the following: (1) Groundwater topography. (2) Permeability values of the soil in the affected area. (3) Accurate evaporation studies. (4) The topography of the base of the bog area. (5) Study of the water systems in the bog area. (6) Water chemistry evaluations of the eco—systems in the bog. (7) Relationships between water chemistry and plants indigenous to the bog...

I therefore urge you to require the applicant to submit a detailed environmental impact statement which addresses the concerns expressed at the meeting.

Yours very sincerely, Edward W. Lavery

My hopes were, first, that our comments to Ray, in writing and in person, would convince him that an impact statement was essential before mining could be allowed to proceed, that a Positive Declaration was a must; second, that our strong, unified, showing would discourage Paolangeli, as with B.R. DeWitt, from pursuing a costly, possibly unsuccessful, impact statement; and third, that Alfred Eddy would be willing to consider more environmentally friendly uses of his land.

Again, as two years earlier, we wait for the Determination of Significance, PosDec or NegDec.

Three weeks later, July 13, 1989, SEQR Positive Declaration; PosDec(2):

> The lead agency, has determined that the proposed action... may have a significant effect on the environment and that a Draft Environmental Impact Statement will be prepared.... Reasons Supporting This Determination: The proposed mining may cause a significant alteration of local groundwater hydrology and thereby negatively affect an adjacent protected wetland known as Malloryville Bog. Increase in heavy truck traffic in this rural residential area is also of concern.
> Raymond J. Nolan

Thus, at the end of our third year at the Bog, we welcomed a second Positive Declaration, PosDec(2), with relief, and we were hopeful that Paolangeli and Eddy would withdraw, choosing not to undertake an environmental impact study.

But, two months earlier, a telephone conversation had introduced a new development that would take us into Year 4 and beyond.

Pileated Woodpecker (*Dryocopus pileatus*) holes

8 BEQUEST

Have a bias toward action—let's see something happen now.
You can break that big plan into small steps
and take the first step right away.
— Indira Gandhi

OUT OF THE BLUE, in May, 1989, spring of our Year 3, I received a surprising phone call. Edward King, an Attorney in Ithaca, identified himself as an executor of the estate of Cornell Professor O.D. von Engeln, with interest in the Malloryville Esker. That call would mark the beginning of a central thread in our story, a thread with which we would be involved through the next eight years.

May 26, 1989. I met with Ed King at his office to pick up some materials he had prepared. Prof. von Engeln (1880-1965) had left in his will instructions to use, after the passing of a last life-income beneficiary, the net trust assets of his estate for one of two land protection projects. The second of the two was protection of the Malloryville Esker. Of course, I knew of Dr. von Engeln's deep appreciation for the esker, but I had no idea, no inkling, of its place in his will. Ed King had contacted me just a few weeks after the death of the last beneficiary, his study of county tax maps and tax parcel ownership having identified my wife and me as owners of a portion of the esker, to explore possibilities.

This revelation seemed to me extraordinarily opportune. At a time of continuing, unresolved challenge, the land still facing its greatest threat, here was an unexpected possibility of funding, 24 years after Dr. von Engeln's death, funding that might further legitimize our efforts to continue the fight against gravel plans, funding for a more definable, more tangible goal of protecting nature by establishing a permanent nature preserve, now, with the backing of von Engeln's name and his bequest. Some skeptics, after all, were still questioning our opposition to gravel mining and our claim of the value of Malloryville's natural history. The goal of protection, for the esker as well as the wetlands, was always on my mind, and this possibility seemed to bring it closer to reality. Plus, the esker, extending west from my property did, in fact, cross the Eddy gravel property, making that parcel important to protection of the esker as well as the wetlands.

And top among my first thoughts, was that the von Engeln funds should go to The Nature Conservancy, long established, highly credible, certainly knowledgeable about nature preserves, and already supportive of our local effort. The new Finger Lakes Land Trust, barely born, just five months from its first organizational meeting, ought not, I felt, be immediately burdened with fighting a gravel mine. Without delay, I talked with Wayne Klockner at his Conservancy office in Rochester, alerting him to the new development.

Prof. von Engeln's will, of 1963, in paragraph "SIXTH," stated:

> Upon the death of the last of said life beneficiaries... I direct that my Trustees retain the services (for just compensation) of Dr. Victor Schmidt of Brockport, New York as scientific consultant in the establishment of a Natural History Preserve of Hendershot Gulf ("Lost Gorge") and the associated Cayuta Lake Outlet Gorges, or, if such venture proves unfeasible, then, for such other similar project as herein below directed... Should

the Hendershot preserve project above specified be deemed inadvisable by Dr. Schmidt by reason of the unavailability of desired site and acreage or the insufficiency of funds, or for any other substantial reason; or to the extent that excess funds are available over and beyond the amounts that can reasonably and efficaciously be expended on the Hendershot Gulf project; then I direct that such funds be devoted, under Dr. Schmidt's direction, to the similar purpose and project of a Reservation of the Malloryville esker and associated bogs. In the execution of such project or projects, I suggest that consideration be given to the erection of suitable markers such as the historic markers set up along New York State Highways, and, if funds permit, making provision for access ways and footpaths into the particular area without disturbance of natural features.

Prof. von Engeln had published a paper in 1945, "Glacial Diversion of Drainage (With especial reference to the phenomenon of the 'Lost Gorge')" in the Annals of the Association of American Geographers, Vol. XXXV, No. 3, pgs. 78-119. In it, he described Hendershot Gulf, for which he appropriately coined the name "Lost Gorge," because it had been overlooked by USGS mapmakers and topographic-map contour lines failed to indicate its presence. He had determined that the gorge, now nearly dry in its midsection with no stream running through its length, and the third of three gorges proceeding from the outlet of small Cayuta Lake (southwest of Cayuga Lake), was formed when glacial ice, for a time, blocked and diverted the lower, present-day lake outlet, forcing the flowing water to cut a new channel through higher ground. Today, at the southern end of DEC's Connecticut Hill State Wildlife Management Area, about 12 miles southwest of Ithaca, the land of Prof. von Engeln's Lost Gorge, is mostly owned and protected by New York State.

May 29, 1989. In Ithaca at Ed King's office, I met with Ed and with Victor Schmidt, the will's designated scientific advisor, who had driven to our meeting, 110 miles, from his home in Brockport. Victor, a geologist, had earned his doctorate at Cornell while studying under, and close friends with, Prof. von Engeln. He had retired from SUNY Brockport where, for many years, he had been a professor teaching geology and other science courses. And Victor was a coauthor, with Cornell University's Verne Rockcastle, of a highly acclaimed and successful series of elementary-school science textbooks, emphasizing hands-on activities for students, as well as a wonderful little book titled, *Teaching Science with Everyday Things*.

At our meeting, I provided details about Malloryville, including its esker and its diverse wetlands, The Nature Conservancy's potential interest, the ongoing threat, and the second SEQR proceeding then in progress. Victor, inquisitive, warm and kindly, had a deep interest in all aspects of natural history, and a day later wrote to me to express his pleasure with our meeting and his eagerness to move forward, quickly. He wrote:

> Dear Bob... It was a pleasure to meet you and to discuss with you the matter of setting up a "von Engeln Natural History Preserve." I am hoping that this can be accomplished in the very near future...
> Sincerely, Vic... Victor E. Schmidt

Then, on June 10, 1989, Victor wrote to Attorney, Ed King recommending Malloryville as their choice for funding, it being excellent in both geology and biology, there being urgency in its need for protection, that The Nature Conservancy should be the organization to establish the preserve, and that Prof. von Engeln be recognized in the preserve and in a special dedication ceremony. Victor wrote:

> Dear Ed... At this time I'd like to summarize four points that seem clear to me:
> 1. Although Dr. von suggested that a sepa-

rate corporation be set up for the establishment and administration of the Preserve, I feel that this would prove impractical. Instead, largely because of the many problems associated with the stewardship of such an area, including vandalism and liability, I think it would be better to place the Preserve under the administration of an established organization. The Nature Conservancy should, I feel, be given prime consideration because of its expertise and experience with the acquisition and protection of natural areas.

2. It is essential that, in keeping with Dr. von's wishes, the geological features of the Preserve not be considered subordinate to the biological, but that both be viewed as interrelated and equally important aspects of natural history. This point may prove to be an obstacle in any dealings with The Nature Conservancy, since its primary goal is the preservation of biologically unique areas. On the other hand, the area including the Malloryville esker and associated bogs is likely to be of considerable interest to the Conservancy because of its orchids and other rare plants.

3. Of the two areas suggested by Dr. von, the one of the Malloryville esker and associated bogs seems to be the more fragile and more urgently in need of protection. This is largely because of the possibility of gravel mining and residential, perhaps even commercial, development...

4. It is important that suitable recognition be given to Dr. von for his contribution and interest in making this Natural History Preserve possible. At the very least the official designation of the Preserve should include his name. Further, at the proper time, the establishment of the Preserve should be marked by an appropriate dedicatory ceremony.

Please do not hesitate to suggest what I can do to expedite the establishment of the Preserve, and continue to keep me posted on the amount of money available for land purchases (or for easements), the ownership and availability of the lands being considered, and your exploratory talks with staff of The Nature Conservancy.

With my best personal regards, Sincerely, Vic... Victor E. Schmidt

Wow! I liked those ideas, and Victor Schmidt's enthusiasm and strong support were wonderfully encouraging. Yet in our meeting, Ed King, as one of the two executors—the second being Fleet Bank, a successor to the First National Bank of Ithaca, its office in Boston—had seemed cool to the idea, with past gravel mining, and the specter of more, in Ed's eyes, dimming Malloryville's appeal. Understandably, neither the von Engeln executors nor The Nature Conservancy would lightly commit to the site in the midst of its confrontation with an unknown outcome. They knew a nature preserve ought to be viable for the long term, defensibility being essential in site-selection criteria. And we certainly faced a defensibility challenge from a neighboring property, a landowner, uncooperative, with very different motives. Doubts, in some eyes, about nature's viability here, recurring skepticism about its future in the absence of forceful counter arguments, could grow to kill our hopes. I couldn't let negative thoughts prosper, and I would continue fighting back with facts and persuasion whenever necessary. Now, exciting to me, was Victor's strong endorsement of The Nature Conservancy as the recipient of the von Engeln trust, and I hoped it would be influential with Ed King, the man who would be the decision maker for the bequest.

Yet, for three months, I heard nothing more from Ed King. Spring turned to summer, and summer brought Ray Nolan's welcome PosDec(2). Then came a memorable lunch at Danny's Place when Andy Zepp and I met Moss Sweedler to introduce him to the Finger Lakes Land Trust and to suggest protection for his fabulous Lick Brook property, thereby planting a seed that would germinate, two years later, with Moss' offer of a trade, Lick Brook for a pond.

Victor Schmidt, on August 12, 1989, wrote to me from his summer home at Blue Mt. Lake in New York's Adirondack Mountains:

> Dear Bob... Before leaving Brockport for the Adirondacks in July, I called Wayne Klockner of The Nature Conservancy about the Malloryville esker and bogs. He was quite familiar with the area and indicated that it is one in which the Conservancy is interested, but that he had not heard from Mr. King.
>
> I also called Mr. King, chiefly to emphasize my feeling that we should get in touch with the Conservancy as soon as possible, largely because of their expertise in acquiring property and easements for conservation.
>
> After I return to Brockport in September I plan to go to Ithaca to refresh my memory of the area, preferably along with you and others. Please let me know if there is a time that is especially convenient for you.
>
> Can you tell me what the present status is of the possibility of gravel mining in the area? ...
>
> Sincerely yours, Vic... Victor E. Schmidt

I called Victor at Blue Mt. Lake to thank him and to fill him in on the good news of the DEC's second Positive Declaration and our hopes that the gravel plans would go away. And we each expressed our puzzlement over Ed King's reluctance to contact The Nature Conservancy.

Year 4: 1989/90

At length, we each received Ed King's letter dated September 21, 1989. Ed had delayed mailing, for three months, a letter of June 14, until September 21, when he had added several more pages (with the new date) and sent it off.

Ed wrote (on June 14, but mailed Sept. 21):

Dear Vic... Thank you for your letter of June 10th and thoughts about acquisitions in Malloryville for The Nature Conservancy providing the most beneficial use of the funds available.

My thinking had gravitated away from trying to buy up outright ownership of much of any land—other than possibly strategic "viewing sites" where the general public might be afforded an opportunity to see and become a little informed about the geologic features which are there to behold. (I have been reliving my youth and the hikes up "South Mountain" to climb the Fire Tower and look over the Allegheny Mountains: a Guest Book was provided, along with glassed-in topographic maps at each of the 4 windows to the world: nothing more.)

The prospect of providing two or three "lookout posts" around the Lost Gorge area seemed much more manageable than trying to buy up acres of the land itself; and the public awareness that might be built by such facilities might itself produce preservation urges in the right people. The Malloryville esker might also be made available to many through the provision of one or more such observation posts—though there is probably no high ground vantage point around there.

There are also ways to preserve other than buying and guarding the land itself. A Permanent Collection of Photographs, videotapes, magazine articles, and the like could be supported and they would "preserve" even after the gravel diggers finally succeeded in tearing much away.

Some such measures could give us much more "bang for the buck" than we could hope to achieve otherwise: you can hardly buy a nice house or more than 50 acres or so around Ithaca for the money this trust will have!

And just how unique are any of these two geologic sites? Is landownership really essential? I have not gone very far yet with the idea of acquiring other interests in land—such as the Conservation Easements, but will get to it in time...

Whatever we finally do, a first step surely must be to realize that "our eyes are bigger than our stomachs," so we had better begin refining and focusing upon projects within the means of our purse.

Then, on September 21, Ed added to the letter:

I think that we should continue to examine both the Lost Gorge/Gulf area and the Malloryville esker site, and develop specific, affordable Preservation proposals for each. I would like to be able do a little something for both areas, if it is feasible...

And after several paragraphs concerning Hendershot Gulf, Ed turns to Malloryville:

Since composing my late-blooming letter of 6/14... (above) I have spoken to Mr. Eddy about our interest in possibly acquiring some of his Malloryville land, and as I told you on the phone last week (?) he is looking for $--Millions for his gravel...

I think we should also be considering whether it is feasible to seek some less expensive Preservation Easements over any of the Eddy land, and to what extent we can afford to require preservation... Would we ask only that a particular, well-defined strip of the gravel... be preserved... Can we do anything worthwhile there with a small amount of money?

Should we also consider purchasing some Preservation Easements from the Beck family? [We have no guarantee that the next generation will have the same preservation instincts as does the present.]...

Perhaps we can and should also consider undertaking some limited-expense projects in both areas: such as the suggested Highway Markers pointing out notable Geologic features...

NEXT STEPS: As for obtaining the help of The Nature Conservancy: it would be premature to approach them until we have selected specific lands and easements and project objectives. I well know how to draw Easements and purchase contracts, and I have also obtained a treatise on conservation easements for more ideas... Thus, I am sufficiently prepared with tools and ideas in that vein to apply to whatever specific project(s) and goal(s) we eventually decide to go after.

Once we decide what we want to try to accomplish, and have developed our own approach to it, we can evaluate whether and to what extent we might want to and could interest the Conservancy in it, whether for financial help and/or expert advice. Why waste their resources in general discussions before we have decided what we want specifically to do? ...

Although gift, estate, and income tax laws generally no longer provide as strong an incentive as heretofore, they too can still prove useful with some potential Sellers and Donors, and I am sure that the Conservancy would lend its expertise in the area if and when we can provide them with specifics for a particular acquisition and the financial situation and goals of a particular Owner whom we would like to convert into a Donor, Seller, or the Grantor of an Easement...

...We must know what is the least we must

do to achieve a credible accomplishment in each area, and we should establish priorities for acquisitions at each site. We must approach this realistically, knowing that we are not going to be able to accomplish all one might wish to at either site...

Meantime, I will try to be ready for a short site trek on short notice whenever it suits all concerned...

Sincerely, Ed King... Edward W. King

Well, that letter was a serious disappointment, certainly not what I was hoping for. Ed King had made no contact with The Nature Conservancy, and his approach seemed to me agonizingly tepid, over cautious, controlling, and very unhelpful. Renewed mining seemed to him a foregone conclusion, while saving only a narrow strip of gravel from ongoing extraction would protect neither the wetlands nor the neighborhood. In fact, in spite of the will's language of, "a Reservation of the Malloryville esker and associated bogs," the value of the wetlands seemed below Ed's radar. And he seemed unaware or unconcerned that the Conservancy had the capacity to match and exceed his funds for the project as well as proven expertise in putting together and managing nature preserves, neither of which were in his experience.

September 27, 1989. Victor Schmidt, sharing my feelings of impatience, wrote to me asking:

Dear Bob, ...would you please sketch on one or both of the enclosed maps the location of the esker, bogs, woodlands, and other significant features? This will help my thinking concerning which properties we should attempt to purchase or get easements on. (If possible, please add the owners' names.)

With my best wishes, Sincerely, Vic

October 12, 1989. Frustrated with Ed King's inaction and

wanting both Victor and Ed to see my maps and hear my thoughts, I wrote a memo to both:

To Edward King and Victor Schmidt: Enclosed are maps and an aerial photo giving an overview and some details of the natural areas at Malloryville. My intent is to provide additional information about the area, and to counter any thoughts that the site is, or soon will be, too far damaged by gravel mining or other development to be worth saving. Such is decidedly not the case! This wonderful and largely unspoiled area must (and will) be protected from destructive activities and permanently (legally) set aside as a nature preserve. Whether money from Professor von Engeln's estate can best be spent here I don't know, but it is important that you thoroughly understand the situation and the nature of the site... before you decide.

The Malloryville esker starts northeast of my brother Ronald Beck's 75-acre kettle and kame pasture and woodland, known locally as "the punchbowl." The esker runs generally south and west through his property, and along Fall Creek. Turning west, it then parallels W. Malloryville Rd. and forms the southern boundary of the 38-acre property belonging to my wife and myself. From here it crosses Alfred Eddy's property to the west and continues a short distance beyond to the point where the road turns to the north.

The photo in Professor von Englen's book (The Finger Lakes Region...) was taken on Mr. Eddy's property (then, a local farmer's pasture) and the view is toward the east. This was the access point for Cornell geology classes. The hike from that point east along the top of the esker and through my property is very nice; the tall, narrow and winding esker is fascinating and impressive, and the transition from open fields to mature woodland adds to the interest.

By blocking any direct stream flow to Fall Creek, the esker is, of course, the prime reason for the development, since the last ice age, of the magnificent wetland complex just to the north, tucked in and among an intricate maze of kames and smaller eskers (see enclosed map). Words and maps simply cannot convey the beauty of the glacier-formed topography, the variety in wetland types and diversity of plant life (including 16 species of native orchids), the peaceful woodlands throughout, and the remarkably pristine quality of the site. Fortunately, the many hiking trails, mostly on dry ground, make experiencing the area easy and enjoyable. In fact, I am often asked by individuals and groups to lead nature walks through the property. Please come for a visit when you can!

My wife and I feel fortunate beyond measure to be able to live in and enjoy every day this unspoiled and endlessly fascinating natural environment. And we welcome others to enjoy, study, and learn from this special place. For instance, just last Saturday, I spent the day here in the wetland with Professor Donald Siegel of the Syracuse University Geology Department. Dr. Siegel, a leader in wetland hydrology research, and a graduate student of his are just beginning a study of the hydrology of this site. He said he chose Malloryville because, for its size, he has "never seen a more diverse wetland complex."

As you know, the unfortunate side of the story is the continuing threat to the esker and to the wetland from proposed gravel mining and other activities on the 110-acre property owned by Alfred Eddy, who himself lives west of Ithaca. The integrity of the wetlands—and its fragile plant communities—is absolutely dependent on its water source, the gravel deposits on Mr. Eddy's land.

In the past three years, we have been successful in stopping a sewage dumping operation and two gravel mining proposals on the Eddy property. Through the State Environmental Quality Review (SEQR) process [with input from Cornell plantations, the county Environmental Management Council, The Nature Conservancy, the state Natural Heritage Program, professional ecologists, botanists and geologists, two attorneys, and numerous concerned citizens], the DEC is now fully aware of the... situation and, I believe, committed to preventing degradation of the natural features of the site. In spite of this, Mr. Eddy is apparently still talking and dreaming (or bluffing) about making millions (!!) from the property (for which I suspect he paid rather little).

Fortunately, gravel mining to date has had little effect on the esker and wetlands..., and the pits are not generally visible even at relatively close distance from the surrounding terrain.

Higher values than profit and greed are at stake here. The desire for short-term financial gain must not be allowed to destroy this irreplaceable natural gem. I am determined to continue doing whatever I can to ensure the long-term preservation of the esker and wetlands, and to find means of permanent protection. Without question, the most urgent need is to acquire control over at least a portion of Mr. Eddy's property including the esker at the south and a buffer area adjacent to the wetland—perhaps 40 acres would be sufficient (?). In spite of his words to the contrary, I am hopeful that Mr. Eddy will soon become more reasonable in his expectations. I welcome your thoughts and help in establishing a permanent nature preserve at Malloryville.   Bob... Robert M. Beck

October 25, 1989, 11:00 a.m. Our letters and phone calls succeeded, at last, in getting four of us together (Ed King, Victor Schmidt, Wayne Klockner and myself) for a meeting at my house and a pleasant hike through the properties, important especially, for Ed to see the land in person. The following day, Wayne wrote to Ed, with copies to Victor and me:

> Dear Ed... I enjoyed meeting you and touring the Malloryville esker site on Tuesday. I am excited by the potential that the Malloryville site offers to meet von Engeln's dream of establishing a preserve around the esker, and I'd like to reiterate that the Conservancy would commit itself to a major project there, involving the acquisition of perhaps as many as 300 acres, if von Engeln's bequest was applied to this site. The bequest would provide the impetus to raise additional funds to complete the project. What is particularly attractive about Malloryville is the prospect of preserving not only significant geological features but also important biological resources, including endangered species, as well.
>
> I look forward to assisting you in your deliberations in any way that I can. I've enclosed some background information on the Conservancy for your information.
>
> Sincerely, Wayne A. Klockner, Executive Director, Central/Western NY Chapters, The Nature Conservancy
>
> PS: I will send you soon our proposal for the Malloryville site including various protection strategies.

Wayne had asked me for local property ownership information. On October 28, 1989, I wrote to him:

> Thanks again for coming to Malloryville this past week. I was very pleased with the events of the

day—the beautiful summer weather, our hike, and the productive discussions with Victor Schmidt and Ed King.

I am herewith enclosing some property information for the parcels of importance in thinking of a preserve of 300± acres. On the enclosed tax map I have written the names of the owners of each parcel. In this memo, I am including tax map numbers, acres, names, addresses, and some comments (knowing full well that you already are familiar with much that I include). I also enclose a... copy of an aerial photo on which I have indicated the esker and wetland areas—much like one I previously sent to Vic and Ed... I hope these materials prove helpful. If you need other information, please don't hesitate to ask.

Bob... Robert M. Beck

October 31. Ed King responded to Wayne:

Dear Wayne... It was indeed a pleasure to meet you and to make that delightful and informative hike with the group through bog and fen and over the eskers! And many thanks for your subsequent letter and The Nature Conservancy material.

After providing details of his search in the county clerk's office for deeds and ownership information on the Eddy property, Ed concluded his letter with:

I look forward to receiving your proposed Conservation Easements on Eddy land, as a starting point for a "fall-back" position or offer if the von Engeln Trustees should decide to acquire any of the Eddy land or an interest therein. If we do so decide, I think we are all agreed that strategically, the first approach should be for a GIFT of fee title to whatever we can get, and [surely] failing that, going for an outright purchase of all of his land at an affordable price; then a back-down to purchase an essential preservation strip; and lastly, a bid for the acquisition of conservation easements only.... Your thoughts on all of this would be appreciated.

Sincerely, Ed King... Edward W. King

Ed King was hanging on tight, stalling, wanting to do land deals and have ownership himself, failing to acknowledge the Conservancy's offer and willingness to undertake, in Wayne's words, a "major project... perhaps as many as 300 acres" and to "raise additional funds to complete the project."

November 22, 1989. As promised, Wayne Klockner mailed his formal Preserve Proposal to Ed King, with copies to Victor Schmidt and me:

Dear Mr. King... Please accept this as a proposal to the von Engeln Trustees to apply the proceeds of the estate towards the permanent preservation of the Malloryville esker and Wetlands Complex. The Nature Conservancy proposes to initiate a protection project at Malloryville to preserve the esker as well as significant biological resources of the various wetlands, which are an integral part of the site's esker-kame-kettle topography. Application of the von Engeln estate to this project would provide crucial seed money not only for initial land protection but also for the Conservancy's fundraising effort to cover the entire project's costs, including additional acquisitions. Site description

The Malloryville site is exceedingly diverse both topographically and ecologically. The esker that meanders through the site is considered the finest example of its kind in the Finger Lakes Region. Also, the site is dotted by kames, or mounds of glacially-deposited till, and kettleholes, depressions left by blocks of glacial ice that melted long ago. Many of the site's wetlands occupy these kettleholes. The Malloryville site, as depicted on the enclosed site map, embraces a prime example of Finger Lakes glacial geology.

The natural amenities of the site have attracted attention for almost a century. Botanists have long recognized Malloryville's diversity of species and wetland types... Authorities from Cornell University wrote about this site...

Here Wayne includes a descriptive paragraph quoted from Cornell Plantations' letter, written 2 1/2 years earlier, to the Town of Dryden and the DEC, and signed by Peter Marks, Robert Wesley and Heather Robertson:

"More recent botanical excursions confirm that today the wetlands of Malloryville have even greater significance. During the last hundred years other equivalent areas of special interest in the region have been damaged or destroyed, making the remaining sites all the more important. Malloryville remains in perfect condition. In addition to the peat bog mentioned by Dudley, Malloryville contains a number of small open seepage marshes or springs that are particularly important because they are the habitat for the rare globeflower. These marshes are very vulnerable to changes in water supply from surrounding land because their continued existence largely depends on upwelling of cold, limey groundwater flowing out of the gravel deposits."

And Wayne continues:

On the enclosed site map, the red line is the proposed site boundary, drawn to include not only the esker and wetlands but also the critical portions of the watersheds that provide a continual flow of pure groundwater to the wetlands. The proposed boundary encompasses 335 acres. Protection strategy

Also enclosed is an ownership map with the proposed site boundary drawn on it. The boundary includes nine key landowners whose property would need to be protected to ensure a defensible preserve.

In order of importance to the site's protection, the ownership is as follows...

Wayne presents a list of nine landowners, the top three, in order, being Gwen and my 38 acres, Alfred Eddy's 109 acres and my brother Ron's 75-acre punchbowl, all together totaling 335 acres within the proposed preserve. And he continues:

The Nature Conservancy would protect these tracts using a variety of methods. The foremost of these is fee simple acquisition either by gift or purchase. For tracts that are primarily buffer to the site's wetlands... conservation easements could be used to prevent development or gravel extraction without the expense of purchasing the tract outright. In all cases, a gift of land would be sought initially.

The protection of the Eddy tract is a priority because of the threat of gravel extraction or home development. The Conservancy agrees that fee simple acquisition of all or the essential portion of the Eddy tract is the most desired option. Management

The Conservancy is prepared to manage the Malloryville esker and Wetlands Complex as a nature preserve. At a minimum, the initial stewardship tasks would include boundary marking and posting, trash removal, and the drafting of a comprehensive management plan. Future stewardship needs are trail layout and maintenance, vegetation clearing and management for clear vistas of the esker and biological monitoring and management of the site's rare species.

The Conservancy proposes to create a stewardship fund to cover the costs of site management.

Project Budget

Here Wayne presents details on estimated land protection costs, administrative costs, a stewardship fund and total project cost, estimated at $250,000.

The Nature Conservancy is prepared to raise the funds for this project to complement the von Engeln bequest. Gifts of land may reduce the required amount for land protection.

Summary

The Malloryville esker and Wetlands Complex offers a diversity of biological and geological features found nowhere else in central New York. The opportunity exists to preserve this special site in a relatively pristine condition.

The nature Conservancy is prepared to launch a major fundraising effort to fund the establishment of a nature preserve at the site, to negotiate the protection of the various tracts with landowners, and to manage the preserve into the future.

We respectfully request that the von Engeln bequest be applied to this project as a challenge grant that would ensure its success.

Sincerely yours, Wayne A. Klockner, Executive Director, Central/Western New York Chapters, The Nature Conservancy

December 3, 1989. Victor Schmidt writes to Wayne Klockner:

Dear Wayne... Thank you very much for sending me a copy of the proposal to the von Engeln

Trustees with regard to the Malloryville esker and Wetlands Complex. It is a well-stated outline of what seems to be a workable plan for action for the preservation of the site... The thought occurred to me that when the Nature Conservancy embarks on a fundraising effort to support this project, it may be wise to make a special appeal to persons who knew Dr. von Engeln, including his students, colleagues, and fellow geologists. At such time I probably will be able to help with some specific suggestions... May I send my best wishes for a happy holiday season?

Sincerely, Vic... Victor E. Schmidt

Victor's support for Malloryville, as the von Engeln estate's science advisor, was strong. Yet, from Ed King, co-executor and Trustee, we would hear nothing more for a long six months.

Following the July, 1989 PosDec(2), we had waited, as with PosDec(1), for the applicant's next move, wondering whether Paolangeli would proceed with an impact statement, or disappear quietly as did B.R. DeWitt. Months, half a year, and more, would pass with no word. That seemed to be good news, no news was good news, and we hoped it would continue. And the time seemed ripe for serious contact with landowner Alfred Eddy, and possibly even negotiation for a land deal. But as far as we knew, Ed King was making no moves.

Then, in June and July, 1990, several letters were written concerning the von Engeln funds. On June 14, 1990, Ed King wrote to Alfred Eddy:

Dear Al... As you will recall, I spoke to you via telephone many months ago about my interest in preserving the Malloryville esker and access for students to it, as was desired by Prof. O.D. von Engeln and expressed in his Will.

I am a Co-Executor and Trustee under the

Will, and we now have a trust fund available to purchase lands or easements in land to try to fulfill Prof. von Engeln's desires that certain local geological features (including this esker specifically) be preserved and made available to students for study.

I know you told me at the time that this was not the best example of an esker in New York State: but it is one which is within a reasonable distance of Cornell University and hence more readily available for study; and it does lie far enough back from the road and any potential, road-front dwelling lots, that your selling it off, or selling the Trust a permanent preservation and access easement in it, would not cost you any good building lots or bother adjacent dwellings or landowners.

As a Trustee, I have to get moving toward some decisions to what projects we are going to devote these funds to; so I would appreciate your early and earnest consideration of this matter, and an opportunity to discuss possibilities with you.

Sincerely, Edward W. King

Victor Schmidt, on June 23, 1990, wrote to Ed King, referring to a letter I have not seen:

Dear Ed, This is in response to your letter of June 15... and our telephone conversation of last evening.

First, in regard to our telephone conversation, I have reread my copy of the portion of Dr. von Engeln's will that deals with the Trust. He clearly had in mind a Natural History Preserve rather than a Geological Preserve, although he viewed the geological aspects of the two areas he suggested as the prime purpose of setting aside these areas. Through my association with Dr.

Von I know that his interest was in Nature in a broad sense, not merely in the geological aspects. I find support for this in the book Cornell Geology Through the Years by Wm. R Brice (a copy of which I have just received from the Dept. of Geological Sciences at Cornell) which refers (on p. 127) to Dr. Von's essay "Shakespeare as an Observer of Nature" in which he drew upon his background gained in wandering through the woods and fields in Ohio, prior to entering Cornell. Also, on p. 83 of Dr. Von's The Finger Lakes Region, referring to the "Lost Gorge" (Hendershot Gulf), I find; "It would be gratifying to have it made a natural history preserve, so that the forest on its slopes and floor would always be spared the lumberman's attack."

The will specifies that a Corporation be formed "...if it should be then deemed advisable... for the purpose of any such project..." this, I should think, would be necessary to protect any property acquired—to post it, protect it from vandalism, draw up regulations concerning its use, etc. Further, I should think that the Corporation should be not-for-profit and chartered by the New York State Board of Regents, and that this would require having a board of directors or trustees, officers, etc. It is my view that, with the Court's permission, it would be more practical to have an established, reputable organization such as The Nature Conservancy protect and maintain the Preserve. It is true that the Conservancy is primarily engaged in the preservation of areas of biological interest, but it also protects geological features when these are part and parcel of the ecology—as they are at the Malloryville esker and associated bogs. I know of no organization that has as its goal the preservation of exclusively geological sites, neither do I know of any organization that could manage the kind of natural history preserve that Dr. Von had in mind better than The Nature Conservancy. I have given consideration to the Finger Lakes Land Trust... but as of now am not certain of the viability....

Finally in regard to our telephone conversation, I will call Wayne Klockner of the Rochester office of The Nature Conservancy on Monday and ask him to send you examples of easements or other agreements or purchases which the Conservancy has made to preserve geological as well as biological areas...

Now let me turn to your letter of June 15, for which I thank you and which I was about to answer when your call came. ...The proposal that I would favor is the one spelled out by Wayne Klockner, Executive Director of the Central/Western New York Chapters of The Nature Conservancy, in his letter of November 22... In this he proposes purchasing and/or getting easements on a total of 335 acres, at an estimated cost, including administrative costs and stewardship funds, of $250,000. To me this seems desirable and feasible, and the Von Engeln Trust could go a long way toward meeting the goal. I agree with you that the Eddy property is the key, and it would seem to be the logical contribution the Von Engeln Trust might make to the entire project.

As I see it, the chief decision that must be made next is on the question of whether we should work with The Nature Conservancy toward this goal. If the Trustees agreed to this, it would seem, then, that the next step would be to get the Court's approval. In regard to this action I plead ignorance, but if the Court's concern is that the intent of Dr. Von's will be implemented, I would anticipate no difficulty in getting its approval. It is true that, as you say, if Dr. Von wanted The Nature Conservancy to have the bulk of his estate he would have said that. Still, he may not have been aware of the Conservancy's existence when the will was drawn; I do not know the will's date, but I read that the Conservancy was chartered in 1951 in the District of Columbia.

I agree with you in that "Lost Gorge will stay put..." and that the Malloryville esker and bogs are much more vulnerable. There is clearly more support among biologists and geologists for the preservation of the Malloryville site than there is for Hendershot Gulf. For example, Richard Fischer, the well-known professor (emeritus) of nature study at Cornell telephoned me some time ago to urge my support for Malloryville, and more recently John Wells, professor of geology (emeritus) at Cornell and my alternate as scientific consultant in carrying out Dr. Von's project, wrote me, "personally I'd like the Malloryville tract" in comparison to Hendershot.

Finally, I see no hurry for the State to acquire land near the mouth of Hendershot Gulf; sooner or later I think the needed public money will be forthcoming... Nevertheless, if the Trustees and the Court agree to the plan to establish the Natural History Preserve at the Malloryville esker and Associated Bogs, once this has been done or is well on the way to being done, I would be willing to give serious consideration to using funds that are not needed for the Malloryville Preserve for helping the State acquire additional land at Hendershot....

Please call me if I can be of any help this coming week, or during the summer... I'm embarrassed by the length of this letter and the number of inked-in changes that will have to be made before I send it. But I'm anxious to get it off to you as soon as possible and I am acting as my own secretary these days, so I know you'll understand.

With my best personal regards, Sincerely, Vic... Victor E. Schmidt

A month later, on July 27, 1990, Ed King wrote to both Victor Schmidt and Wayne Klockner (bold emphasis is Ed's):

Gentlemen... Alfred Eddy is ready to talk turkey about our acquiring some or all of his land! To aid your thinking about negotiating strategies, I will now bore you with the details:

Much to my surprise, Alfred Eddy telephoned me 10 days ago and asked me just how much land I wanted to acquire for preservation of the esker. I told him I was not sure—that personally I thought a strip of 100 feet or 150 feet along the east side would do nicely; **but** that I had not studied the land closely enough to be sure that such a strip would cover the esker and pit area, **and** that I would have to contact my "science advisors" to get their opinions and advice in any event.

He said that he had to know soon just how much land I wanted. I sensed that he might be thinking of marketing the property or developing residential lots. I had forgotten the details of Wayne's outline proposal as to the Eddy land: hence the stall for time to look into it, while also not appearing too eager to jump. Eddy said he had land surveyed recently and would be glad to show me the survey, and I said that would be helpful.

After our conversation, I dug out Wayne's proposal and was surprised to see that he had recommended that we go for Eddy's whole 109 Acres! So I got out tax maps and topos and a large aerial photo covering a good area of the Township, and I proceeded to do some plotting (—both map-wise and strategy-wise) to decide how best to approach Eddy, and whether to ask for 109 Acres! I decided to tell him the following:

"My scientific advisers have told me that we should have access to the gravel pit area itself as well as to the intact portions of the esker; that the esker runs right across the Eddy land (as well as northerly into it); and that accordingly, they think we should consider acquiring the whole 109 Acres and try to work with the Nature Conservancy to set up a viable, large area project there."

When I called Eddy's office back last Monday, Al was out of town but his wife said he'd be back Tuesday and that she would have him call me. She seemed to know what it was about. He did not call: so I decided I'd better hit him with 109 Acre proposition quickly, before he committed himself to listing the property, or selling to someone else. So I called him this morning and related the above to him.

He said that I was catching him off guard with that 109 Acre request! "Do you realize how much gravel is in that land? How valuable it is? Do you have that much money?" he asked. (I did not respond directly or challenge him on the value of the gravel or raise any question about getting a permit to extract it. I said merely that we are not interested in gravel as a commodity, but in **preservation** of the land in its pristine condition, but that some felt that the gravel pits provide excellent opportunities to examine the various types of rock, gravel, sediment, etc. in the area: and for those reasons, the Cornell Geology Dept. advisor [meaning Art Bloom] encouraged acquisition of the open pit area as well.

Al said the Nature Conservancy probably wouldn't be interested in the esker as much as they were in the bogs and plants—and that we'd have to deal with other people [Beck] to get that land or easements on it. I told him that it was my understanding that Beck would be willing to work with the Conservancy to that end. And I also told him that "the Conservancy people" are willing to sit down and discuss land acquisitions with us and Mr. Eddy, once I get as much detail as I can; and that for that purpose I'd like to see his Survey Map for starters. He has promised to get a copy to me; said he did not have one there—that his Geologist... had the map.

We talked of access to the northerly lot or portion of his land. [The gravel pit road provides the only way into it.] We also discussed the topography [undulating] and the zoning [Residential]. He several times again expressed his surprise at my talking about buying the whole thing, and said "your advisors probably don't know the value of that gravel." He also said "even if you are not interested in developing the land, you still have to pay the real value of it"— 980,000 [?] cubic yards, I think he said!

But as we talked and the wheels whirred, he suddenly said (and then repeated) in effect "Maybe it could be set up or arranged so that I could take out that large mound of gravel [on the north lot?]. Maybe that would work."

So his price to us [whatever it might be: he didn't say!] might be moderating in his mind, in exchange for the reservation of some mineral rights. (We might also, at some point, try to pull the price down further by suggesting that he retain some of the land at the south end suitable for residential building lots: e.g. along the Malloryville Road frontage (where he had 545 feet from Beck westerly to a house lot [c. 170' front x 285' deep] which he sold off some time ago.

And perhaps even more building lots along the west side could be cut out for him, in order to bring his price down, when it comes down to it.

Meanwhile, what easements/lands would Bob Beck be willing to give or devote to the project to make our dealing with Eddy Sensible? What should we be asking of him? Shouldn't we ask Bob Beck (and his brother?) to commit themselves to **re-purchase** this Eddy land **from the Trust**, subject to Von Engeln purpose conservation easements on it? (The Trust might then have money left for Lost Gorge Acquisitions, and even after that (we hope) some money left over to invest to produce a little income for some support to such projects. (Another nice feature: a residual trust fund would also continue to generate some small Trustee fees... which might "keep [me] in cakes and ale" as Prof. von Engeln put it!

I will enclose a couple copies of maps and my sketches of the Eddy lands for your immediate reference. I'd also like your several, quick reactions to my questions concerning Beck participation.

I am **not** sending a copy of this to Bob Beck, and I have not told him of this sudden development: but I have no objections to either of you revealing it to him, if in the process of sounding him out about participation. Since Eddy and I have already addressed the possibility of Beck participation, I no longer have the fear that Bob's appearance in any way might jeopardize getting a deal with Eddy. (**But of course**, any agreement for or talk of the Becks buying Eddy land back from the Trust should be kept **confidential**: I don't know how Al would react to that thought. His price will be high enough, I'm sure, without giving him an incentive to push even higher or harder than usual!)

Sincerely, Ed... Edward W. King

Well, Ed was thrilled with his efforts of the moment, yet nothing more happened. I had asked to talk with him, once, about the timing and importance of the DEC's second Positive Declaration, but he declined to see me. By his refusal, I was puzzled and disappointed, and I troubled him no more.

And I didn't understand Ed's strange suggestion in his letter, secretive and kept from me—(Was I an adversary, motives suspect, not to be trusted? Wasn't it I who had spearheaded efforts to protect the lands, to protect the possibility even of a future nature preserve here?)—and his suggestion that I repurchase Eddy land from the von Engeln Trust, that I buy back whatever bit of land he could acquire from the gravel property, as if I had disposable cash readily at hand. Had I such resources, he ought to have known, I could have purchased the Eddy tract myself, saving a decade or so of hassle and headache for all concerned.

One time, after a meeting at DEC with Ray Nolan, landowner Alfred Eddy had asked of me, "Why don't you make an offer?" but I couldn't answer, nor could I breathe even a word to him of von Engeln or Nature Conservancy possibilities. I, as instigator of obstacles in his gravel-mine path, had best provide no information, better that he not know of my association with either Ed King or The Nature Conservancy.

A hopeful, possible, window of opportunity was closing. A year had passed since PosDec(2). The time had been an opportunity for serious discussion with Alfred Eddy, a time before Alfred would become fully committed with the DEC in a third-round of gravel plans, a time when The Nature Conservancy had offered to lead a major effort to establish a 300-plus acre preserve at Malloryville, a time when Victor Schmidt, with enthusiasm, had counseled prompt acceptance of the Conservancy's challenge. But Ed King, while admirably protecting the von Engeln funds and keeping the Lost Gorge option open, seemed stuck in thinking small, avoiding Victor's sensible and farsighted advice, and forgetting, in his communication with Alfred Eddy, the lay of the land and even essential points in Wayne Klockner's bold Proposal. Though it was possible, maybe probable, that no talks with Eddy would have been fruitful, still, as we were approaching the end of our Year 4, it seemed a lost opportunity. Soon another gravel application would intervene and five more years would pass before Eddy was approached again in serious effort to negotiate a land deal.

Skunk Cabbage (*Symplocarpus foetidus*) flowers in ice

9 NegDec

Even if you are on the right track,
You'll get run over if you just sit there!
— Will Rogers

IN THE PREVIOUS October—1989, early in Year 4—I received a letter from Jim McNamara, a graduate student of Prof. Don Siegel at Syracuse University. Jim wrote to ask for my permission to undertake a hydrogeology study in the wetlands for his master's dissertation. He would be installing piezometer pipes at numerous sites in the swamps, fens and bog to learn about groundwater flow and chemistry in the functioning of the diverse wetlands, and taking a core sample for study from the bog. I heartily approved, eager to learn more, myself, about what makes the place tick, how such diversity came to be, and how it is maintained. Jim's study and my association with Prof. Siegel and some of his colleagues and students over the coming years, would prove most helpful in our opposition to yet another, a third, gravel mine proposal.

In early November, 1989, Jim installed his piezometers, rigid, half-inch inside-diameter, gray PVC pipes, 1–4 meters (about 3 to 13 feet) in length and open at the bottom, in small clusters called "piezometer nests" at fifteen locations in the wetlands. And with help from his wife, Lori, he surveyed the sites, determining elevation differences between the nests. Then he began collecting data, sampling the water to measure pH, specific conductance and chemistry, recording the height of water in the tubes to determine groundwater movement, up, down or horizontal, as well as hydraulic conductivity, and returning repeatedly to observe seasonal changes.

Eleven months later, on October 5, 1990, I joined Jim, Don, Prof. Paul Glaser from the University of Minnesota, and several students, to extract a core sample from near the center of the bog, carefully, in a procedure that I was assured would not cause any significant damage to the wetland. With a tall, hand operated, core-drilling, tripod apparatus, we started removing 3-inch diameter by 18-inch long plugs of peat, starting at the green sphagnum-bog mat, and proceeding downwards, 18 inches at a time. These peat cores were laid out, end to end in order, in white PVC pipe split lengthwise, opened and lined with kitchen plastic wrap, to seal and contain the core for transport back to the lab. We had no idea how deep it might be to the gravel bottom of the glacial kettle in which the bog had grown, and we quickly ran out of lengths of threaded iron pipe needed to go deeper.

Saturday morning, I quickly called hardware stores, hoping to find one with threaded pipe. In luck, I reached an Agway storeowner who said he could help if, between customers, he could find time to thread both ends of his sections of unthreaded pipe. We drove six miles to the store and, with the owner's cooperation, obtained what we needed. Back at the bog, adding pipe, length-by-length, retrieving cores and boring deeper, we found the kettle's solid bottom at 10 meters below the soles of our boots, 33 feet, 12,000 years of darkness, below the acid bog's sunlit lush green surface.

And later, studies of the plant remains in the peat core combined with radiocarbon dating of core layers revealed that the surface plant community, growing ever higher with increasing peat depth, transformed from alkaline fen to acid bog, 4100 years ago, as mineral-rich groundwater reaching the surface from below, lessening with height, became less influential as rainwater from above became more important.

May 16, 1990, Year 4. From my house, I hear activity beyond the wetlands. Seven test pits are dug and vertical 4-inch diameter white PVC pipes are installed as test wells on the upland Eddy gravel property. Five months have elapsed since Wayne Klockner's Preserve Proposal to Ed King, six months since Jim McNamara began his study in the wetlands, and nine months since PosDec(2). I would soon learn that Brayton Foster is working as geological consultant for landowner Alfred Eddy, and Eddy is now considering applying for a permit directly, this time to operate the mine himself rather than leasing the land to another operator, Paolangeli having decided not to pursue an impact statement. Apparently, Eddy and Foster are taking up Ray Nolan's DEC offer, from a year earlier to Paolangeli, when Ray wrote, "In an effort to avoid requiring the preparation of a dEIS I am asking you to consider preparing a complete hydrological study of the area so that any negative effects on the wetland from the proposed mining activities can be identified." That study, apparently its intent, could empower Ray to issue a NegDec, rather than an appropriate PosDec requiring a dEIS. SEQR rules then, by my understanding, would require neither public comments, nor an impact statement (dEIS), nor further review, before approval of mining permits by New York State's DEC.

Meanwhile, neither the von Engeln bequest, its commitment to Malloryville yet to be decided by Ed King, nor The Nature Conservancy's Preserve Proposal to him, each being sensitive and confidential, could become public, nor included even in my person-to-person talks with Ray Nolan at DEC. With Ray, I felt comfortable in saying only that The Nature Conservancy had a strong interest in seeing the site protected. Premature talk of any specifics, might be viewed by Ray as inappropriate, unfair speculation not to be acknowledged, in a DEC review, and such talk, getting back to von Engeln's Ed King, likely would alienate Ed's thinking towards Malloryville.

Uncertain as the situation was, we would have months to

wait, nearly half a year, mid May to early November, for Brayton Foster and Alfred Eddy's next move.

Year 5: 1990/91

Dated November 5, 1990, a fat envelope arrives at the Tompkins County Environmental Management Council (EMC), with a cover letter from Brayton Foster:

> Enclosed is a copy of a DEC Mining Permit Application to be submitted next month for the Eddy property adjoining the Malloryville Bog in the Town of Dryden. Included in this application is a hydrogeologic study of the property done this past summer.
>
> To ensure that the adjoining bog is not disturbed by mining the operator will limit the maximum annual mining rate to one half that of peak historic levels, not approach the bog closer than previous mining, preserve the groundwater barrier in the middle of the Eddy property, mine only above the water table and not use groundwater for any processing operations at this site.
>
> The total material to be removed during the next 20 years is approximately 800,000 cubic yards compared to the approximately 600,000 cubic yards removed during the last 20 years...
>
> Your comments will be attached to the permit application.
>
> Very truly yours, Brayton P. Foster, Consulting Geologist

As an active member of the EMC, I was among the first to read the proposed, not yet submitted, application. Foster and Eddy's strategy made sense: forestall criticism by presenting their mining plan to the County EMC for review, in advance of formal submission to the State DEC; gain valuable public support, perhaps even the endorsement of the County, by proffering the plan as an entirely benign, small scale operation wholly

compatible with the neighborhood and with the adjacent wetlands. On the surface, to anyone unfamiliar with the place,
unaware of the depth of controversy, all might seem well, a
reasonable source of gravel for needed construction, an application worthy of support. Yet, to others willing to take a deeper look at the natural environment and its neighborhood, to
those familiar with and concerned about protecting things of
lasting value, the plan to extract gravel for twenty years at that
particular location, is revealed as something quite other than
benign, something undeserving of the support or approval of
either the County or the State. And, importantly, in the application's Groundwater Flow hydrogeologic study, the dubious
conclusions of a subsurface dam and two groundwater flow
systems on the Eddy tract, and that mining would have no
impact on the wetlands, struck me as going far beyond what
the meager data could support.

At the December 17, 1990 monthly meeting of the Tompkins County EMC, a resolution, with the customary "Whereas"
list, was presented and passed with unanimous approval of the
20 members present:

> RESOLUTION... Recommending Protection of
> Three Unique Natural Areas at Malloryville:
> Whereas, at Malloryville, three Tompkins
> County Unique Natural Areas—Malloryville Bog
> (with Swamp/Fens/esker, DR-3), North Mallo-
> ryville (DR-4), and Malloryville Fen (DR-34)—are
> highly rated and of regional significance,
> Whereas, the geology of the area consists of
> unusually striking kame, kettle and esker topog-
> raphy and includes the Malloryville esker, de-
> scribed by von Engeln in The Finger Lakes Re-
> gion: Its Origin and Nature (1961) as perhaps the
> best example in the Finger Lakes Region,
> Whereas, as a consequence of the complex
> topography, diverse natural community types
> occurring in close proximity to one another (bog,
> fens, mineral-rich wooded swamps, mineral-

poor wooded swamps, marsh, marl springs, streams and upland forest),

Whereas, the wetlands in the Unique Natural Areas include rare community types and contain at least 32 rare or scarce plant species, some of which depend upon the upwelling of cold, mineral-rich groundwater from surrounding gravel deposits,

Whereas, alterations in the quantity, location or quality (pH, mineral content, nutrients or pollutants) of groundwater flowing into the wetland areas would have significant impacts on the wetland communities and species present,

Whereas, in reviewing two gravel-mining proposals for an adjacent site in the past 3 1/2 years, the DEC—as lead agency—twice concluded that mining may have large and important impacts on the environment (SEQR positive declarations...),

Whereas, the Tompkins County EMC in two resolutions... requested and obtained the discontinuation of the septage disposal operation adjacent to Malloryville Bog,

Whereas, because of the complexity of the site it is difficult, if not impossible, to predict either the groundwater flow into the wetlands or the impact that gravel mining or other development projects would have on the flow and on the wetland communities and species that depend on that flow,

Therefore, be it resolved that, in view of the rarity, quality and significance of these Unique Natural Areas and their unusual scientific and educational value, it is the desire of the EMC that irreversible damage to these areas not be risked as a result of development decisions,

And further resolved, that caution be observed in land-use planning for these areas and adjacent land and that development be denied

for any purpose or projects that pose any danger whatsoever to the long-term protection of the Unique Natural Areas at Malloryville.
Approved 20-0-0.

As always, the EMC resolution was directed to the Tompkins County Board of Legislators, and in addition this one was mailed to Brayton Foster, to the Town of Dryden and to Ray Nolan at the DEC.

Dated January 15, 1991, the Eddy/Foster Application was formally submitted to the DEC and included in the application was the EMC's Resolution to which Foster responded by writing:

> ...the operator shares the Environmental Management Council's goals of preserving adjoining unique natural areas. The limiting activities outlined... combined with the histories of overgrazing, previous mining and the hydrogeologic understanding presented in this application will allow gravel mining to proceed with confidence.

At that point, I was hopeful that Ray Nolan would announce receipt of a complete application and would request comments from the public for his review in determining significance, PosDec or NegDec. But Ray wasn't ready, and he told me, "Not yet..." for comments. We waited through January and February, then Ray wrote to Brayton Foster on March 4, 1991:

> Dear Mr. Foster... As I mentioned to you during our last meeting I have provided a copy of your report regarding the above referenced project to Frank Trent, a DEC geologist in our Kirkwood office. I appreciate your advising me that there is no particular urgency with this project. This will allow the Department to thoroughly review your initial submission and develop a set of additional

information needs prior to submitting a completed application to the public review process.

In order to maintain a reasonable parallel with the time frames pertinent to the application review I am providing you with the enclosed notice of incomplete application...

You should be aware that additional information needs and concerns may be identified during the public comment period which will follow the Department's acceptance of either a complete application or a dEIS.

If you have any questions regarding this letter feel free to contact me...

Very truly yours, Raymond J Nolan, Sr. Environmental Analyst

March 6, 1991. Memo from Frank Trent of DEC to Ray Nolan:

I have reviewed the report titled Groundwater Flow at the Eddy Property... A Hydrogeologic Study prepared by Brayton P. Foster, Consulting Geologist... This report suggests that the groundwater flow regime within the proposed gravel mining area has little impact on the adjoining Malloryville Bog. For the following reasons I do not believe that this report satisfactorily supports that conclusion.

This report suggests that the groundwater hydrology of the site and the adjoining Malloryville Bog is rather complex. It suggests that two or more discrete groundwater flow regimes are present at this site, yet only uses six data points (monitoring wells 3, 5, 6 and 7, the residential water well at the Geiger-White house and an elevation of Fall Creek.) This is not sufficient data in order to support the varying groundwater flow directions suggested by this study. At a minimum, I suggest that these additional monitoring wells be drilled...

Locations for five additional wells are suggested, and Trent states how they should be installed, using a drill rig rather than placing the pipes in dug test pits, as had been done with the first seven wells. And Frank Trent continues:

> Since the test pits were only 18 to 20 feet deep the groundwater table was not encountered in wells 1, 2 and 4. The statement in the report regarding the groundwater table in the vicinity of these three wells being about 35 to 40 feet below the ground surface is not supported by the data from these wells. All one can conclude is that the groundwater table in this area is at least 18 to 20 feet below the ground surface.
>
> ...hydraulic conductivity values can and should be obtained from wells installed as I suggest. This is particularly critical as regards characterizing the lateral moraine which is hypothesized as forming a subsurface dam. The report "projects" this moraine as extending across the site in the subsurface. Actual hard data must be collected in order to demonstrate this. That is why I have suggested that at least two monitoring wells be installed in this deposit.
>
> The report cited the existence of a number of springs and seeps within the Malloryville Bog. An effort should be made to locate and map these springs and seeps. The elevations of them [sic] should be surveyed as they define the groundwater table at those points.
>
> All of these data points should be used in order to prepare a contour map of the groundwater table for purposes of determining the direction(s) and velocity of groundwater flow... The elevations of all data points used should be surveyed.

April 29, 1991. Nearly two months after Frank Trent's

memo, Ray wrote a letter to Brayton Foster:

> Dear Mr. Foster: As you know I have received comments from Frank Trent regarding your groundwater flow study at the Eddy property... Mr. Trent suggests that, at a minimum, five additional monitoring wells be drilled as follows...

Ray's letter then quotes, word for word, Frank's nearly two-page memo specifying the suggested wells before concluding with:

> The application will remain incomplete pending resolution of the questions surrounding the ground water conditions at the site.
> Very truly yours, Raymond J. Nolan

I didn't know to what extent this was common practice in SEQR reviews: the lead agency, here the DEC, asking the applicant to collect and analyze data to "avoid requiring" an impact statement, then, with the applicant's continuing claim of no environmental harm still unconvincing (meaning there may well be adverse environmental impacts), asking for still more data instead of declaring a PosDec, the aim seemingly of further maneuvering to declare a NegDec. That accomplished, no nasty impact statement is required, messy public input is minimized, controversy quietly avoided. That scenario may, in fact, be common in environmental reviews, yet Malloryville's complex, unique and sensitive wetlands were already known to the DEC, known by Ray Nolan to be defended by professional botanists, wetlands ecologists, and hydrogeologists, respected scientists who were speaking out against the risk of removal of upslope gravel. But those comments were in DEC's files of the two previous mining applications, not in the current file. To Ray, were those many letters just out-of-sight, out-of-mind and inconvenient, or legally untouchable, or were they perhaps merely the occasional comments of transient environmentalists not likely to be around, not likely to be heard from again, this time? I couldn't see into Ray's mind. Clear to me, however, was the need to call the application complete, to request public comments, to acknowledge the environmental risks, to declare a PosDec, as in the DeWitt and Paolangeli reviews, and thus to require a dEIS encouraging full scientific and public input.

May 3, 1991. Brayton Foster, at the behest of landowner Alfred Eddy, writes to Ray Nolan, presenting inaccurate, misleading information concerning the Town of Dryden's interest at Malloryville, distorting facts to protect their DEC application:

> Dear Mr. Nolan... The Alfred C. Eddy property at Malloryville in the Town of Dryden, Tompkins County has had a Special Use Permit for the mining of gravel on this property... One of the conditions of this permit is that mining (no specified quantity) must continue each year for the permit to remain in effect. Small quantities (less than 1,000 tons) have been mined on this site each year to preserve the Special Use Permit. Since a mining permit application is now being considered by your office which may not be completed for some time the applicant wishes to notify the Department that small quantities will be mined to preserve the Special Use Permit of the Town of Dryden.
>
> I do not want this technical point to further complicate the permit process while the mining permit application is being reviewed...
>
> Brayton P. Foster, Consulting Geologist

Well, that technical point was incorrect, a falsehood. Then, in my fifth year at my home, gravel mining on the Eddy property had not occurred since I moved in and did not continue. Alfred Eddy's Special Permit had long since expired, and he had no Town of Dryden gravel-mining permit in effect. Henry Slater, of Dryden, had earlier made that clear and Mahlon Perkins, the Town Attorney, would do so again.

Andy Zepp, after spearheading the establishment of the Finger Lakes Land Trust as his graduate work at Cornell, next had accepted employment with The Nature Conservancy at the Central & Western NY Chapter office in Rochester, under Executive Director Wayne Klockner. Soon, however, Wayne would be leaving to become The Conservancy's State Director in Maryland, where earlier he had been second in charge, and I was concerned his Malloryville Proposal might be neglected with change in personnel, and with the von Engeln bequest in limbo.

But our Conservancy Chapter Board hired David Klein as our new Executive Director, and in my interaction with him I was pleased that he immediately took interest in keeping the project alive. In fact, David's keen understanding of my interest and his unwavering support throughout the next years was always, for me, a source of immense comfort and encouragement. And Andy Zepp, as Director of Land Protection, would take the lead, together with his numerous other projects, in the effort to create a Conservancy preserve at Malloryville. From his time in Ithaca, Andy knew me, and he knew the challenges we were facing in defending against the series of gravel mining proposals.

After renewing contact with Ed King of the von Engeln estate, Andy invited Kate Hubbs, of the Conservancy's New York State office, to meet with him (Andy) and myself on a site visit here. Kate was the statewide Director of Preserve Design and she was familiar with Wayne's Preserve Proposal. Now it was important for her to see the place first-hand, including the Eddy tract in an effort to answer Ed King's question about how much of the Eddy land would be essential to a viable preserve. To that question there was no easy answer, but I urged, and they agreed, that neither Ed nor The Conservancy should consider settling for only a narrow buffer strip.

July 18, 1991. Andy Zepp wrote to Ed King:

Dear Mr. King: I am writing in order to follow up on our most recent conversation regarding the Eddy property in Malloryville. After a field inspection, Kate Hubbs, the Conservancy's New York Director of Preserve Design, decided that no determination concerning a minimum adequate buffer for the wetland could be made with currently available data. Kate did suggest, however, that such a determination might be possible once Eddy has provided the data requested by NYSDEC as part of the mining permit application process.

I will continue to monitor the DEC permitting process and will contact you once we have more information. Please do not hesitate to contact me in the meantime if I can be of assistance in any way.

Sincerely, Andrew E. Zepp

Year 6: 1991/92

Again days and weeks become months, summer, fall and winter pass, then, on March 2–4, 1992, five new test wells on the Eddy property are drilled and installed by Northstar Drilling Co., using 2-inch diameter PVC pipes 26-50 feet deep, grouted to the surface, ten months after Ray Nolan and Frank Trent's instructions to Brayton Foster for more test wells, 14 months since the mining application was submitted, 22 months since the first seven wells had been installed.

June 25, 1992. Brayton Foster sends his hydrology report supplement to Ray Nolan. From Foster's letter to Ray, I quote a few relevant excerpts. Foster writes:

Dear Mr. Nolan: Enclosed are well logs for 5 new observation wells installed in March... These wells are at the locations suggested by Mr. Frank Trent...

Well #12 does change the... conclusion regarding flow of water under the old south pit area. While the gradient is still southwestward the present interpretation does not define any groundwater barrier with the adjoining bog to the east...

While the additional drilling has changed and expanded our understanding of the geologic system present on this property it continues to support the basic concept of groundwater being delivered or "leaked" to the bog through an extended time period...

Very truly yours, Brayton P. Foster

July 17, 1992. Frank Trent sends a memo to Ray Nolan concerning the Foster supplement reporting on the five new wells. Trent notes that Foster's supplement changes the interpretation of the application's previous Groundwater Flow report in a critical way, changing perhaps the central argument in the application, that there are two groundwater tables separated by a "subsurface dam," a change that, to me, appears to seriously weaken Foster's certainty of no environmental impact. And yet, Trent, perplexingly, concludes that mining "should have a negligible impact" on the wetland. Frank Trent writes:

>...The groundwater table map suggests that there are not two distinct groundwater tables at this site as previously reported. This map suggests that groundwater flows from both the northern and southern parts of the proposed gravel operation will impact the Malloryville Bog. ...Provided that the till deposits are not disturbed it appears that gravel mining at this site should have a negligible impact on the hydrology of the Malloryville Bog.
>
> Frank Trent

But wait! Haven't these new data weakened the argument? While Brayton Foster, the applicant's consultant, understandably continues his push for approval of mining, isn't DEC skepticism appropriate here, serious caution necessary, when further study and additional facts clearly weaken, even undermine, key components of the original argument, an argument proclaiming, with overly-confident statements, no environmental harm will be done? In SEQR, shouldn't that revelation, such uncertainty in a complex situation, almost certainly trigger a PosDec, require an impact statement, especially when the resource at risk is a rare, fragile, irreplaceable natural environment?

Year 7: 1992/93

Four full months later, Ray Nolan writes to Town of Dryden's Supervisor, Jim Schug, complying with the state's amended Mined Land Reclamation Law, enacted 14 months earlier. The new amendments had potentially returned to local governments considerable power to control the location of mining through local zoning ordinances and power to regulate some aspects of a mine's operation through local laws of general applicability, that is, through laws only incidentally affecting mining, but not the specifics of the mining process itself. In the SEQR process, the state could agree or disagree with local government input and would incorporate local concerns that it agreed with into permit conditions if a permit were issued. Yet as before, DEC authority would supersede and preempt all other local laws.

November 16, 1992. Ray's letter to Dryden Supervisor Jim Schug:

> Dear Mr. Schug: On September 1, 1991 a revised Mined Land Reclamation law became effective because of actions taken by the New York Legislature and Governor Cuomo. Section 23-2711.3 states: "Upon receipt of a complete application for a mining permit... a notice shall be sent by the Department, by certified mail, to the chief administrative office of the political subdivision in which the proposed mine is to be located

(hereafter, 'local government'). Such notice will be accompanied by copies of all documents which comprise the complete application...

(a) The chief administrative officer may make a determination, and notify the Department and applicant, in regard to:

(i) appropriate setbacks from property boundaries or public thoroughfare rights-of-way,

(ii) manmade or natural barriers designed to restrict access if needed, and, if affirmative, the type, length, height and location thereof,

(iii) the control of dust,

(iv) hours of operation and,

(v) whether mining is prohibited at that location. Any determination made by a local government hereunder shall be accompanied by supporting documentation justifying the particular determination on an individual basis. The chief administrative officer must provide any determinations, notices and supporting documents according to the following schedule:

(i) within thirty days after receipt for a major project...

(b) If the Department finds that the determinations made by the local government pursuant to paragraph (a) of this subdivision are reasonable and necessary, the Department shall incorporate these into the permit, if one is issued. If the Department does not agree that the determinations are justifiable, then the Department shall provide a written statement to the local government and the applicant, as to the reason or reasons why the whole or a part of any of the determination was not incorporated."

Ray then concludes:

Enclosed you will find a complete Mined Land Reclamation application submitted by Alfred C.

Eddy.... As the Chief Administrative Officer you must notify this office, pertaining to the above referenced section of the Law, by 30 calendar days from the date of this letter. If you have no concerns, we would like a statement so stating that determination. If nothing is received from you by the 30 day timeframe, we will assume you have no interest.

Sincerely yours, Raymond J. Nolan, Sr. Environmental Analyst

November 16, 1992, the same day as his letter to Town Supervisor Jim Schug, Ray Nolan issues two SEQR documents:

NOTICE OF COMPLETE APPLICATION... Project is a Type I action and will not have a significant effect on the environment. A coordinated review with other agencies was performed and a Negative Declaration is on file...

Raymond J. Nolan

November 16, 1992, NegDec:

NEGATIVE DECLARATION: Notice of Determination of Non-Significance... The New York State Department of Environmental Conservation, as lead agency, has determined that the proposed action described below will not have a significant effect on the environment and a Draft Environmental Impact Statement will not be prepared...

REASONS SUPPORTING THIS DETERMINATION:

1. All topsoil will be removed and stockpiled for the purpose of reclamation.

2. The facility will be operated during normal working hours and not on Sunday.

3. After mining has taken place, the area shall be reclaimed as per the submitted reclamation plan,

topsoil replaced and a vegetative cover planted to hold topsoil in place.

4. A permit, if issued, will include conditions as necessary to mitigate any potential adverse effect on the permitted area and its resources.

Based on the submittal of the long EAF and in mining and reclamation plans, the project will not have a significant effect on the environment for the following reasons:

5. The project conforms to zoning regulations in the town's land-use plans.

6. There will not be any significant additional use of energy for the project.

7. There will not be any solid waste generated nor hazardous waste produced.

8. No protected wetlands or watercourses will be impacted. A hydrogeological study has been conducted and reviewed. No impact to quality or quantity of water entering the Malloryville Bog is expected to occur as a result of this proposal.

The mining will occur at the southerly end of the Malloryville esker which is owned by the applicant and not now protected by any existing state law...

Raymond J. Nolan

So, after our team effort had won two welcome PosDecs, in Year 1 and Year 3, concluding the DeWitt and Paolangeli reviews, now, in Year 7, two-and-a-half years into the third gravel mine application, we find ourselves confronted by a shocking new hurdle, a wholly unwelcome, unreasonable NegDec, Ray Nolan's Determination of Non-Significance, no significant adverse effect on the environment, a SEQR Notice to which we will need to mount a determined, powerful response, an unjustifiable DEC Determination that could not be allowed to stand.

Meanwhile, in that same time period in our story, say during the three years leading to Ray's NegDec—to put events in perspective—we were not simply waiting for a next move during some very long intervals of uncertainty. Rather, diverse, parallel work and events had continued, filled with excitement, challenge, accomplishment and sadness of their own:

Jim McNamara and Don Siegel's wetland hydrology and bog-core study began, progressed and concluded with a research paper about to be published in the Journal of Hydrology. Barbara Bedford and Robert Wesley, with others, studied Malloryville's fens in a New York Natural Heritage Program research project. Wayne Klockner of The Nature Conservancy prepared his Preserve Proposal for Ed King, co-executor of the von Engeln estate. I continued my volunteer work with The Nature Conservancy's chapter board and its Stewardship Committee. With my county Environmental Management Council, we completed a detailed, 800-page inventory of Unique Natural Areas of Tompkins County. Gwen and I welcomed our first child—a boy, Nathan Robert. We carefully designed and had built an addition to our small house to accommodate our family, doubling its size while keeping it appropriate to the place, and I milled and installed custom interior wood trim. I worked as the Finger Lakes Land Trust's first Executive Director and secured Lick Brook by searching for and finding the right pond for a swap with Moss Sweedler. And, with great sadness for us all, my father at age 93, lost his life in a car accident as a passenger returning from a dinner out with a friend, having brought to my house, early that June morning, filets of fish he had freshly caught from his own farm pond.

Bog Rosemary (*Andromeda glaucophylla*)

10 RESOLVE

It is our attitude at the beginning of a difficult undertaking
which, more than anything else,
will determine its successful outcome.

— William James

I HAD THOUGHT that a Determination of Significance, the Positive or Negative Declaration (PosDec or NegDec), would be preceded by a public comment period, appropriately preceded by comments as normally requested in a Notice of Complete Application. I had thought that public comments would be seriously considered prior to making that important Determination. A NegDec means "end of review," no dEIS required, project cleared for approval. Yet, curiously, Ray Nolan had issued his NegDec on the same day—the same date— as his Notice of Complete Application (long delayed, for nearly two years). Under pressure from Alfred Eddy and Brayton Foster, and apparently the DEC, Ray had proceeded to make his decision without written comments (the single exception being the County EMC Resolution when the application first appeared two years earlier). And though he had declared it to be a "coordinated review" with other agencies, he had not notified or received any information from the Town of Dryden. As it should have, though, the Complete Application notice did specify a comment period, but strangely, to occur after Ray's NegDec, too late to influence his decision.

Given all he knew, what was Ray thinking? Was he truly serious? Was he simply lazy, taking the path of least resistance at the moment, push from our side temporarily relaxed, the environment be damned? Was it incompetence? Was his NegDec a ploy to avert a lawsuit from the applicant, knowing that Malloryville's defenders would fight back to ultimate success? Or was it an entertaining hurdle placed in our path, somehow meant to test our resolve, win or lose? I didn't understand Ray, but I knew what we had to do. To do nothing was to accept defeat. I was angry. Then, in our seventh year of effort, we would reappear, in his face, with renewed resolve in spades. To comment now, was to insist that a done deal be undone, that the NegDec be reversed, that the review be reopened, that our concerns be taken seriously, that we be heard: we were not going away.

Yet, considering that the newly amended Mined Land Reclamation Law gave local governments additional power over gravel mine siting, I suppose we could have had faith that the Town of Dryden's strong opposition alone, somehow, could have stopped the current mining proposal, regardless of Ray Nolan's handling of the SEQR process. But I didn't know how that would work. If we failed to respond to the NegDec, would the Town and we have to file a lawsuit to begin a potentially expensive and long fight in the courts against a gravel mine that the DEC had already approved? Not wanting to think about that, I knew we could not relax. We had to stick with SEQR and deal with the current NegDec.

Rescind was a new word for me, a legal term of many synonyms. In my thesaurus I found, "revoke, repeal, retract, cancel, reverse, overturn, overrule, withdraw, annul, nullify, void, invalidate, quash, abolish, vacate." That's what needed to happen. Our immediate task was to have Ray Nolan's NegDec rescinded. But, reminiscent of an earlier statement from a DEC official that there was "no history anywhere of a gravel mine harming a wetland," I was told that, for gravel mines in New

York State, a Negative Declaration had "never been rescinded." I didn't know about that, but clearly our work was cut out for us.

We needed to do more than we had done before with success, in the DeWitt and Paolangeli reviews. Immediately, I would re-contact members of our team, reactivate our coalition, assure them that we were in this fight to win, and I would provide them with the new information they would need to write new letters. As before, I sensed that all our letters to DEC from the previous two SEQR reviews would be forgotten or ignored, as though irrelevant, as this was another, a different application. We needed to write again, responding in a third critical rally of letter writing. Then I would request help from our Town and County officials and our elected local and state representatives, I would seek to contact higher-level DEC officials, and I would alert the media for newspaper coverage. Together, we would pull out all the stops to put pressure on the DEC, to put them in the public spotlight, to compel them to do the right thing.

November 30, 1992. Among the first to write was Betsy Darlington of Ithaca who got directly to the point, with clear, forceful eloquence, in saying to Ray precisely what many of us were thinking. Betsy wrote:

> Dear Ray: I was astonished to see that you had issued a neg. dec. for Alfred Eddy's gravel application next to Malloryville Bog! If ever a case deserved a full-blown dEIS, this is it. It's too bad that you have never taken Bob Beck up on his offer to show you the bog. Perhaps then you would have a true appreciation for this extraordinary place. Given the complex hydrology that is likely to exist at the site, how can a few test wells prove beyond a shadow of a doubt that the mining will have no impact on the bog? And, given the ecological importance of the bog, this is no place to take any chances. It's not like a court of law where guilt must be proven beyond a rea-

sonable doubt. Unless you can say absolutely that no harm would come to the bog, there should be a positive declaration. I do not believe that you can say that.

Too much is at stake here, Ray. We look to the DEC to protect important resources like Malloryville Bog, for the benefit of the public at large—the people of the State of New York. Yes, it's more time-consuming to issue a pos. dec., and yes, it irritates the applicant. But you are not there to serve the applicant. What are we to think when the DEC so clearly shirks its responsibilities to the public?

This case has come up repeatedly for years. Are you just getting worn down and tired of hearing about it? If that's the case, the message to those who would despoil our significant resources is, "Just hang in there! The DEC will eventually get tired of us and let us do what we want!"

Please, Ray, I urge you to reverse your decision!

Sincerely, Betsy Darlington
Cc: Pat Reixinger, DEC-Albany; Jim Schug, Dryden Town Supervisor

December 10, 1992. The Tompkins County EMC wrote:

Dear Mr. Nolan: ...Our organization contacted you concerning the bog and its protection some two years ago, asking that activities which might have a harmful effect be restrained. A copy of the resolution which we drew up and sent at that time is enclosed.

The Negative Declaration which your agency has issued concerning the permit request is distressing in light of the local people and organizations which have been and are concerned with the preservation of this bog over the years. We hope that an opportunity for additional comment from those with technical background and experience in particular, will be possible in the near future...

The Town of Dryden had grown, in a few years, from disinterest in protecting Malloryville's wetlands to become a central, active supporter of our cause. Henry Slater's early letters were important in turning back the DeWitt and Paolangeli proposals, and early on he had requested the involvement of Town Attorney, Mahlon Perkins. And when Jim Schug was newly elected Town Supervisor, I had met with him and gained his support. Then Ray Nolan's recent letter to Jim on November 16, announcing the Complete Application, triggered a serious face-to-face meeting, on December 15, 1992, between Town Attorney Perkins and Ray.

On December 19, 1992, Mahlon Perkins wrote to Ray, addressing some deficiencies and blatant errors on Ray's part:

> Dear Ray: Thank you for taking time on December 15 to review the above application and the environmental review which was conducted by you and the Department. As I told you, my meeting with you was in my capacity as Town Attorney for the Town of Dryden where the 33 acre unconsolidated surface mine is proposed.
>
> The Town was not aware that an application was viable or pending or that an environmental review was being conducted until the Notice of Complete Application was received by the Town Supervisor in November. The Notice is dated November 16, 1992 and was received by the Town Supervisor along with your letter of November 16, 1992 on November 19, 1992. Accordingly, pursuant to Environmental Conservation Law §23-2711(3)(a)[2nd(i)] the last day to respond is today. This is true notwithstanding the statement in the last paragraph of your November 16

letter to the Supervisor which required a response by December 16.

The Notice of Complete Application also requires the submission of comments in writing by December 28 and this letter should be taken as a response to that Notice and the request for a response solicited in your November 16 pursuant to ECL §23-2711(3).

Since the comments of the Town are required to be solicited pursuant to ECL §23-2711(3) the Town is an involved agency and should have been involved (initially) in the SEQR review. Notwithstanding this omission (which the Town does not hereby waive) the Supervisor has instructed me to contact you with comments from the Town.

I am enclosing a copy of Section 806 of the Ordinance which pertains to quarries, excavations and topsoil removal in R-C zoning districts.

The town is an involved agency but had no knowledge of the ongoing environmental review until the Notice of Complete Application was received by the Supervisor on November 19, 1992. Pursuant to 6 NYCRR 617.10(a)(3) the Notice contained a copy of the Negative Declaration.

The Town, therefore, has not had sufficient opportunity to comment on the reasons supporting the Negative Declaration or to review the materials which were forwarded to the Supervisor along with your letter or which were subsequently obtained by the Town and which are apparently part of the DEC file. (As you know, this project involves a significant amount of local controversy because of its proximity to the Malloryville bog. The significance and importance of the bog is well documented. Your own file is replete with documentation.)

However, we will comment on the one statement in the Negative Declaration. (5. The project conforms to zoning regulations and the town's land use plans.)

Mr. Eddy's original DEC permit expired...[more than 7 years ago]. Based on correspondence in the file the applicant has alleged that he has continued to remove less than 1,000 tons of material per year from the site. The Department does not have jurisdiction over such small operations but regulation of such an operation is still governed by the provisions of the Town of Dryden Zoning Ordinance Section 806.

In 1981 Mr. Eddy received a Special Permit from the Town, executed the requirement Agreement with the Town and filed a surety bond, all as required by Section 806 of the Town of Dryden Zoning Ordinance. Section 806(6) requires that the surety bond be renewed annually. Section 806(7) provides that the discontinuance of the operation for a period of 12 consecutive months requires a new Special Permit application (and hearing). The Town's position is that any rights Mr. Eddy obtained under the original Special Permit terminated because of the failure to renew the surety bond and because of the discontinuance of operations for periods in excess of 12 months. Such discontinuance is supported by observations of local neighbors and Town personnel. Accordingly, the conclusion of number 5 in the Negative Declaration is false.

In May of 1988 [more than 4 years ago] the zone in which the Eddy property is located was changed from a R-C zone to a RB-1 zone. Mining is allowed in a R-C zone but is not permitted in a RB-1 zone. Mr. Eddy could continue to mine after the zoning change if he continued a valid, existing non-conforming use at the time of the zone change. Such non-conforming use cannot be expanded into other areas without a Special Permit under the provisions of the Town of Dryden Zoning Ordinance. There is an important distinction to be drawn here. For Mr. Eddy to preserve his rights to a non-conforming use, the use must be lawful. The use cannot be lawful if the surety bond was not renewed. Since there is no existing, continuing lawful non-conforming use, accordingly, the Town feels that there would now have to be a change in the zoning classification in order for Mr. Eddy to recommence mining at this site.

Because of such a need and local controversy and importance of the site, the Town believes that an environmental impact statement should be prepared which should address all of the factors involved in such application, not just the relationship between the hydrogeology and the Malloryville bog.

Since mining is prohibited at this location, the Town feels that it does not now need to make the determinations required by Environmental Conservation Law §23-2711(3)(a)(i)-(iv). In the event that the applicant is able to demonstrate to the Town that he has a valid existing non-conforming use and that no Town approval is required to expand such non-conforming use into other areas, or if the applicant is able to obtain a change in zoning classification which would not prohibit mining, and if the Department then intends to issue a Permit, the Town reserves the right to comment on the aspects of the Permit under which local government input is sought under ECL §23-2711(3).

I should also advise you that the Town may consider taking action against Mr. Eddy for the violation of the conditions of his 1981 Permit, Agreement and apparent willful violation of the provisions of the Town of Dryden Zoning Ordinance including the unlawful removal of material while no surety bond was in effect.

Thank you for your historical prospective and analysis in this matter. If the Town has other or continuing concerns regarding the environmental review, it may take you up on your offer to attend a Town Board meeting and brief the Town on the extent of the environmental review, specifically with respect to the relationship of the hydrogeology and the Malloryville bog.

Very truly yours, Mahlon R. Perkins

December 21, 1992. At 2:00, around a dining-room table at Barbara Bedford's house, several of us, Barbara, Robert Wesley, Donald Siegel, Ted Lavery and I, met for a strategy meeting. Barbara and Robert, together, Cornell wetlands ecologist and botanist, knew the wetlands intimately as did Professor Don Siegel, hydrogeologist at Syracuse University. Don's student, Jim McNamara, had completed his hydrogeology study and we were waiting for his paper to appear in print, and reprints to be available, that very month in the Journal of Hydrology. And Environmental Attorney Ted Lavery of Skaneateles, who had attended a meeting called by Ray Nolan in the Paolangeli review and had written a letter at that time, joined us at my request.

We talked briefly about the two previous SEQR reviews and turned our attention to the current situation, the dire seriousness of the NegDec and the urgency in responding to it. Without delay, we would again put our thoughts and arguments in writing to the DEC, as we had in years before, while adding important new knowledge gained since, this time insisting the Negative Declaration be rescinded. At some point in our talk, Ted offered that he should proceed in obtaining a stop work order to halt gravel mining. That seemed out of place, not relevant then, as mining was not occurring. We needed to focus on the immediate problem, to prevent the situation from ever progressing to that point. First, we needed to prevent the DEC from approving permits. I was not willing to even contemplate conceding, then only to fight an operating mine later. Feeling a little annoyed with Ted, and perhaps too hasty in response, I said something like, "But who's working for whom, here?" That probably didn't go over well and likely soured the relationship between Ted and me. As happened, I had reluctantly lent to him, upon his strong and repeated insistence, my treasured copy of von Engeln's book, *The Finger Lakes Region*, an early printing hard cover I had purchased at Cornell many years earlier. Later, when I asked, several times, Ted could never find it. I never got it back.

Donald Siegel had given me, for my review, a draft of his detailed letter critiquing the application. Then, slightly revised, he sent it off to Ray Nolan. Here, I have included Don's entire letter, and those of others, not because all the details are essential in following this story, but rather because of their absolutely crucial, vital, importance in determining the story's outcome, and to illustrate the awesome degree of thought, effort and dedication that he and others put into our defense of Malloryville, busy professional people, generously, unselfishly, without pay, volunteering their valuable time and expertise for a special place they felt worthy of their support, for a cause they believed in.

December 23, 1992. Professor Donald Siegel wrote to Ray Nolan:

> Dear Mr. Nolan: This is a letter report expressing my opinion on the hydrogeologic setting of the Malloryville Wetland, near Freeville, New York, and the extent to which proposed mining of gravel adjacent to the wetland may affect the wetland functions. I request that you reconsider the Negative Declaration issued on the proposed gravel mining... in light of my concerns.
>
> My report consists of three parts. The first part briefly describes my scientific credentials and experience upon which my opinion is based. The second part reviews the current scientific understanding of the hydrogeologic setting of the Malloryville Wetland. The third part critiques the report, prepared by Mr. Brayton Foster, on the

potential effect of gravel mining on the Malloryville Wetlands.

Part I. Professional Experience and Training

I hold BS and MS degrees in Geology from the University of Rhode Island and Penn State University, respectively, and a PhD in Hydrogeology with a minor in Civil Engineering from the University of Minnesota. Prior to my current position as Full Professor of Geology at Syracuse University, I was a Hydrologist and Geochemist for the US Geological Survey. I have studied wetland hydrology, geochemistry, and ecology for over 20 years, and have numerous publications related to wetlands in peer-reviewed scientific journals. I have served as an expert for the Environmental Protection Agency on wetland litigations and have been a scientific peer reviewer for EPA wetland research programs. This year, I received the Geological Society of America's Birdsall Distinguished Lectureship in Hydrogeology, for which I will be traveling extensively in North America to present talks on wetland groundwater hydrology.

Part II. The Hydrogeology and Ecology of the Malloryville Wetland

The following information is abstracted from my scientific paper on the hydrogeology and ecology of the Malloryville Wetland, to be published in December 1992 by the Journal of Hydrology (McNamara et.al, 1992) [Hydrogeologic controls on peatland development in the Malloryville wetland, New York (USA), J.P. McNamara, D.I. Siegel, P.H. Glaser and R.M. Beck, Vol. 140, pp. 279-296]. The study from which this paper was written was done to determine why five very distinct and different wetland vegetation communities occur in such close proximity in a hydrogeologic setting that typically lends itself to only one vegetation type. Enclosed is a pre-print draft of the report. As soon as I receive copies of the printed paper, I will forward several of them to you.

The Malloryville Wetland, adjacent to the Malloryville esker occupies a series of what are called "kettle" depressions created by large blocks of ice that broke off a continental glacier thousands of years ago. A core of peat and underlying sediment which we collected in the center of one of the basins in the wetland shows that ponds originally filled the basins when the glacial ice melted. These ponds, underlain by sand, later filled in with sediment and organic matter to form the soils sustaining vegetation communities today.

Hydrologically, the Malloryville Wetland is a closed system; water only enters it as direct precipitation and groundwater seepage from adjacent thick sand and gravel deposits. The groundwater that enters the wetland originates as percolating (infiltration) precipitation that falls on the upland ridges surrounding the wetland. The amount of groundwater seepage to the wetland is substantial enough on its western and northern margins to support numerous springs that form creeks flowing to a pond. The fact that groundwater upwells at wetland margins is unequivocally shown by water level measurements in groundwater monitoring wells located throughout the wetland (McNamara et. al. 1992). However the driving force (hydraulic head) that causes groundwater to enter the wetland changes seasonally as the water table rises and falls under the surrounding mineral soil uplands.

To evaluate the groundwater flow regime in the wetland, my students and I installed 15 piezometer nests from which we measured water levels monthly for about one year. Groundwater clearly discharges from the flanks of the Malloryville esker to the wetland, and then flows generally north-northeast. In the northern part of the wetland, groundwater moves in the opposite direction, from the north to southwest. The viability of the wetland and its diverse plant communities depends upon the amounts of groundwater delivered to the wetland and how the relative proportions of groundwater and rain water change the chemical characteristics of the surface water used by the plants. In one place, located in the southern part of the wetland, bog vegetation has formed over the more typical fen vegetation.

Bogs are unusual in "kettle" depressions in western New York. Measurements of groundwater levels at the bog site show that during part of the year water moves upward towards the bog surface, whereas during other times water moves downward. The unique bog is very old. Radiocarbon dating of the peat shows that the bog began to grow about 4,100 years ago, probably as a response to a fen peat buildup. This unusual bog ecological system is delicately balanced with respect to the hydrology of the wetland. Even a few percent change in the amount of groundwater delivered to the bog may cause it to cease to grow and cause fen vegetation to reestablish at the site (e.g. Siegel and Glaser, 1987). The unusual character of this wetland, discussed in [our] paper, has already received international attention through the scientific "grapevine," even before [the] paper was in press. For example, this past fall a group of Swedish geologists and ecologists from the University of Uppsala requested and got a visit to the site during their tour of significant wetlands and geology of the Northeast.

Part III. Review of Report of B. Foster on the Hydrogeology of the Malloryville esker

This report discusses a project to determine the potential effects of sand and gravel mining on the hydrology of the Malloryville Wetlands. I first want to say that the Foster report was very ably reviewed by Mr. Frank Trent of your office, and I will be reiterating some of his concerns. He and I agree on several deficiencies of the Foster report. Unfortunately, Mr. Trent apparently was unaware of the hydrogeologic study that my students and I did on the Malloryville wetland. Had I known that the proposed mining was being re— reviewed by DEC, I would certainly have sent him a copy of the paper. In any case, I definitely would welcome discussing the wetland and esker hydrogeology with Mr. Trent and getting his opinions on the hydrogeology of the site in view of the results of our study.

With respect to the Foster report, I find that it contains both significant conceptual errors and a project design that precludes accurate determination of what hydraulically might happen should sand and gravel mining proceed.

The major problems of the report are as follows:

1. The report concludes that there are three, independent "water tables" in the vicinity of the wetland; one under the hills to the west, one under the wetland, and one to the south. This is conceptually incorrect. The hydrogeologic setting of the Malloryville Wetland is that of a classic inseepage wetland. Groundwater is recharged (replenished) on uplands and discharges (upwells) to the wetland. Otherwise, the groundwater seeps would not occur at the base of the hillsides at the western wetland margin, especially on the southwestern side. Indeed, pore-water pressures are such that there are areas of "quicksand" associated with the seeps. There is only one continuous water table, found at depth under the

uplands and near or at the wetland surface. If there were multiple water tables, zones of dry or partially dry soil would occur below and above soils saturated with water. Multiple zones of saturation have not been at all demonstrated.

2. The report suggests that most groundwater under the uplands west of the wetland bypasses the wetland. This is not the case; much groundwater moving from the uplands located adjacent to the wetland ends in the wetland. Indeed, from a wide literature of wetland-groundwater interactions, it is highly likely that most of the groundwater recharged to the eastern side of the esker winds up in the wetland.

3. Because the hydrogeologic interpretation by Foster is conceptually so flawed, the conclusions within it are untestable and probably unsound. The following information is needed to evaluate the extent to which gravel mining may affect the Malloryville Wetland vegetation:

a. Data on the vertical directions of groundwater flow in the sand and gravel deposits under the proposed mined area and along transects to the wetland. This information, routinely obtained from piezometer clusters in hydrogeologic studies of all kinds, is critical for any calculation of how much groundwater enters the wetland from the potentially affected upland.

b. Data on how much recharge occurs in the upland area. This data is obtained from temporal data on groundwater level changes coupled with precipitation data. Knowing the recharge rate is especially important because removal of overburden in the mining operation conceivably could increase the recharge potential to the uplands because of the loss of soil moisture storage. With loss of soil moisture storage, the water table under the upland could rise with attendant increase in groundwater discharge to the wetland springs. If groundwater seepage increased, fragile ecosystems could be flooded and even the hydrologic function of the bog could be changed. The water table mound sustaining the bog is only a inch or two above the surrounding regional water table! It is essential to scientifically evaluate how much recharge from the eskers surrounding the wetland ultimately gets to the wetlands within the context of the actual groundwater flow system in the wetland area... Numerical simulation models for groundwater flow is one method routinely used to predict the sensitivity of complex wetland systems to changes in watertable configurations.

c. Additional test hole drilling is needed to evaluate the subsurface stratigraphy. Only by such drilling (not shallow test pits)—and installation of piezometer clusters—can it be determined if the buried till is a "hydraulic dam," as suggested by Foster.

d. The hydrogeologic controls over how much groundwater flows to the wetlands at discrete springs should be determined. The hydrogeology of the Malloryville wetland and associated eskers is complex. Groundwater discharge to the wetland is focused, in part in springs that clearly provide much of the nutrients and water fluxes to the wetland system. Groundwater flow is not "diffuse" and slow, rapid enough to create overpressured "quick" sands near the side of the wetland where mining is proposed to take place. Major questions that need to be scientifically addressed include: 1.) Why do the springs occur where they do? 2.) To what extent will mining influence the preferred pathways that focus groundwater discharge to the springs? Specific plant community structures and groundwater geochemical techniques might be useful to evaluate the hydrodynamics behind the spring occurrences.

In summary, the Foster report in my opinion does not in a significant way evaluate the groundwater flow field associated with the Malloryville wetland, nor the potential effects of mining on the wetland hydrology. The wetland vegetation clearly is sensitive to small changes in the groundwater flow regime, shown by the succession of rare bog vegetation over fen vegetation in a place where such a succession would seem to be precluded. The wetland and esker system has been known to be vegetationally and geologically unique for over 100 years. It is equally unique hydrogeologically, as shown by the acceptance of the McNamara paper by an internationally renowned, peer-reviewed technical journal. I urge that additional studies, some of them quite standard, be made to evaluate the potential environmental impact of the wetland system by the proposed mining.

Please feel free to contact me on this matter at your convenience. As I said earlier, I would welcome discussing the hydrogeology of the site with Frank Trent as well.

Sincerely yours, Donald I. Siegel, PhD, Professor of Geology, Syracuse University

December 24, 1992. Cornell geologist Art Bloom wrote to Ray Nolan:

Dear Mr. Nolan: Yet again, as I did on August 14, 1987 and on June 7, 1989, I express my concern about a proposed gravel mining operation near Malloryville. Copies of my earlier letters are enclosed, and I reemphasize the comments therein. ...I find it surprising that any gravel mining operation in an area draining into the wetlands at the head of Fall Creek would be permitted without requiring an environmental impact statement and subsequent review of that statement.

Sincerely, A.L. Bloom

cc: Mr. James Schug, Town of Dryden Supervisor

December 28, 1992. At their Cortland field office, I met with Carl Schwartz of the US Fish and Wildlife Service, United States Department of the Interior. Carl agreed to write to Ray Nolan:

Dear Mr. Nolan: ...The Service is concerned that the proposed project may have a detrimental affect on an adjacent unique natural area—the Malloryville Bog and Fen. ...Due to the complexity of the topographic relief, numerous diverse natural community types occur in close proximity to one another—bog, fens, mineral-rich and mineral-poor forested wetlands, emergent wetlands, marl springs, streams, and upland forests. Needless to say, this is an extremely valuable and unique wetland complex.

The Malloryville Fen has been identified as being strongly minerotrophic, an area influenced by water that has been in contact with soil or bedrock, and which is richer in mineral-nutrient elements than rainwater. Conditions within the watershed such as size, deposit, and relief, affect the amount and chemical properties of the water flowing into the bog... The extraction of gravel adjacent to this unique area may indeed have an irreversible, detrimental affect...

Wetland ecosystems are threatened by continued loss and degradation, 56 percent of our Nation's wetlands have already been lost. The Service has estimated that New York State alone has already lost more than 60% of its original wetlands. The Nation's appreciation of the ecological, social, and economic values of wetlands has increased dramatically throughout the last decade. The Service urges the NYSDEC to carefully consider the proposed project. The loss of the Malloryville Bog, especially in view of its high quality, scientific and educational value, and diversity would be devastating to the Finger Lakes Community.

Thank you for the opportunity to provide comments on the proposed project. Please advise us of action taken pursuant to our recommendation or changes in the proposal...

Sincerely, Carl Schwartz, acting for Leonard P. Corin, Field Supervisor

cc: J. Schug, Supervisor, Town of Dryden, Dryden, NY

December 28, 1992. Andy Zepp of The Nature Conservancy:

Dear Ray: I am writing in regard to your department's... issuance of a negative declaration for environmental impacts associated with the resumption of mining at the Eddy property in Freeville, New York. This proposed action is of concern to The Nature Conservancy in that the subject property borders the Malloryville wetland complex, an outstanding natural area that has been recognized through the Conservancy's Natural Areas Registry Program.

The... wetlands are of special significance in that they harbor an array of different wetland habitats as well as several rare plants in a very localized area. Any alteration of the hydrology within this complex could have a profound effect on the species and habitats present.

As proposed, the impacts associated with further mining of the Eddy property are by no means clear. Of particular concern is the nature of groundwater flows from the Eddy property into the adjacent wetland complex. I do not feel that current studies have adequately addressed how removal of overburden will affect the amount of groundwater recharge which takes place in upland portions of the Eddy property. Even a slight change in recharge levels could raise nearby wetland water levels and have a dramatic impact on associated vegetation.

In light of the questions which are associated with any significant alteration of lands surrounding the Malloryville wetlands, I strongly urge that additional hydrological information be gathered before any decision is made concerning the application in question.

Thank you for your consideration. Please do not hesitate to contact me if you have any questions about my comments.

Sincerely, Andrew E. Zepp, Director of Land Protection

December 26, 1992. My letter to Ray:

Dear Ray: I disagree strongly with your recent Negative Declaration.... To issue this permit would be a failure in the responsibility of the Department of Environmental Conservation to the people of New York State.

In this letter I request that you reverse that determination. In stating my reasons for this request, I reemphasize much of what I have said to you previously in person and in my letters to your office dated 7/28/87 and 5/30/89 [5 1/2 and 3 1/2 years ago, commenting on the two previous applications].

Protection of the extraordinarily diverse and fragile environmental complex... demands either that this permit be denied outright—based on ample information already available—or, at very minimum, a draft Environmental Impact Statement be required. Your determination of "no significant effect on the environment" is unconscionable, especially in light of the following facts:

1) the long-recognized biological and geological significance of the site.

a) Three New York State protected wetlands (GR-12, GR-13 and GR-10) are adjacent to and downslope from the mining site,

b) Two of the wetlands (GR-12 and GR-13), because of their rare plant species and rare community types... are highly ranked as "scorecard" sites by NYS DEC's Natural Heritage Program and are registered with The Nature Conservancy's Natural Areas Registry Program,

c) All three wetlands and their adjacent uplands have been designated by Tompkins County as Unique Natural Areas... The wetland complex known as Malloryville Bog (immediately east of, downslope from and paralleling the mining site for approximately 1300 ft.), has been recognized and studied by botanists and visited by naturalists for over 100 years for its remarkably rich and diverse plant life and natural community types... As you know, my wife... and I own and live at this site.

d) The prominent Malloryville esker, running adjacent to all three wetlands, also extends across the mining site. The esker has long been recognized for its distinctive features. It has been studied by geologists and used as a field trip site by classes from SUNY-Cortland and Cornell University (for over 90 years)...

2) the documentation from the NYS Natural Heritage Program, The Nature Conservancy, the Tompkins County Environmental Management Council and numerous letters of botanists, geologists and others attesting to the unique significance of the site provided to your office over the

past six years in response to two previous mining applications at this site: Your reluctance to open the files and review this documentation and your insistence that scientists and others resubmit their letters for each application (now for the third time, and on short notice) has been frustrating and seems unfair.

3) the expert testimony presented by scientists from Cornell and Syracuse Universities at the informal hearing called by you in June 1989 [3 1/2 years ago] and instrumental in your Positive Declaration of 7/13/89 [PosDec(2)] (Unfortunately, no transcript of the meeting was prepared),

4) the two previous Positive Declarations issued by your office (8/7/87 & 7/13/89) for earlier mining applications at the same site. Each required that a draft Environmental Impact Statement be prepared and in each case the applicant chose not to proceed.

5) the questionable conclusions and self-contradictory nature of the hydrology study provided by the applicant.

a) Your statement that: "no protected wetlands or watercourses will be impacted." (Your reason #8 "supporting this determination") is disputed by highly qualified scientists including Professors Donald Siegel, Hydrogeologist in the Geology Department at Syracuse University and Barbara Bedford, Wetlands Ecologist in the Department of Natural Resources at Cornell University, whose familiarity, in both cases, with this particular site stems from their own research there. For example, Dr. Siegel's serious reservations about the adequacy and conclusions of the applicant's hydrology report are based on his intensive and long-term studies of the hydrogeology of Malloryville Bog and a paper by him and his students to be published this month in the Journal of Hydrology. (Please see the written comments sent directly to you by Drs. Siegel and Bedford.)

b) The 12 test wells on the mining site were installed by the applicant in 1990 and 1992 at your request, "In an effort to avoid requiring the preparation of a dEIS." These are your words in a letter, dated 5/3/89, to the previous applicant, and offered to and accepted by the current applicant. It seems to me that this short-circuiting of the SEQR process—your avoidance of a scoping session, avoidance of a dEIS, and consequent minimization of public input—is, in this case, improper and unfair. We are dealing here with a rare, complex, fragile, and irreplaceable ecosystem. Public input must be encouraged.

c) Also, I must ask why the supplement (dated 6/25/92) to the applicant's 1990 hydrology study—reporting data from 5 of the 12 test wells, and clearly weakening and contradicting the 1990 conclusions—was not included in the [applicant's] spiral-bound completed application?

6) Zoning in the town of Dryden specifically prohibits gravel mining at the project site and surrounding neighborhood (zoned R.B.-1, residential and agricultural, since 1988). This is directly contrary to your statement that: "The project conforms to zoning regulations and the town's land use plans." (your reason #5 "supporting this determination.")

7) The levels of truck traffic and machinery noise would severely impact our quiet rural neighborhood (far more than existing farm operations); in the application and Environmental Assessment Form, statements to the contrary are preposterous and simply wrong.

In conclusion, I repeat my request that this permit be denied outright or, at minimum, a dEIS be required. The esker and wetlands... have been studied, enjoyed and valued by scientists, teachers, students and the general public for over 100 years. Gravel mining adjacent to the esker and immediately upslope from the wetlands threatens irreparable harm to both. In view of the quality and significance of this site and your responsibility to consider the long-term public good, I believe that the Department of Environmental Conservation ought to actively assure protection of these irreplaceable natural treasures.

Sincerely yours, Robert M. Beck

cc: James Schug, Supervisor, Town of Dryden; Robert Bendick, Deputy Commissioner for Natural Resources, DEC

December 26, 1992. Barbara Bedford and Robert Wesley, based on their intimate experience with the site, write a stunning, comprehensive, truly outstanding letter, a letter that, even if standing alone, ought to be seen as more than sufficient to force reversal, rescission, of Ray Nolan's NegDec:

Dear Mr. Nolan: We are writing in regard to your Notice of Complete Application and Negative Declaration... Our comments, which express grave concern and dismay at your conclusions, follow.

We believe you have made a serious error in judgment in not requiring an environmental impact statement (EIS) for a mining project that may cause irreparable damage to the Malloryville Bog and associated wetlands, a unique and valuable site both geologically and botanically. An EIS is warranted for several reasons.

First, the Malloryville Bog and associated wetlands are significant at local and state levels. They are remarkably diverse and include excellent examples of several rare and uncommon wetland types and many rare and scarce plant species. The area has been officially designated by the Tompkins County Environmental Management Council and the Tompkins County Board of Representatives as a Unique Natural Area. In total 7 different wetland communities are recognized. The New York Natural Heritage Program recognizes the area as containing high quality examples of five element occurrences, features they consider of statewide significance. These include rich sloping fens, rich shrub fen, rich hemlock-hardwood peat swamp, dwarf shrub bog, and the rare globeflower, *Trollius laxus* ssp. *laxus*. The wetland flora is very species rich. In a survey we conducted with the Natural Heritage Program of 21 of the few high quality fens remaining in the state, we found the Malloryville Bog to be one of the richest. Just one small area (5 meters by 20 meters) contained 103 different species of plants. All of the wetlands on the site taken together contain even more species. This degree of biological diversity is highly unusual, especially in an area of less than 26 acres.

In point of fact, there are two additional unique natural areas that may be affected by the proposed mining activity. One lies immediately north of the Malloryville Bog complex and the other just south of Malloryville Road. Both of these areas, likewise, have been officially designated by the Tompkins County Environmental Management Council and the Tompkins County Board of Representatives as Unique Natural Areas and one of them has been recognized by the New York Natural Heritage Program. If we included these areas in our analysis, the total species richness and number of rare and uncommon species present would be phenomenal for an area totaling less than 200 acres. We estimate that the total number of species present in the wetlands alone approaches 200. By The Nature Conservancy's method for recognizing ecological rarity and significance, these sites together would contain more than 15 element occurrences. Further research is likely to uncover more rarities.

Second, the unique nature of the wetlands is dependent on the quantity and quality of groundwater moving from the surrounding uplands and discharging in a number of springs and seeps at the margins of the wetland. Their very character is defined by their hydrology, i.e., the amount of water they receive, when they receive it, and what that water contains. Historically, the hydrology of the Malloryville wetlands has been determined by the geology and topography of the surrounding landscape. Any activity on the uplands that may alter flows of water to the wetlands may destroy their unique characteristics. Given the thousands of years over which these wetlands have developed, their destruction is essentially irreparable.

Third, the topography and geology of the site are complex and do not lend themselves to easy analysis. All of the different wetland communities in the complex occur within the same hydrogeological setting, which seemingly should cause them to be quite similar, yet several distinct types have developed. The exact nature of the mechanisms that control the development and maintenance of the wetland communities is still only partially understood. It is, in fact, a subject of our current research program. As scientists who have spent their careers studying wetlands, we do not see how the potential harm to the Malloryville Bog and its associated wetlands possibly could be evaluated without an extensive and thorough EIS.

We urge you seriously to reconsider your determination and reverse your Negative Declaration. Our interests in this site are scientific, as well as personal. In our combined experiences, we have seen few wetlands as topographically and biologically diverse, or as beautiful. There is a very real potential that the proposed mining activity will cause them irreparable damage. They deserve a formal, systematic and intensive review.

We would be pleased to answer any questions you may have regarding the Malloryville Bog and associated wetlands...

Sincerely, Barbara L. Bedford, F. Robert Wesley

cc: Robert L. Bendick, NYDEC; Patricia Reixinger, NYDEC; James Schug, Town of Dryden Supervisor

January 5, 1993. Barbara Bedford takes the initiative to write, with her usual precise and direct eloquence, an excellent letter to Robert L. Bendick, Deputy Commissioner for Natural Resources, New York State Department of Environmental Conservation (DEC):

Dear Mr. Bendick: You may recall hearing me speak at the May 1991 meeting of the Board of the Adirondack Park Agency. I am using that occasion to seek the attention and power of your office in a highly significant matter currently before the Cortland Office of the DEC. Despite considerable evidence to the contrary, Mr. Ray Nolan of that office has issued a Negative Declaration in the case of a gravel mining operation that has the potential to cause irreparable damage to one of the most unique and pristine wetland complexes in the State.

I enclose a copy of the letter my colleague, F. Robert Wesley, and I sent to Mr. Nolan expressing our concerns, and requesting that he reverse his decision. Mr. Nolan's files contain extensive additional testimony to the significance of the site. I also enclose a copy of a letter to Mr. Nolan from the owner of the affected wetlands, Robert M. Beck of Freeville, who wishes to protect them.

In twelve years of living in New York State, I have never before involved myself with a wetland regulatory case. And I do not write to you lightly now. I believe this case is truly significant and worthy of your attention and mine, as well as that of all those who are concerned with protecting the State's remaining biological diversity and natural heritage. Please call me... if I can provide you with any additional information.

Sincerely, Barbara L. Bedford
cc: Robert Beck; Raymond J. Nolan

Would our elected representatives to New York State government be willing to listen and provide help? Marty Luster, NYS Assemblyman from my district, was a smart, hard-working and popular legislator and an unusually strong advocate for the environment. I called him and he agreed to meet with me to hear my concerns.

January 13, 1993, 2:30. In his office in Ithaca, I met with Marty and an assistant where they listened to my case, reviewed the documents I brought, and asked many probing questions. Within a day, Marty then wrote to Ray Nolan, sending copies of his letter to the DEC's Regional Director and to the State DEC Commissioner; January 13, 1993:

Dear Mr. Nolan: I have been contacted by several individuals who have expressed concern over the negative declaration issued in connection with the above application concerning gravel mining at Malloryville in the Town of Dryden, Tompkins County.

I have reviewed a number of documents in connection with this application and have interviewed Robert Beck, one of the owners of the portion of the property that might be adversely affected by the proposed operation. Without pretending to expertise that I do not possess, I am concerned about the fact that the negative declaration was issued despite the history of this parcel. Apparently two prior applications for mining permits have been made in recent years, both of which resulted in positive declarations and a discontinuance of the application by the owner of the mining site. I am puzzled by the change of circumstances which must be shown to exist that now have resulted in a negative declaration. I understand that the current application is a somewhat smaller proposal than the two previous endeavors, but I am reluctant to believe that a decrease in the size of the operation, standing by itself, could cause the reversal of policy apparent in your action.

I have also reviewed a quantity of scientific data presented to me, all of which indicates, at the very least, extraordinary caution before this permit is granted. In view of the history of this parcel and the current scientific information in your possession, I would strongly urge you to reverse the negative declaration and require a full environmental impact statement so that the issues raised by the opponents of the project can be seriously considered and an in-depth investigation can be had.

My concern at this point is that the process be fair and open and that all individuals having an interest be given ample opportunity to present their case. The negative declaration precludes that type of extensive and detailed examination.

I look forward to your response.

Sincerely, Martin A. Luster, Member of Assembly

cc: C. Thomas Male, Regional Director, DEC; Thomas C. Jorling, Commissioner, DEC; Robert Beck

January 25, 1993. Prof. Don Siegel, in a letter to Ray No-lan, commented on Brayton Foster's supplement to his hydro-geological study, data from five additional test wells, the data Frank Trent had reviewed but which, weakening their case, inexplicably, or with intent, was not included in the Complete Application. I had alerted Don to its presence, and he had requested the supplement from Ray:

> Dear Mr. Nolan: I have looked at the additional test hole and water level data you sent me on the hydrogeology of the Eddy Property near the Mal-loryville Wetland. The information unfortunately does not change my conclusions that the hydro-geologic study by Mr. Foster has significant problems.
>
> The most important issue is that the hydro-geologic study does not address the unequivocal groundwater discharge that sustains the springs located along the western edge of the Malloryville wetland. The groundwater discharge is suffi-ciently great enough to prevent the springs and their streams from freezing during the winter. The pore pressure generated by one of the springs has even created a quicksand. Because of these point sources of groundwater discharge, it is erroneous to conclude that the wetland is sustained by "extended" groundwater leakage through material with low permeability. From my experience in wetland hydrogeology, I have to conclude that the Malloryville wetland is a clas-sic groundwater "flow-through wetland" that de-veloped over kettle depressions formed in sand, gravel and perhaps till. These types of wetland settings are similar to the hydrogeologic settings of lakes in kettle depressions and receive most of their groundwater discharge at their edges rather than through their surface area. The material beneath the peat at the raised bog site is sand

and gravel, suggesting that at least part of the wetland depressions formed over course-grained material (McNamara and Siegel, in press).

The proposed sites for gravel mining west and northwest of the Malloryville wetland logically are the recharge areas for the groundwater system that discharges to the wetland. Were the wetland not sustained largely by groundwater influx, then fen and rich swamp vegetation would not be maintained (excluding the very unusual raised bog) especially, given the meters of naturally acidic peat that underlies much of the wetland. The driving head gradient that sustains the springs is large enough to maintain surface water flow throughout the year. I suspect that the flow paths to the springs are quite short and I am also concerned that any accidental spillage of fuel during mining might rapidly reach the wetland.

The Foster Report shows that the glacial stratigraphy is complex, and it is probable that hydraulic head under the northwestern glacial drift is hydraulically connected to the sand and gravel deposits located immediately west of the wetland where the springs are found. Only a very thin continuous permeable strata within deposits of otherwise lower hydraulic conductivity would be sufficient to move a large amount of water (see Freeze and Cherry, 1979). It would be difficult to characterize the recharge area for these discrete flow paths and the amount of groundwater recharging to the wetland without at least: 1.) additional stratigraphic studies, especially in the nearshore area of the wetland, 2.) a measured seasonal water budget leading to determination of recharge rates, 3.) geochemical studies to trace probable flow paths, and 4.) calculations of groundwater flow rates, residence times and directions. There is especially little information on the configuration of the water table immediately west of the wetland. Additional definition of the water table here is critical to further understanding the flow system under the proposed mining area. Given the uncertainties in the stratigraphy, detailed studies would have to be done in the wetland, including drilling of test holes. It would be difficult, if not impossible, to conduct such a study without impacting the wetland ecosystems. Because of this limitation, McNamara and I used computer simulations to determine how sensitive the wetland might be to changes in the topography of the water table. The results of the work strongly suggested that the wetland is delicately poised to its groundwater hydrology.

I reiterate my position that too little is known about the hydrogeology of the Malloryville wetland to allow mining of gravel from its probable recharge area. Such mining could very well seasonally impact the volume of water provided by the springs that substantively sustain the wetland system. It is also possible that mining activities could accidentally affect the quality of the groundwater discharging to the wetland. I urge the DEC to insist that a full EIS be done to evaluate all aspects of the Malloryville wetland hydrogeologic and ecologic system before gravel mining is allowed. Much like the status of the Marcell Bog in northern Minnesota, the Malloryville wetland has many scientific and ecologic aspects that could make it a "benchmark" wetland for the northeastern United States.

I would be happy to discuss this with you at your convenience.

Sincerely yours, Donald I. Siegel, Professor of Geology

January 25, 1993. On the same day as Don Siegel's additional comments, Ray Nolan wrote to landowner Alfred Eddy stating his plan to arrange a small meeting for discussion amongst the three geologists, Brayton Foster, Frank Trent and Don Siegel:

> Dear Mr. Eddy: This letter confirms my conversation with Brayton Foster earlier today.
>
> Mr. Foster has indicated that you agree to a suspension of the statutory time frame for review of the above referenced application. I have suspended that time frame as of the date of this letter.
>
> As you know, there is still no agreement as to the hydrological characteristics of the proposed mine site and the potential negative affects mining might have on the nearby Malloryville Bog. I am arranging a meeting between the three involved geologists to discuss the situation.
>
> After that meeting I will be able to determine the validity of the previously issued Negative Declaration and the need for further hydrological investigation of the site.
>
> Your continued cooperation in this matter is greatly appreciated. If you have any questions regarding this letter please feel free to contact me directly or through Brayton Foster.
>
> Very truly yours, Raymond J. Nolan

January 30, 1993. Ithaca's daily newspaper, The Ithaca Journal printed a front-page story titled "Wetlands dispute in Dryden: Naturalists say bog is threatened by mining," featuring a photo of me in the woods, and spelling out pretty clearly the controversy. Alfred Eddy is quoted as saying, "It would be low key—no cement plants or anything like that. We're farmers. We're not out to hurt the bog." Town Supervisor, Jim Schug, said, based on what he's heard and read, "There are a lot of people opposed to this, here." And the article continues (excerpts):

Nolan ultimately will decide whether or not to give Eddy DEC approval. Thus far he's waiting for more environmental data. "Make no mistake, we're concerned about that bog, and we're not going to make any careless decisions," Nolan said. "We have embarked on a procedure to get at the truth."

This procedure, however, is another reason Beck and others are concerned. They maintain Nolan should have required Eddy to produce a Draft Environmental Impact Statement. But he did not.

Nolan claims that with the previous mining on the land, the only missing information is a reliable hydrology, or water-flow study. Thus, he maintains a full DEIS is unnecessary at this point. "All the other information we need we already have in our files," he said. "The issue now is the hydrology."

Nolan said he's reviewing the various hydrology reports and is several weeks away from making a determination.

Meanwhile Beck is waiting anxiously. "This area is special enough so we should not be taking this kind of risk," Beck said. "If these plants disappear, there's no way you can get them back again."

Well, from Ray Nolan, we seemed to be hearing a bit of double talk. Of course, Ray had already written his NegDec, his declaration of no impact, and the only reason, the sole reason, he was now "reviewing various hydrology reports" is because we were in his face with letters brimming with details challenging his flawed NegDec.

Feb 17, 1993. I wasn't invited to Ray's meeting with Foster, Trent and Siegel, but I wish I could have witnessed it, secretly. Prof. Don Siegel's detailed, extensive, incisive, written comments had been central in forcing Ray into a reconsideration of his NegDec, and Don's presence at the meeting, as representative and spokesman for the wetlands, would be instrumental in determining Ray's next move.

March 1, 1993. Ray Nolan wrote to Alfred Eddy:

Dear Mr. Eddy: The public comment and technical review period for the above referenced project has concluded. With your concurrence the Department has suspended the statutory time frames in order to provide opportunity for further discussion of the hydrological information provided by your consultant, Mr. Brayton Foster, and Dr. Siegel of Syracuse University.

The Department has carefully considered all of the information thus far provided and has determined that the mining activity you propose may have a significant impact on the Malloryville wetland complex adjacent to your property. Accordingly, the Department hereby rescinds the previous Negative Declaration and has prepared a Positive Declaration pursuant to 617.6(i)6NYCRR. The decision to rescind the original Negative Declaration is based on information received during the review period which indicates that the characteristics of the Malloryville wetland may rely significantly on groundwater discharge from the gravel deposit you propose to mine. The hydrogeological information at hand does not adequately characterize the existing groundwater flow pathways, residence time in the gravel deposits or seasonal discharge rates. Disruption of one or more of these characteristics may significantly alter the quantity and quality of water reaching the wetland with irreversible changes to the rare plant communities located there. These rare communities depend upon a delicately balanced interaction of water volume, pH and dissolved minerals.

The Department's decision to rescind the Negative Declaration and replace it with a Positive Declaration means that a draft Environmental Impact Statement (dEIS) must be prepared by you. The dEIS should focus on the hydrogeological relationship that exists between the gravel deposit you propose to mine and the Malloryville wetland.

This decision will become effective 30 days from the date of receipt of this letter unless additional information that addresses the issues identified above is brought to the Department's attention.

If you have any questions regarding this letter please contact me at the above location.

Very truly yours, Raymond J. Nolan

Hallelujah! With great relief and renewed exhilaration we received word that the NegDec was to be rescinded. A major hurdle had been surmounted. A remarkable outpouring of support from many generous, caring, thoughtful, dedicated people had kept our fight very much alive. Midway through Year 7, we were promised another Positive Declaration, PosDec(3), mining permits would not be granted any time soon, and we would wait to see if Alfred Eddy would proceed, or not, with a dEIS.

In January, 1993, I had called New York Senator Jim Seward to request a meeting such as I had had with Assemblyman Marty Luster. Senator Seward declined, but was willing to talk on the phone. On March 4, 1993 he wrote to me:

Dear Bob: I enjoyed speaking with you recently regarding a gravel pit application for a parcel near your property. Your concern was about the DEC determination, that based on the facts presented at the time, no Environmental Impact Statement would be required for the permit application. As you know, this determination may be changed if further information shows a need for an EIS.

When the State Environmental Quality Review Law (SEQR) was enacted, the public comment period was built into the permit process as the opportunity for additional facts and information to be introduced and considered. Evidently, Dr. Siegel from Syracuse University has been instrumental in contributing additional information and raising questions about the relationship of the proposed gravel mine to the hydrology of the Malloryville Bog.

I have been advised by Mr. Ray Norton [Nolan], Regional DEC biologist, that DEC was going to host a meeting of scientists, including Dr. Siegel, to review all the data. Perhaps by the time you receive this letter, a decision will have been made on whether to reverse the negative declaration for an EIS or to grant the permit.

I can certainly understand your deep concern about protecting the unique properties of the bog. I feel confident that by following the SEQR process, as required by law, the public will be assured of ample opportunity to introduce pertinent information and express concerns and any decisions made by DEC will be well documented and considered.

I believe that it is vital for state agencies in New York to serve the public by carefully following proscribed [prescribed?] procedures for any action which they may take. Thank you for calling so that I could be aware of your concerns and have the opportunity to follow up on them with DEC.

Sincerely yours, James L. Seward, State Senator

I did appreciate Senator Seward's contact with the DEC in

response to my phone call, and was thankful for any help he may have provided. In reading his letter, however, I found myself in strong disagreement with one of his statements. I found I could not agree with his fourth-paragraph sentence, calmly advising confidence in the SEQR process, stating that "the public will be assured of ample opportunity to introduce pertinent information and express concerns," and that "any decisions made by DEC will be well documented and considered." My recent experience had been quite different. We had followed the SEQR process, and prior to Ray Nolan's NegDec, we were not at all "assured of ample opportunity" to introduce our comments. And that NegDec decision made by the DEC was most definitely not "well documented and considered." Ray Nolan did not invite public comments on Brayton Foster's hydrology study (at Ray's request, done "to avoid requiring... a dEIS"), or on the Complete Application until after he had declared his NegDec in spite of his knowledge of long-term public concern, controversy, and the involvement of reputable scientists who would have introduced essential "pertinent information" prior to his decision. We had to intervene, after the fact, to have the ill-conceived NegDec rescinded. That, I believe, is not how SEQR is intended to work.

At that point, had we blinked, mining permits likely would have been granted, soon, and the DEC itself, in failing to properly implement SEQR, would have failed in its responsibility to protect the environment. My experience does not give me comfort in trusting the system to protect the environment if public input can be so easily shut out. In New York State, SEQR is essential to environmental protection, the best we have, perhaps equal to the best modern civilization has produced, but more often than acknowledged, extraordinary public diligence and hard work are necessary to ensure that the system functions as it should.

March 22, 1993. Brayton Foster writes to Ray Nolan:

Dear Mr. Nolan: On behalf of the applicant I request the Department not rescind the Negative Declaration as proposed in your 3/1/93 letter to Mr. Alfred Eddy as no significant new information was presented during the comment period which ended 12/28/92. Dr. Donald Siegel's comments based on his review of only part of the application and supplements was received by the Department on 12/29/92. In subsequent comments Dr. Siegel continues to speculate that groundwater MAY flow from the proposed south pit area southeastward toward the Malloryville wetland but provides no supporting data in his 1992 Journal of Hydrology publication or at our 2/17/93 meeting with you in Cortland.

Brayton Foster presents further discussion, and then concludes with:

The last sentence in the second paragraph of your 3/1/93 letter to Mr. Eddy which implies the groundwater regime is "delicately balanced" appears misleading given the survival of the water delivery system for thousands of years with the accumulation of several meters of wetland sediment (peat) and its accompanying water level changes. Using Dr. Siegel's depth/age profile it appears the bog is rising at approximately 3.9" per century ($1\pm$ cm/ per 10 years) by natural processes. It requires a robust water delivery system to accommodate these ongoing changes, climatic variations, previous mining, and significant land use changes which include topsoil erosion leaving the Malloryville Bog and wetland in its present unstressed condition.

I will attempt to provide more information on any of these topics during the time frame suspension that the Department feels are necessary.

Very truly yours, Brayton P. Foster, Consulting Geologist   cc: Alfred C. Eddy

June 10, 1993. A story in The Syracuse Post Standard's Tompkins/Cortland edition (excerpt):

> DEC Orders Study of Gravel Pit Plan. Fears voiced by scientists have led the state Department of Environmental Conservation to reverse its finding that a gravel pit operation won't harm neighboring wetlands.... "It's a major step in the right direction," said Beck, a biologist who owns most of the wetlands and has spent the last six years fighting plans for a gravel pit.
>
> It has also been a long fight for landowner Alfred Eddy of Ithaca. Eddy, who is applying for the third time to use the land as a gravel pit, said he will talk to his consultants about the next step.
>
> Eddy insists the mining operation would not harm the nearby wetlands, and he is willing to spend more time and money on studies to prove that point. "I would just like to hear an answer," he said Wednesday.
>
> No amount of data will prove to Beck that mining isn't a danger to the wetlands.
>
> "It's not an ordinary cattail marsh," he said. "This site is extremely sensitive, extremely complex... It's a really exceptional place."
>
> Beck, whose efforts have attracted the attention of state legislators, said he wishes the state would do more to protect high-quality wetlands.
>
> He wonders what would have happened to these wetlands if they weren't owned by a biologist and weren't close enough to Cornell to attract the attention of its scientists.
>
> "Almost certainly, they'd be gone," Beck said.

Well, I didn't actually say to the reporter, "No amount of data will prove that mining isn't a danger to the wetlands," yet, plainly, I gave that impression. Undeniably, it was pretty close to what I was feeling, given the circumstances. And while I may have said of the wetlands, "Almost certainly, they'd be gone," that was an exaggeration, degraded likely, but not gone. I am not a hydrologist, and I never claimed to fully understand the hydrology arguments on either side. Nevertheless, considering that my wetlands and their obvious flowing springs were at the base of the slope immediately adjacent to the Eddy tract to be mined, had made, in my eyes, arguments by Alfred Eddy's paid consultant, that no harm would be done, suspect and thoroughly unconvincing. His data did not provide, for me, any confidence of no harm.

Besides, it seemed unfair that the DEC and Ray Nolan had narrowed the environmental review down to the uncertainties of hydrology alone, when many reputable scientists had argued that the risks are simply too great at that location, and many others, including the Town of Dryden and nearly all neighbors, were strongly opposed for entirely valid reasons aside from hydrology, reasons enough from the very beginning to discourage mining and to at least require a dEIS to explore all issues. But since, at the DEC, hydrology was said to be the sole issue, I felt extremely fortunate to have had Professor Donald Siegel speaking hydrogeology for our side, countering the arguments of our opponents with stunning detail, agility, brilliance and commitment.

August 26, 1993, SEQR Positive Declaration; PosDec(3):

> The New York State Department of Environmental Conservation as lead agency, has determined that the proposed action... may have a significant effect on the environment and that a Draft Environmental Impact Statement will be prepared....
> Reasons Supporting This Determination:
> 1. Review of this proposal indicates that the hydrology of Malloryville Bogs may be altered and cause irrevocable changes in the Bog's unique characteristics. Data must be developed to re-

spond to this concern.

2. The impacts associated with increased heavy truck traffic on rural roads of the area must be identified and addressed.

3. Local residents have expressed concern over possible devaluation of their properties.

Raymond J. Nolan

Resolve

Amanita mushroom (poisonous)

11 dEIS

Endurance is patience concentrated.
— Thomas Carlyle

WOULD ALFRED EDDY and Brayton Foster choose to prepare an impact statement as required by the new Positive Declaration, the NegDec having been rescinded, or would they discontinue their pursuit of mining at this location, as had Paolangeli and B.R. DeWitt four years and six years earlier? Now, as then, we would need to wait and see, hopeful that gravel-mining plans would go away.

Year 8: 1993-94

But the timing seemed right for Ed King to talk again with Eddy about possible purchase of his land with von Engeln funds. On September 17, 1993, Andy Zepp wrote to Ed King:

> Dear Ed: I have enclosed a copy of the recent decision by the NYSDEC which will require a full (draft) environmental impact statement (dEIS) before any mining can be undertaken on the Eddy property at Malloryville. Given the added costs of an impact statement, perhaps Eddy will be more receptive to a cash purchase offer at this time.

221

Please give me a call if you would like to discuss the situation further prior to an approach to Eddy. I look forward to speaking with you again.

Sincerely, Andrew E. Zepp, Director of Land Protection, Central & Western NY Chapter, The Nature Conservancy

January 25, 1994. Four months had passed, then Andy called Ed King and wrote a memo for the Conservancy's file:

Spoke with attorney Ed King today regarding Malloryville, the Eddy tract, and the von Engeln bequest. King has not had any contact with Eddy since the DEC required an EIS for any gravel mining. He admitted that it was not a high priority.

King requested that I provide him with a draft easement which would protect the portion of the Malloryville esker on Bob Beck's property.

At the end of the conversation, King agreed to contact Eddy once he had obtained information about Eddy's right to appeal the EIS decision. AZ

March 31, 1994. Three more months passed. Nothing. Then Andy met with Ed King in Ithaca. Andy's memo to TNC file:

I met yesterday with Ithaca attorney Ed King to discuss the status of protection efforts at Malloryville Swamp & Fen as well as the von Engeln bequest funds. For several years now, both TNC and Bob Beck have been urging King to utilize the bequest funds to purchase the 100+ acre Eddy property which is adjacent to Malloryville Swamp. Bob Beck has also agreed in concept to the idea of donating a conservation easement over his property if the Eddy tract is secured.

Though partially mined, the Eddy property

contains important buffer to the wetland complex. Eddy has sought additional mining permits, but his efforts have been stalled when faced with the cost of a required environmental impact statement. King approached Eddy prior to his last bout with the DEC mine regulators. I have been urging King to approach him again re. a sale of the property.

As originally proposed by Wayne Klockner..., the von Engeln funds would be used to purchase lands as part of a greater protection effort which would protect the wetlands as well the impressive glacially influenced topography. Von Engeln specifically left the money to protect the Malloryville esker.

While meeting with King, I let him know that Ron Beck (Bob's brother) was no longer utilizing his 75 acre pasture next to Bob's. Since this property also includes part of the esker, and I have never walked on it, I suggested that we schedule a field trip once the snow melts. King agreed and I will try to set something up for the end of April.

The field trip will provide us with an opportunity to clarify TNC's interest in this area while at the same time give us a chance to get King moving forward to expend the bequest monies. AZ

But Ed King seemed unwilling to either re-approach Alfred Eddy or to release the Von Engeln funds to The Nature Conservancy which would give Andy and Director David Klein the go-ahead to establish the Preserve (rather than Ed attempting to do it himself), nor did Ed participate in Andy's suggested field trip.

May 10, 1994. Andy Zepp and David Klein did, however, come to Malloryville, meeting me at my house, on a warm and sunny spring day for an invigorating hike. They were interested in seeing the northeastern section of the 300+-acre potential preserve as Wayne Klockner, four and a half years earlier, had proposed. Of the three Tompkins County-designated Unique Natural Areas here, the one named North Malloryville consists mostly of upland mature hardwoods on kames and esker and cool Hemlock swamp, each rich in wildflowers and wildlife, on tracts owned by Cornell engineering professor Tony Ingraffea and my brother Ron Beck. We set out through a section of my property, crossing my footbridge, then over my hardwoods kame near the spot where I, alone in dark evening twilight, had encountered a Bobcat a few years earlier. Then we climbed the high kame on my brother's 75-acre punchbowl property, following the fence line between his and the Eddy parcel. At the top, we paused to admire the view to the south while I related my adventure there, as a boy with my younger brother Rick, stamping out the hot, rapidly-spreading fire from someone's deserted campsite, and the surprise $2.50 government checks we received later.

Continuing through the punchbowl we hiked up and down hill through inviting spring woodlands while skirting denser brushy areas, the favored habitat for Ruffed Grouse. On their annual "partridge"-hunting excursions with their well-trained bird dogs, my veterinarian-cousin Albert Beck and his son Patrick regularly chose the punchbowl as a favorite destination, driving from their distant homes. Next, we carefully traversed a swamp and hopped, at a narrow point, a stream, locally called Spring Brook. Then we entered the 68-acre Ingraffea parcel, a tract of mature woodlands on complex hill and valley terrain formed by glacier meltwater, at the northeast end of the Malloryville Esker. Then we turned south, walked up the end of the big esker and followed the path along its top, looking down on a Hemlock swamp to our right, and to our left, immediately below, the flowing water of Fall Creek paralleling the base of the esker. There, before arriving at a natural breach in the esker where the woodland stream we had crossed earlier flows through, we were thrilled with the sight and calls of an adult Osprey flying low beneath us, over the waters of Fall Creek. We continued on the esker top along the easternmost extent of the punchbowl property, then dropped down and followed the old railroad bed which at that point intervenes between the esker and Fall Creek, the three for a time paralleling each other, side by side, and completed our walk back to the road at my driveway, the spot where Professor von Engeln and his students got off and back on trains on their field trips from Cornell. There, reflecting on a most pleasant outing, I sensed that both David and Andy agreed that North Malloryville had to be included in a future nature preserve.

June 22, 1994. Notice of Completion of Draft EIS:

> A Draft Environmental Impact Statement has been completed and accepted by the NYS DE-PARTMENT OF ENVIRONMERNTAL CONSER-VATION, as lead agency, for the proposed action.... Comments on the Draft EIS are requested and will be accepted by the contact person until August 15, 1994.
> Raymond J. Nolan

Before June 22, I didn't know for sure if we would or would not be seeing a Draft Environmental Impact Statement. But then, ten months after PosDec(3), the answer appeared. Alfred Eddy had not conceded. The time, once again, had arrived when I would contact our supporters, our team, with the information they would need, this time to respond to a dEIS with our fourth major round of letter writing. As before, sensing that inaction or poor response on our part would be perceived by the DEC as weakness or loss of interest, I knew we could not relax, but needed to respond yet again in force. In truth, even now, I felt that our long years of effort could easily end for naught, that we could still fail despite all of our letters contained in the DEC files of the two previous mining applications and those in response to the NegDec in the current SEQR proceeding, that if we became complacent now, Ray Nolan would be freed to bend again to the pressures from Eddy and Foster for their gravel mine.

Nearing the end of our eighth year, a mutual trial of endurance would continue, an absentee landowner doggedly pursuing profit from his land while wishing for our disengagement (maybe we would lose interest, or move away); we rallying once again, speaking and writing deeply-felt words in defense of un-despoiled nature and a peaceful neighborhood, still here, wide awake, our resolve intact.

Yet, that dEIS, 51 pages plus appendices and maps, presented very little that was new. But that fact, perhaps, should not have been a surprise, since, after all, the application itself, before Ray Nolan's NegDec, had already contained the hydrology study that Ray, much earlier, had requested to avoid requiring an impact statement.

Still, I found interesting and disturbing Brayton Foster's attempt to use a large spring snowmelt, clearly shown in his dEIS photos as water flowing, on the surface from the northern area to be mined, directly into the northwest corner of my wetlands, as support in the dEIS for their mining application (but soon Don Siegel, in his comments to Ray Nolan, would effectively deal with that particular argument). In fact, that identical surface flow path was no surprise to me, nor was it to former resident Richard Zelinsky who had reported it at a Dryden Town Board hearing for Eddy's gravel mine six years before my arrival. And I had reported it to my county Environmental Health Division, as problematically leading downslope from Paolangeli's DEC and County approved septage lagoon, through the septage spreading field, to my wetland.

July 7, 1994. I wrote to David and Andy at The Nature Conservancy:

> Dear David and Andy, The dEIS from Alfred Eddy/Brayton Foster which you should have received contains no big surprises. The only new data they provide are groundwater levels from last year's... heavy spring melt.
>
> Enclosed here are comments from Barbara

Bedford, Don Siegel and myself...[concerning the NegDec] The comments on the wetlands, hydrology, esker and zoning are still valid.

In the dEIS, Foster is wrong in his statements that the portion of the esker shown in the photograph from von Engeln's book is gone because of previous mining. Not so. It remains intact, though quite overgrown with vegetation.

Foster does not mention Natural Heritage Program data on the wetlands. I am requesting from Natural Heritage that their data on Malloryville Swamp/Bog and Malloryville Fen be sent to Ray Nolan (once again, for his current file).

Ray... tells me that it is increasingly probable that, after comments are in, he will pass this issue on to an administrative law judge who will hold an adjudicatory hearing for final determination.

Thanks! Bob

Again, I engaged in contacting our supporters and copying and sharing documents for their use in writing comments to DEC. I started composing my letter right away and mailed it a few weeks later.

August 12, 1994. My letter to Ray Nolan:

Dear Ray: With this letter, I wish to comment on the Draft Environmental Impact Statement [dated by Brayton Foster 3/1/94, with DEC Notice of Completion 6/22/94] for the proposed Alfred Eddy gravel mine....

After reviewing the dEIS I remain deeply concerned about the potential for irreversible degradation of the Malloryville wetlands (immediately downslope from the proposed mine) and the certain negative impacts on our quiet rural neighborhood. (Please see my earlier letters—dated 7/28/87, 5/30/89 and 12/26/92—to your office in response to this and two previous mining applications at the same site. Enclosed is a copy of my 12/26/92 letter concerning the current application.)

My wife and I own the property containing the wetland complex known as Malloryville Bog and a portion of the Malloryville esker. We chose to make our permanent home and raise our family here specifically because of the unspoiled surroundings of remarkably diverse wetland communities and fascinating kame, kettle and esker topography—all, a legacy of the last ice age.

Although this is our home, you must understand that our interest in protecting this local environment is more than a "not in my backyard" response to unwanted development. Because of the area's highly unusual biological and geological richness, it's best human use is as an un-degraded natural resource for public enjoyment, education and scientific research. Currently, in fact, the Malloryville wetlands and esker are actively being used for such purposes.

For example, the site is the focus, as you know, of wetland hydrogeological studies being conducted by faculty and graduate students at Syracuse University and is the subject of a scientifically important paper (referred to in the dEIS and which you have in your files) on the formation of peatlands published in the Journal of Hydrology in 1992. Botanical and ecological research at Malloryville, on wetland communities and species, is being conducted by faculty and graduate students at Cornell University and by the DEC's New York Natural Heritage Program.

Further, in recent years I have been asked by dozens of individuals and numerous groups (including school and university classes and eight or so different organizations) to lead interpretive walks around and through the maze of wetlands and wooded uplands, and on the long, snaking esker ridges (enclosed are: a list of groups that have recently visited Malloryville and a map of my property showing the network of hiking trails).

My comments on the dEIS follow:

1) Biodiversity: The dEIS does not state the facts or significance of the highly unusual biodiversity of the adjacent wetlands, nor the rarity of the natural communities and species present, nor the designation of the three adjacent sites by Tompkins County as Unique Natural Areas (other than to include, at the end of Appendix C, the... resolution of the Tompkins County Environmental Management Council urging their protection). Consequently, I have requested that current printouts on Malloryville be sent to you from the New York State (DEC) Natural Heritage Program and the Tompkins County Unique Natural Areas databases.

2) Hydrology: The dEIS conclusions drawn from the applicant's hydrology data are challenged independently by three professionals, at Cornell and Syracuse Universities, with knowledge and experience in hydrology (please see their comments sent directly to you). The dEIS fails to demonstrate or provide adequate assurance that the wetlands would not be adversely impacted, possibly seriously and irreparably by upslope gravel mining.

3) Traffic, Noise and Dust: Our neighborhood is rural, quiet and peaceful. Traffic on West Malloryville Road is very light and local agricultural activities are not objectionable. The dEIS totally fails to convey the dramatic increase and massive impact of noise, traffic (and probable dust) from the proposed excavation, dry processing and dump trucks on the quality of our neighborhood. For example, the proposed increase from the current average of fewer than one (usually

light) truck per hour to the passing in front of residences of a heavy dump truck every 5 minutes (12 trips per hour, 100 per day) would represent a major negative impact, unacceptable in our neighborhood.

Further, the dEIS is misleading because on most maps several of the private residences adjacent or very close to the proposed mine and haulageway are simply not shown: for example, absent in Figs. 1, 3 and 13 are the four residences that would be most impacted, including one adjacent to each side of the haulageway.

4) Local Zoning and Previous Mining Permit: The applicant has provided false and misleading information to the DEC over the past several years concerning local land use plans and the status of his previous local mining permit. Current Town of Dryden zoning at Malloryville prohibits mining without a zoning variance and town officials have stated in writing that the applicant's previous permit expired [in 1982] and any continuation is illegal (see their letters in your files).

5) Need for Gravel: Contrary to statements in the dEIS, there are four other gravel mines within about 6 miles of the proposed site and several others within Tompkins County.

In conclusion, because of the quality and significance of the natural features at Malloryville and the quality of the neighborhood, a gravel mine is simply inappropriate at the proposed location. Therefore, I request again that the New York State Department of Environmental Conservation, acting on its responsibility to assure protection of our remaining natural heritage and to consider the long-term public good, deny this permit to mine gravel at Malloryville.

Sincerely yours, Robert M. Beck

cc: James Schug, Supervisor, Town of Dryden;

Robert Bendick, Deputy Commissioner for Natural Resources, DEC

Again, in the next pages, I include many of the letters written in defense of Malloryville's unspoiled wetlands and quiet rural neighborhood as vivid testimony to the continuing commitment and extraordinary depth of support in this long series of environmental reviews.

July 11, 1994. Betsy Darlington, again with her usual directness, wrote to Ray Nolan:

> Dear Mr. Nolan: It is abundantly clear from all of the evidence that has been presented that the proposed gravel mining would pose a significant risk to the Malloryville Wetland as well as to the unique natural areas to the north and south of it. These resources are of exceptional quality and must be protected on behalf of the people of the State.
>
> There is no way that you or anyone else could state categorically that the mining would not damage (or even destroy) the wetlands, whether from changes in hydrology or pollutants or both. The hydrology reports differ in their conclusions, but the one from Mr. Foster does not appear credible in light of studies conducted by Donald Siegel.
>
> To permit the gravel mining would be to experiment with a rare, complex, and fragile ecosystem that took thousands of years to develop. Does the State really want to risk damaging or destroying it? It is hard to imagine any justification for taking such a risk. Nothing short of an absolute certainty that no harm would come to the wetlands could possibly justify granting a permit. Clearly, such certainty is impossible. Indeed, Siegel's, as well as Barbara Bedford and Robert Wesley's, studies all indicate that there is significant risk of damage.

It is amazing that, given all the evidence, the DEC hasn't simply banned mining in that location, and keeps considering one permit application after another. This wastes the time (and money) of the applicant, of those seeking to protect this unique wetland, and of the State.

You owe it to future generations to deny the permit once and for all, and to make it clear that you will not entertain future applications.

Sincerely, Betsy Darlington

cc: Pat Reixinger, DEC; Robert Bendick, DEC

July 14, 1994. Ken and Mary Kay Welgoss, neighbors and school teachers, wrote to Ray Nolan and Jim Schug:

...As residents of West Malloryville Road, we feel that allowing a gravel pit to open in this area would be extremely detrimental to the wetlands, the neighborhood, and our overall quality of life.

Specifically, we object to the noise, dust, and danger to young children and pets that would result from a large volume of trucks going into and leaving the gravel pit. While our scientific knowledge is limited, it is also our understanding that the owner of this property has not sufficiently proved that the gravel pit would not adversely affect the water supply of the wetlands. This is an area of exceptional natural beauty and, as we understand it, of singular value for scientific study. Therefore, we feel strongly that it should not be violated. Finally, we recently learned that our home, as well as homes owned by three of our neighbors, was not represented on a map of the gravel pit area submitted with the... request. These residences are located right at the entrance of the proposed gravel pit. Whether or not this was a deliberate effort to minimize the perceived impact this gravel pit would have on individuals living in the neighborhood, the fact remains that this is a residential area and we all would be seriously affected... For these reasons, we encourage you to deny the request...

Thank you very much for your consideration of our concerns...

Sincerely, Kenneth Welgoss; Mary Kay Welgoss

July 15, 1994. I contacted the US Fish and Wildlife Service Cortland office, and they forwarded their previous letter by Carl Schwartz to Ray.

July 23. Professor Donald Leopold, highly respected botanist and wetlands ecologist at SUNY College of Environmental Science and Forestry (SUNY-ESF) in Syracuse, and my colleague on the Conservancy's chapter board (now Distinguished Teaching Professor and Chair of his ESF department) stated his views in a powerful letter to Ray Nolan:

> Dear Ray: I wish to express my strong opposition... The dEIS does not demonstrate that the proposed project would not have serious consequences on the unique Malloryville Bog wetlands and the overall character of the biological and geological resources of the area. Short-term economic gain for few individuals could result in serious degradation of New York's natural heritage that has developed over thousands of years.
>
> I write to you as a teacher and researcher in wetland ecology, former Chair of The Nature Conservancy's Central New York Board of Trustees, and current Editor of the Natural Areas Journal, a journal received by thousands of professionals whose goal is to preserve the special attributes of natural areas. I also write to you as someone who has visited the Malloryville wetlands, as well as dozens of peatlands throughout the eastern U.S.
>
> I have had an opportunity to review all of the

letters that Drs. Don Siegel and Barbara Bedford have written to you regarding this project, beginning with their reaction to your Negative Declaration of 11/92. I find it incredulous that this project is still being considered after the opinions written by Drs. Siegel and Bedford. Dr. Siegel is one of the most highly respected peatland hydrogeologists in the world, and he has published an important peer-reviewed scientific paper based on the work he and Jim McNamara did at Malloryville (I was a reader on Jim's committee). Dr. Bedford and her colleagues have spent much time in minerotrophic wetlands in New York and are in an exceptional position to comment on the importance of the Malloryville wetland in relation to minerotrophic wetlands elsewhere in New York. Based on my own visit to this area and minerotrophic wetlands throughout the Northeast, I would concur with information in Dr. Bedford's letters to you that Malloryville "Bog" has one of the richest floras of minerotrophic wetlands in New York. The rich flora is due to the great variation in water chemistry, ranging from near ombrotrophic to very minerotrophic areas. These conditions could be greatly altered by gravel mining.

The operation of the proposed gravel mine here could damage one of the most unique natural areas (including the geological and biological features) in central New York. Why take a chance with such a special area for such a common product?

Please give the most serious attention to the professional opinions offered by Drs. Siegel, Bedford, and me. I do not believe any group of professionals with similarly strong credentials could justify even the thought of a gravel mine at the proposed location near the Malloryville wetlands.

Respectfully submitted, Donald J. Leopold

August 4, 1994. Jim Hanson, Commissioner, and Katie White (now Katie Borgella) of the Tompkins County Department of Planning wrote to Ray:

> Dear Mr. Nolan: The Tompkins County Planning Department staff has reviewed the Draft Environmental Impact Statement (DEIS)... and has prepared comments for your consideration.
>
> Please find attached a copy of the introduction and pertinent sections of the inventory of Unique Natural Areas of Tompkins County. As stated in the introduction, the areas included in the inventory "provide the community with a valuable resource, providing sanctuary for rare plants and animals, and helping to maintain the diversity of natural communities in our region." The main concern of the Planning Department is that three of the unique natural areas in the county (No. DR-3, DR-4, DR-34) could be seriously impacted by a gravel mining operation on the Alfred C. Eddy property. As you can see from the enclosed report, the areas contain significant numbers of rare or scarce species, as well as unique examples of those types of ecological communities in our region.
>
> While the hydrogeology of the site is best left to experts to analyze, we request that you take all precautions possible to ensure that the Malloryville Bog system is not negatively impacted by the proposed gravel operations. We were particularly concerned by the following comments in the letter to you from Professor Donald Siegel, dated December 23, 1992: "The viability of the wetland and its diverse plant communities depends upon the amounts of groundwater delivered to the wetland and how the relative proportions of groundwater and rain water change the chemical characteristics of the surface water used by the

plants" and "The wetland vegetation is clearly sensitive to small changes in the groundwater flow regime, shown by the succession of rare bog vegetation over fen vegetation in a place where such a succession would seem to be precluded."

Although we are not hydrogeologists, Brayton Foster's argument (pages 31 and 46)—that the April 1993 natural recharge of the site will far exceed any recharge that could occur as a result of groundwater mounding, so therefore the removal of the gravel will not impact the regional groundwater table—seems to lack substance. Isn't there a large difference between a temporary seasonal snow melt and a permanent alteration of groundwater flow and height due to reduced load? Wouldn't the potential permanent rise in the wetland groundwater table have the same amount of seasonal flow added to it as it always has? We do not feel qualified to comment on these questions, but hope that you will look at the issues of ground and surface water levels in the bogs seriously. As you are well aware, wetlands are very fragile ecosystems, and even small changes in water composition and flow can greatly impact the health of those systems.

Although there will be no County-wide impacts associated with the increased traffic in the area of the project, it appears that there will be a big impact on West Malloryville Road. That road is very narrow and winding in sections, and all truck, automobile, and farm machine operations will have to use caution. Additionally, the road's (and the neighborhood's) rural character will be disturbed by the noise levels associated with large trucks hauling gravel at a rate of 12 trips per hour.

We also want to bring to your attention, in case it hasn't been already, that mining is not a permitted activity under the Town of Dryden's zoning ordinance, and that a variance would be required.

Thank you for the opportunity to comment on the Malloryville Pit DEIS. If you have any questions, please contact Katie White [Borgella]....

Sincerely, James Hanson, Jr., Commissioner of Planning

cc: James Schug, Town of Dryden Supervisor

August 6, 1994. Hydrogeologist Don Siegel, as he had done before, put his thoughts into an extraordinarily thorough, detailed letter to Ray Nolan, a remarkable letter, like his others, for which I remain profoundly grateful, far beyond words:

Dear Mr. Nolan: I have reviewed the Draft Environmental Impact Statement and Mined Land Use Plan for Alfred C. Eddy, and would like to express my comments on the technical merit regarding potential hydrogeologic effects of future mining on the status of the adjacent Malloryville wetland. As you are aware, I am familiar with the hydrogeology of the setting (McNamara et. al, 1992) and have addressed the technical merits of previous applications to mine the site both at meetings and in letters to you on December 23, 1992 and January 25, 1993. In summary, I find that that the opinions expressed in this Draft Environmental Impact Statement and the additional data provided by it did not significantly address the major issues I have raised: 1.) Does the applicant sufficiently characterize the hydrogeologic setting of the wetland? and 2.) Can the applicant show that vegetation in the wetland, acknowledged as one of the most unique in the State, will not be affected by changes in the hydrology caused by mining?

The applicant has not sufficiently characterized the hydrogeologic setting of the wetland and adjacent uplands. I am perplexed that the applicant still insists that groundwater is moving northwest to south-southeast through and under the wetland. This direction is almost perpendicular to the direction that surface water and groundwater moves in the wetland soils. McNamara et. al (1992) and McNamara (1990) report monthly profiles of hydraulic head at 15 piezometer locations in the five different wetland communities in the Malloryville wetland. In their study, they clearly show that the hydraulic gradients in the saturated peat are towards the small pond and natural creek that flows to Fall Creek. The wetland is not "perched" above the regional water table; mineral soil beneath the peat is sandy and saturated. There is no evidence to suggest that the wetland soils are not in hydraulic communication with the regional groundwater system. Consequently, there must be a groundwater divide located under the steep esker immediately south of the Malloryville wetland. The overall direction of groundwater flow in the wetland towards the creek and pond from west to east is consistent with the existence of a hydraulic divide.

Even more perplexing is the applicant's insistence that there is virtually no groundwater discharging west to east from the southern part of the Eddy property to the wetland, despite the numerous springs discharging on the western side of the wetland. The applicant proposes an hypothesis that each spring is the termination of an individual long flow path from the northern part of the Eddy property. This hypothesis is untenable. In fact, the applicant does not even know what the elevation of the water table is in the southern part of the Eddy property because most of the wells fail to intersect the water table; they are dry. The applicant's interpretation (EIS Map #3) drawn with equipotential lines oriented perpendicular to the wetland, forces groundwater to move parallel to the wetland boundary, and the wetland water table (and water surface in the wetland) to dip to the south; it simply does not (McNamara et. al, 1992).

Furthermore, parts of the hydrogeologic discussion in the applicant's EIS are misleading with respect to the hydrogeologic setting of the Eddy property and wetland. For example, the esker crossing the southern part of the Eddy property is still intact and has not been mined away. Cross-section A'-A" in Map #4 does not show this esker because the section fortuitously passes through the driveway cut into the esker. Also, the Geiger-White well is located south of the esker, separated from other monitoring wells by the esker's ridge of high ground. A groundwater mound would logically occur under this ridge locally diverting southward groundwater flow towards the wetland. How much groundwater is diverted to the wetland depends upon the height and persistence of the mound relative to the regional water-table gradient upon which the mound is superimposed. The cross-section B-B' (Map #4) is also misleading. This cross-section shows considerable distance and relief between the proposed north pit and the wetland. However, had the cross-section been drawn a little to the west, it would have been clear that the wetland is much closer to the proposed pit and directly down the topographic and hydraulic gradients from it.

I proposed at a meeting with you and the applicant an alternative hypothesis (my Figure 1) wherein water-table contours are parallel to the boundary of the wetland. I am surprised that the applicant did not address the issues raised by my diagram. Let me repeat them. For almost 30 years, a water-table configuration such as I have drawn has been recognized as occurring in hydrogeologic settings consisting of kettle depression wetlands and lakes in outwash, kame deposits and esker complexes (e.g. Krantz and Medlin, 1991; Anderson and Munter, 1981; Meyboom, 1967; Williams, 1968; there are many others). The applicant's hypothesized water-table map, if correct, would not only be the first one of its kind for hummocky glacial terrains; it would also violate the fluid mechanics governing flow systems in wetland-lake settings (Winter, 1976 and numerous subsequent reports on modeling results confirmed by USGS field studies). If correct, the applicant's interpretation would also contradict direct observations of the water table configuration in the wetland itself (e.g. McNamara et. al, 1992). Contrary to the Draft EIS, most springs discharging on the western flank of the Malloryville wetland are the discharge zones of flow paths originating at water table mounds under the western kame and surrounding eskers. Springs discharging to the northwest part of the wetland probably are from flow paths similar to that described by the EIS; springs on the southwest probably come from a flow system recharged at the southern part of the Eddy property. A water table configuration drawn consistent with that ubiquitously determined for other similar wetlands and lakes implies that changes in the hydraulics of local flow caused by future mining could lead to changes in the unique vegetation communities.

Unfortunately, it is impossible to determine with any precision the orientation and location of flow paths from which the springs derive because there is so little information on the glacial stratigraphy and depth to confining beds or bedrock on the southern part of the Eddy property. With better and deeper stratigraphy, at least some modeling could be done to determine the configuration of probable flow paths and how discharge rates might be affected by mining. Indeed, I am also struck by the lack of any piezometer nests at all to show how hydraulic head changes with depth in the proposed mined areas. With this data, now routinely obtained in hydrogeologic studies, alternative hypotheses can be tested; without it, the issues become that of best professional judgment.

Wetland vegetation communities change because of changes in saturation, nutrient input, and chemical composition in the pore-water quality in the sorption zone during the time of maximum growth. The applicant presented no information addressing these issues, nor any understanding or discussion of how diverse the wetland vegetation is in the Malloryville wetland. Most of the rarest wetland flora at the site is found near the springs on the western side, not at the bog community. However, the applicant focused his hydrologic arguments only on the issue of whether future mining can affect the bog. The raised bog is scientifically interesting because the McNamara et. al (1992) study presented a new hypothesis explaining how bogs can form in environmentally hostile places where groundwater discharges upward. McNamara et. al (1992) used a computer model to determine the sensitivity of the flow system to a building groundwater mound in the bog area (the EIS discussion shows poor understanding of how this model was done, but that misunderstanding is not an important point to address in this letter). With respect to the bog, the crux of the EIS hydrologic arguments to support mining is that during spring snowmelt, the increase in water-table elevation under the kame is very large (many feet), whereas no similar increase in the elevation of the water table occurs in the wetland. Therefore, it was concluded, the wetland is drained sufficiently well enough by the pond and stream to not affect the saturation state of the bog. It is also argued in the EIS that mining cannot logically affect the bog because bog vegetation has occurred at the site for thousands of years.

I have few arguments with these conclusions because the maximum wetland water height and the efficiency of the wetland to move water during spring snowmelt is not a major concern. The site obviously has been wet enough for 1,000s of years to support a wetland that drained to a natural creek, long before the pond was installed. The critical issue is not the wetland's efficiency to move water, but rather, what affects will changing hydrology have on the nutrient budget and pore-water chemistry in the sorption zone of the plants. This issue is particularly acute for fen plants which germinate considerably after snowmelt. The critical time for fen wetland plants is during their early-mid growing season, not during snowmelt. Nor is it relevant that water levels return to mid-summer levels independent of the volume of spring snowmelt to the wetland. What is important is how might mining affect the water and chemical delivery system to the upper peat during middle spring to early summer. That the wetland drained efficiently during snowmelt is irrelevant to the question of how mining could affect the plants.

Were gravel mining to occur as proposed, there would be less unsaturated material to retard and attenuate rainfall. It stands to reason that the elevation of water table mounds would be higher than now with greater recharge to the water table. Winter (1976), Siegel (1983) and others have shown that only a few cm increase in the elevation of a groundwater mound can seasonally change the hydraulics of a wetland in a dramatic way. Whether the groundwater mounds under the north and south proposed mining areas will increase or decrease with mining can be addressed (and is routinely done so) by numerical or analytical flow models. Of course, the results of the models would have to be calibrated (tested) against the known configuration of the mounds, for which we only have direct data on the north end. Second, the increase in the hydraulic gradient caused by the higher mounds would necessarily increase the discharge of mineralized groundwater and upward hydraulic gradients under the peat along the wetland western edge where most of the unique wetland vegetation is found. The amount of increase in discharge could also be evaluated if details on the deeper stratigraphy and hydraulic head at the Eddy property were known such that at least conceptually reasonable flow paths to the wetland could be evaluated.

Increasing the amount of groundwater flow would increase concentrations of solutes and nutrients to the root zone. Root-zone water is a mixture of surface water from rain and upwelling groundwater. Bog and fen vegetation are generally highly controlled by pH; only a few % increase in mineralized water can change pore-water pH to where bog vegetation no longer thrives (Siegel, 1983). It is my understanding that much less is known about the nutrient and chemical controls over rich fen vegetation than is known for bog vegetation, but **the fact that this fen vegetation is so rare argues to a narrow range in controlling factors**. Indeed, ecologists recognize the rarity of the fen vegetation at the Malloryville wetland. For example, Cornell Plantations (letter, March 27, 1987) argues that Malloryville fens

"...are very vulnerable to changes in water supply from surrounding land..." In summary, I find the EIS unacceptable with respect to resolving the critical hydrologic issues related to the wetland. Little additional information on hydrology is presented except for records during snowmelt, a non-critical time for wetland vegetation. [Here Don includes citations for the nine publications mentioned in his letter.]

I include a copy of my cv for your information.

If you have any questions on this statement, feel free to contact me.

Donald I. Siegel, Professor of Earth Sciences

August 8, 1994. Dennis Swaney, Cornell scientist with expertise in hydrology, and fellow EMC member with me, wrote to Nolan:

Dear Mr. Nolan, I am writing as a concerned citizen, and a representative of the Tompkins County EMC from the Town of Dryden, regarding the impacts of proposed gravel mining operations on Malloryville Bog. I am currently employed by the Cornell Center for the Environment, where I am involved in computer simulation of environmental systems, particularly the transport of dissolved substances through watersheds. I have had an opportunity to examine a copy of the draft EIS for the proposed gravel pit, and am troubled by some apparent methodological problems.

The consulting geologist who has prepared the draft EIS has prepared a map (map #3) which purports to show contours of the water table elevation of the regional aquifer on the basis of a dozen or so monitoring wells, a household well, and the elevations of local water bodies. Unfortunately, the network of wells is situated such that most of the measurements fall directly on the proposed mining site, and not between the mining site and the potentially affected wetlands. The contour map for these areas therefore seems largely speculative: the well data would allow other interpretations of the groundwater contours than those provided by the consultant. The fact that the contours of this map seem to bear no relationship to the local topography (map #1) makes these extrapolations even more suspect.

Real groundwater flows are affected not only by the gradient of the groundwater contours, but by the variability of local hydraulic conductivity. While the consultant has measured conductivity in a few locations (perk tests) he does not attempt to map this highly variable parameter, and consequently his indication of the direction of groundwater movements (figure 17) is not well supported.

The directions of groundwater movement implied by map #3 and figure 17 also fail to account for overland flow and "quickflow" (the flow beneath the soil surface which occurs following precipitation or snowmelt), which are generally assumed to follow local topographic contours. While the draft EIS documents the occurrence of significant overland flow from the proposed mine area following snowmelt, noting that it quickly drains through the affected wetland, it fails to address the impact of changes in the quality of this water. Common sense dictates that the placement of a mining site uphill of and within a few hundred feet of a wetland is not a good idea. Soil loss associated with the operation of heavy equipment is known to be a significant contributor of nutrients and sediment to surrounding water bodies if allowed to be transported in run-off waters. Given the sensitivity of these wetlands

to such impacts, and the placement of the mining site relative to the wetlands, it would seem
that surface and shallow subsurface flows may
represent as great a threat to the wetlands as are
the potential groundwater impacts.

I urge you to consider both of the above
points in your review of the draft EIS.

Sincerely, Dennis P. Swaney

cc: James Schug

August 9, 1994. Mahlon Perkins, Attorney, Town of Dryden writes to Nolan:

Dear Ray: Please allow this letter to serve as
comments from the Town of Dryden in connection with the Notice of Completion of Draft EIS...

I previously wrote to you on December 19,
1992 requesting that this matter be the subject
of a dEIS and outlining in general the position of
the Town.

The dEIS has two items which the Town con-
siders to be an error.

The first item occurs on page 6, section 2.B.1
Past Mining History. The Town takes exception
to the statement, "Mining at rates of less than
500 yards per year has continued since 1985"
and the conclusion, "since gravel mining has
continued at rates below 1,000 tons per year the
mining on the Eddy property is a pre-existing
use." That statement and conclusion are contrary to the facts and the Town of Dryden Zoning
Ordinance. Neighbors and Town personnel dispute the continued removal of material from the
site.

Prior to the adoption of the New York State
Mined Land Reclamation Act amendments effective September 1, 1991, this mine was the subject of a special permit application by Mr. Eddy
to the Town of Dryden. A Town permit was is-

sued to Mr. Eddy on April 8, 1981 and he filed with the Town Clerk a $5,000 surety bond. The surety bond was for a period of one year and the permit was valid so long as a surety bond remained in effect. The surety bond lapsed after its initial term and was not renewed and accordingly any rights Mr. Eddy acquired under the permit also lapsed. Therefore, any use of the property under the terms of that permit since its expiration has not been lawful and cannot constitute a lawful pre-existing use.

The zoning was changed in 1988 to RB-1 which does not allow mining as a right or with a special permit although mining may be allowed if the applicant can obtain a use [zoning] variance. The RB-1 zone does not prohibit mining.

Assuming _arguendo_ that Mr. Eddy were to be able to prove an existing lawful non-conforming use, (and therefore does not need to obtain a variance) he must still comply with the Town of Dryden Zoning Ordinance Section 1701 (special permit) since he intends to extend or enlarge the alleged lawful non-conforming use.

The other item in the DEIS which is in error is contained on the copy of the Full Environmental Assessment Form dated January 21, 1991 specifically the response to question B 25. The special use permit previously issued has expired. Therefore, as set forth above, the applicant will need to obtain either a use variance or in the event the applicant can demonstrate a lawful non-conforming use then he will have to obtain a special permit.

Notwithstanding the foregoing, the Town reserves the right to comment on the conditions to be attached to any permit under ECL §23-2711(3).

Thank you for your consideration of the Town of Dryden comments.

Very truly yours, Mahlon R. Perkins, Town of Dryden Attorney

August 10, 1994. Professor Peter Marks and Nancy Ostman write to Nolan:

Dear Mr. Nolan: We are writing to you again about the Malloryville Bog area.... We are reiterating our concern for the integrity of the area and have enclosed our letter from June 6, 1989, which summarizes the historic, scientific, and educational value of the Malloryville wetlands...

We remain concerned that gravel mining on the Eddy property would adversely affect the... wetlands by altering the water supply and are asking you to carefully consider the potential consequences of the current mined land use plan. We have reviewed the data presented in the DEIS and are not convinced that the data collected, and the time period over which it was collected, is adequate to determine the effects of the mining proposal on the groundwater that sustains Malloryville Bog. It appears that our concerns are shared by Barbara Bedford, Wetlands Ecologist in the Department of Natural Resources at Cornell and Donald Siegel, Hydrologist in the Geology Department at Syracuse University.

In conclusion, our review of the DEIS for Malloryville suggests that the impact of the gravel extraction proposed on the water supply to and on plant communities of the valuable... wetlands can not be resolved using the data included in the DEIS report. We remind you that a very high quality natural area is at risk, and that damage to the site would be irreparable and a significant scientific and educational loss. Other sites like this one have been destroyed in the past, and rare species found on those sites have been extirpated. It is our responsibility to protect the few pristine sites like Malloryville Bog that remain. Thank you for your consideration.

Sincerely, Nancy L. Ostman, Natural Areas Program Director, Cornell Plantations; Peter L. Marks, Chair, Ecology and Systematics, Cornell University

August 10, 1994. Brenda Werner, a Malloryville neighbor, wrote to Ray Nolan:

Dear Mr. Nolan: ...I recently moved to my present home... I had carefully chosen the location, as a home purchase is a considerable investment. What attracted me to the location includes: peacefulness, safety for playing children, and air low in exhaust fumes and dust (all a result of light traffic flow and almost nonexistent truck traffic) and the natural beauty and uniqueness of the surrounding bog land. As an environmentalist and outdoorsman, I enjoy birdwatching, botany, as well as jogging and cross-country skiing. In addition, I had understood that the local zoning prohibits such business activity as mining, and this knowledge also influenced my choice of home.

I feel that a [gravel] mine would considerably and detrimentally alter the environment. Mining and trucking activity would create considerable dust and noise. Heavy truck traffic would create an unsafe situation for children (as well as joggers and cross-country skiers) and would have a negative impact on the road. The dust, truck and equipment noise and mining activities would affect the quality of the surrounding bog land and the wildlife within. A mine would not be a suitable business activity for the current zoning. I would not consider purchasing a home next to a mine, and am certain that the present owners will have difficulty selling the home, and at a reasonable price.

I appreciate the opportunity to voice my opinion regarding the future of my neighborhood. I would hope that you would seriously consider my concerns over this matter. Thank you.

Sincerely yours, Brenda G. Werner
cc: James Schug, Town of Dryden

August 12, 1994. Scott Sheavly and Marcia-Eames Sheavly, former Malloryville neighbors, send a letter to Nolan:

Dear Mr. Nolan, Due to our growing family we have recently moved into a larger house in Freeville. However, during the five and a half years we lived in our house at... West Malloryville Road, which we continue to own, we developed a fondness and deep sense of appreciation for the... area and we continue to be concerned about the preservation of the West Malloryville neighborhood and the adjacent Malloryville Bog.

We have reviewed the Draft Environmental Impact Statement prepared for the proposed gravel pit... Based on the positive declaration issued by you last fall, the EIS is supposed to address the effects of increased road traffic, noise, and the effect on property values. Regretfully, the EIS contains significant misleading, inaccurate, and subjective findings, and fails to satisfy the requirements set forth in the positive declaration. Additionally, the EIS does not satisfy our concerns about the impact of a noisy industrial operation in the center of a rural residential and agricultural neighborhood.

The EIS states that road traffic... will "only double..." ...the claim that traffic will "only double" defies common sense and fails to consider the weight, noise, and danger posed by dump trucks every five minutes...

The EIS also fails to assess the impact of noise. The EIS states that noise from mining equipment and trucks will be mitigated by trees, low hills and distance and its noise can be compared to similar noise created by farm equipment. While it cannot be disputed that vegetation, terrain and proximity to sound directly impact how far sound carries, the EIS provides no supporting evidence to quantify this statement. One cannot make a reliable assessment of the impact of noise without data supported by decibel readings at various nearby locations. Furthermore, unlike the proposed mine, farms were present when we and other residents purchased our property, and are permitted under current zoning restrictions while the mine is not. The farms do not create excessive noise and are not a nuisance. Accordingly, the presence of farms and farming equipment is not an issue.

Finally, the EIS claims that there will be no impact on the value of nearby properties. This bold claim is made by a geologist, not an expert in real estate appraisal. Consistent with other misleading and inaccurate statements within the EIS, this claim is based entirely on a subjective opinion, not substantive evidence.

Clearly, the Draft EIS for the proposed mine does not adequately address the impact of the mine on the West Malloryville Road neighborhood. West Malloryville Road and the surrounding neighborhood is a wonderful place to walk, bike, play, and live peacefully without the intrusiveness of an industrial mining operation. We wish to keep it that way. We request that the permit for the proposed mine be denied.

Sincerely, Scott Sheavly, Marcia Eames-Sheavly cc: J. Schug; H. Slater

August 12, 1994. Ron Schassburger concludes his strong letter to Ray with the following:

> I believe it to be of the utmost importance that the following be recognized:
> • the Malloryville Bog area is unique both geologically and biologically, concentrating in a relatively small area tremendous diversity of landform, habitat and species assemblage,
> • it has been recognized as such for more than one hundred years, and has been and continues to be of inestimable value both scientifically and educationally,
> • to even threaten, let alone disturb this area, would indeed be tragic for all of those who would make use of this site now and for posterity,
> • the burden of proof must rest on the shoulders of those who would put such a valued environment at risk—they must demonstrate with certainty that their operations will not affect this area,
> • and if such certainty cannot be provided it is only prudent that a permit for their operations not be granted; to do otherwise is gambling something of tremendous value to many for small economic value to few.
> Sincerely yours, Ronald M. Schassburger, Ph.D.

August 13, 1994. Barbara Bedford and Robert Wesley write to Ray Nolan:

> Dear Mr. Nolan: ...Our comments which express serious concerns with the project and the shortcomings of the DEIS follow... [Here they restate much of their information from previous letters, and continue.] ...the topography and geology of the site are complex and do not lend themselves

to easy analysis. We do not consider that the DEIS accurately characterizes the hydrogeologic setting of the Malloryville wetlands, particularly the hydraulic gradients and the resulting groundwater flows. Since Mr. Foster's findings disagree with published scientific data from these wetlands (McNamara et al. 1992), we can only conclude that the interpretation presented in the DEIS is wrong. Also we do not feel that the applicant can show, based on this DEIS, that the vegetation of the Malloryville wetlands will not be affected by changes in the hydrology caused by the proposed mining activity.

We urge you to reject this DEIS and this application, as there is a very real potential that this proposed mining activity will cause the Malloryville wetlands irreparable damage. In our view the scientific, natural history and aesthetic value of this site is too great to justify the risk of this loss.

We would be pleased to answer any questions you may have regarding this matter. Please don't hesitate to give us a call.

Sincerely, Barbara L. Bedford, F. Robert Wesley

August 14, 1994. Rebecca Schneider, a Cornell wetlands ecologist/hydrologist, wrote to Nolan after Barbara Bedford had suggested that I contact her:

Dear Sir: I am writing regarding the impacts of proposed gravel mining operations on the hydrogeologic processes of Malloryville Bog. My opinion is based on a strong academic and research background in wetland studies. I have a doctorate degree from Cornell University in Ecology and a Masters degree in Environmental Sciences from the University of Virginia. For the past ten years, I have conducted numerous research projects which examined the interrelationship of wetland plant communities with their hydrologic and geochemical environment.

A main conclusion of the March 1994 Draft EIS (by Mr. Brayton P. Foster) is that "the groundwater delivery system for the adjoining wetland will not be impacted by the proposed mining..." (p. 3, par. 2). Mr. Foster bases his conclusion primarily on water level data and soil profile data collected from a series of groundwater wells. These data are summarized in the form of a map of the potentiometric water surface across the site (Map 3) and as a figure showing groundwater flow patterns (Fig. 17, p. 38). The DEIS goes on to state that these flow paths are in direct contradiction to those proposed by McNamara et al. in their 1992 journal article and disprove the author's statement that the bog is supported by regional groundwater flow.

A careful review of Mr. Foster's data on water wells and well locations raises a strong concern that his interpretation of the groundwater flow system is unjustified and therefore that his conclusions may also be invalid. Specifically, Fig. 17 shows groundwater flow paths that run southwest and parallel to wetland GR12 in the southern portion of the site. These flow paths are based on the positioning of the water table elevation lines on Map 3. I believe that the positioning of the lines in this portion of the site is not the most probable or accurate one. Water levels were only observed in well 10 (height = 1113.3) and in well 12 (height = 1088.7) throughout the study. A more accurate drawing of the potentiometric surface would show water surface lines between these two wells that run almost parallel to the GR12 wetland boundary with a steep gradient to account for the lack of water in wells 1, 2 and 4. Such a reinterpretation of the water table surface would result in groundwater flow lines leading more directly into wetland GR12. This is a more probable configuration given the overall topography of the land outside of the Eddy property (Figure 12, p. 19) and agrees with the data and conclusions of McNamara et al. 1992.

Given this potential flaw in the interpretations regarding the groundwater flow system of the Eddy property, I believe that the resulting conclusions of the DEIS, e.g. that there will be no impact on the groundwater flow to the adjacent wetland, should also be viewed with considerable caution.

Yours truly, Rebecca Schneider

Year 9: 1994/95

Entering the ninth year in our story, our comments on the dEIS completed, the comment period ended, I now wait for Ray Nolan's DEC response.

September 7, 1994. Ray writes to Brayton Foster:

Dear Mr. Foster: Enclosed please find copies of all responses received by the Department during the public comment period for the above referenced document. Please review these comments and provide the Department with your response to them as soon as you are able.

You will note that concerns are raised over safety issues, noise, dust, etc. These should be specifically addressed in your response to the dEIS, if appropriate, or by additional information gathered by you.

The concern for the future integrity of the Malloryville wetland remains the most significant issue, as you will note in many of the comments.

At this point I believe that a public hearing is likely with the primary focus on the hydrogeological issues.

I will not commence the public hearing pro-

255

cess until receipt and review of your response to comments is accomplished. However, if your client requests commencement of the hearing process immediately the Department will proceed accordingly.

If you have any questions regarding this letter please feel free to contact me.

Very truly yours, Raymond J. Nolan, Environmental Analyst

After 4 1/2 more months, during which Alfred Eddy had not requested a hearing, autumn had come and gone, and Witch Hazel trees by the wetland edges had bloomed, displaying their curious, thin and twisted yellow petals, the last flowers to appear before winter, Ray Nolan received, on December 27, 1994, Brayton Foster's written responses to our comments.

Again, we hear nothing as weeks turn to months, almost five months through winter's cold, with precise, straight-line Fox tracks in the snow, and into spring with Peeper and Wood Frog choruses and woodland wildflowers in bloom, then Ray Nolan writes a pivotal letter to Eddy and Foster, a letter marking, in our long journey, the closest the DEC had gotten—in truth, the closest in writing it ever got—to actually denying Eddy's gravel mine permit.

April 25, 1995. Ray Nolan's letter to Alfred Eddy and Brayton Foster:

Dear Mr. Eddy and Mr. Foster: This letter follows recent discussions with Mr. Foster regarding the above referenced mining permit application. The file for this application consists of the original application, supporting documents, initial public comments, the draft Environmental Impact Statement (dEIS), comments received from the public following the public review of the dEIS, and the applicant's response to those comments.

As you know, the Department's original Determination of Non-Significance [NegDec] was based on initial review of the application and was rescinded as a result of comments received from the public. Those comments indicated a potentially serious impact to the nearby Malloryville fen/bog complex (the wetland) resulting from significant changes to local groundwater hydrology caused by removal of material from the adjacent esker (the project site). The dEIS was then submitted and accepted for public review. The public comments received raised issues concerning the wetland and potential impacts to its hydrology as a result of the proposed mining. The applicant's response to those comments did not resolve that issue.

The Department has determined that public comments, in this instance, raise a substantive and significant issue. Resolution of this issue may result in the denial of the permit or imposition of significant conditions thereon. Accordingly, pursuant to Uniform Procedures and State Environmental Quality Review (6NYCRR Part 621 and Part 617) the Department will hold a public adjudicatory hearing on this application and action.

Here, in the middle of this letter, I welcomed Ray's words: "...public comments, in this instance, raise a substantive and significant issue," and "Resolution of this issue may result in the denial of the permit...," words clearly in our favor. Yet, I was disappointed with words that still seemed too ambiguous and noncommittal. They were not the definitive statement I believed appropriate and would like to have read, saying simply and directly, "Permit denied."
Ray's letter continues:

The public adjudicatory hearing will be held according to the Permit Hearing Procedures contained in 6NYCRR Part 624. Pursuant to 624.11 the applicant must pay for the cost of physical accommodations, publishing required notices and stenographic services. The process begins with our submittal of a Hearing Request to the Department's Office of Hearings. The Office of Hearings would then publish and serve notice of the hearing, and thereafter proceed to conduct the hearing.

Prior to submittal of the Hearing Request, we could attempt to arrange a meeting with you, Department staff, and the commenters, with a view toward potential resolution of this matter without a hearing. If you agree that such a meeting may prove beneficial, please sign the bottom of this letter indicating your consent to delay the commencement of the hearing beyond the deadlines established in Uniform Procedures, and return to me (an extra copy of this letter is enclosed). I will then set up the meeting.

If I have not received your consent to delay by May 9, 1995, I will assume that you do not wish such a meeting, and I will submit the Hearing Request.

If you have any questions regarding this letter please contact the undersigned as soon as possible.

Sincerely, Raymond J. Nolan, Environmental Analyst

Periodically, for seven or so years, sometimes at frequent intervals, I had visited Ray at his Cortland DEC office, mainly to review his Malloryville files for new items and to photocopy what I needed. After his NegDec, he had become less welcoming for a time, but that period came and went, and now he seemed happy to see me. We talked about the meaning of a formal "adjudicatory hearing," a legal proceeding overseen by an administrative law judge, all parties to be represented by lawyers. And we talked about his plan to convene a less formal meeting, "with a view toward potential resolution of this matter without a hearing," words reminiscent to me of his previous informal meetings, beginning six years past in the Paolangeli review before PosDec(2), first privately between me, Paolangeli and Flumerfelt, then one among all interested parties at a larger meeting, and another 28 months ago, among only geologists after his NegDec in the current review. At all three, Ray seemed hopeful that we would compromise allowing mining plans to proceed. But, in each, our firm stance produced outcomes in our favor. Now, Ray was again seeking resolution through some form of compromise.

Alfred Eddy, having consented to a delay in the adjudicatory hearing, I, and others, then received Ray's letter setting the date for his informal meeting, a meeting that would prove important to future events.

June 26, 1995. Ray Nolan letter to me:

> Dear Mr. Beck: The Department of Environmental Conservation, in agreement with Mr. Alfred Eddy, has determined to conduct a meeting between NYS DEC staff, Mr. Eddy, and those individuals who have provided comments during the review of the draft EIS prepared for Mr. Eddy's mining proposal.
>
> The goal of this meeting is to determine if there is an opportunity to approve Mr. Eddy's application and issue a permit with conditions that would protect the Malloryville Bog from negative impacts.
>
> If it is determined that the draft permit proposed by Department staff is acceptable to all parties the need for an adjudicatory hearing can be avoided. Failure to resolve existing concerns over Malloryville Bog's future protection will result in the Department proceeding with an adjudicatory hearing in this matter.
>
> The meeting is scheduled for Thursday, July 13, 1995 at 10 a.m. in the conference room of NYS DEC's Cortland Sub-office, 1285 Fisher Ave., Cortland, NY 13045-1090.

The Department looks forward to your continued participation in this matter and it appreciates your past contribution.

Very truly yours, Raymond J. Nolan, Environmental Analyst

July 10, 1995. Professor Don Leopold, botanist/ecologist of SUNY-ESF, wrote in a fax that he could not attend the meeting and made his views known, again, in a direct, forceful, uncompromising response to Ray's letter:

Regarding your letter of June 26, I have been away the past two weeks trying to finish a book, and cannot attend this meeting. I would have appreciated knowing about this meeting more in advance. Such short notice suggests that the meeting was arranged for Mr. Eddy's convenience and to minimize attendance by those who have consistently spoken against his mining proposals. The idea of this meeting is ludicrous anyway, if the goal is indeed "to determine if there is an opportunity to approve Mr. Eddy's application and issue a permit with conditions that would protect the Malloryville Bog from negative impacts." If the New York State Department of Environmental Conservation wants to truly protect Malloryville Bog then the decision should be a simple one of denying the permit for mining. You undoubtedly have enough evidence from prominent experts in their fields to overwhelmingly argue against the mining near Malloryville Bog. I suspect that few if any of these experts are making any money by taking this position. I hope that the NYS-DEC will not let an economic argument that benefits very few win out over our responsibility to fully protect something so unusual for future generations. Donald J. Leopold

Unlike Ray Nolan's desire for compromise, neither I nor

my colleagues were likely to welcome a "draft permit," agreeing to "a permit with conditions," implying compromise that would make mining acceptable, so that, "the need for an adjudicatory hearing can be avoided." If Ray's meeting would not produce a compromise, then we should expect him to submit an adjudicatory "Hearing Request" and we should begin preparation without delay.

I had learned that participants in an adjudicatory hearing are required to apply in advance for party status and are advised to be represented by an attorney. I talked with Judy Rossiter, an attorney in Ithaca with whom I had worked when she did pro bono work for the Finger Lakes Land Trust, and who had suggested to me the ultimate pond that Lick Brook owner, Moss Sweedler, after visiting many others on outings with me, happily found to his liking. Judy was unable to represent us, but recommended I talk with Attorney Dan Hoffman of Ithaca.

Dan Hoffman then, for a nominal fee, agreed to work with us and, for the purpose of the hearing, suggested that we form an informal group, which we would call "Friends of Malloryville." And Dan agreed to start by attending Ray's scheduled informal meeting at DEC in Cortland.

July 13, 1995, 10 a.m. Ray's informal meeting turned out to be a pretty big deal. Although he didn't call it a hearing, and no transcript was kept (again), numerous DEC personnel attended, including Ray and several of his colleagues and superiors— Frank Trent, Engineering Geologist; Joe Moskiewicz, Mined Land Reclamation Specialist; Ralph Manna, now Regional Permit Administrator, Division of Regulatory Services; William Gallagher, Asst. Regional Attorney; and facilitator Ward Dukelow. Of course Alfred Eddy and Brayton Foster were there. For our side, more than 20 neighbors were present and ready, when asked, to speak in defense of their homes and neighborhood. I sat with attorney Dan Hoffman, and attending also were Town of Dryden's Supervisor, Jim Schug and Zoning Officer, Henry Slater. And importantly, invaluable scientists, friends, stalwart colleagues, Donald Siegel, Barbara Bedford and Robert Wesley were there.

The printed agenda included seven sections:

    I.   Introductions
   II.   Purpose of Meeting
  III.   Establish Ground Rule
  IV.   Brief Statement by Project Sponsor
   V.   Historical Background & Update on Status and Department Position
  VI.   Brief Comments by Attendees
 VII.   Discussion of Issues/Identification of Alternatives to Proposal and Necessary Conditions to Protect Malloryville Bog

Ralph Manna took charge and did an excellent job in laying out the purpose and plan of the meeting, while Ray, mostly throughout, stayed in the background. Ralph and others certainly knew in advance, from the history of the case, the arguments and positions of both sides. He probably had been told that Eddy wasn't quitting and likely would sue the DEC if he didn't get mining approval. And Ralph probably figured we likely wouldn't give our consent to even limited mining. Though we hadn't threatened legal action, Ralph probably knew we would proceed with that, if mining were approved. And, as the meeting progressed, my feeling grew that Ralph supported our cause and really wanted to avoid placing sensitive wetlands at risk of degradation.

The crux of the meeting came last, with the first part of agenda item VII, "Discussion of Issues," when Don Siegel brilliantly, with hydrological detail, countered Brayton Foster's arguments that the proposed mining posed no threat to the wetlands. Our side should never have been asked or expected to prove that harm would be done, that the wetlands, absolutely, would be degraded. That was not our goal, and not the intent of SEQR. Rather, our need was to state the risks, and to make apparent the deficiencies, the weaknesses in the applicant's arguments, to punch holes in his assertive statements and rationalization claiming his project would cause no adverse impacts, no environmental harm. With scientific expertise and great skill, Professor Siegel had made the day. And as we expected, the last part of the agenda, "Identification of Alternatives to Proposal and Necessary Conditions to Protect Malloryville Bog," seemed pointless and was not discussed, as neither side was willing to make concessions.

Without compromise at the meeting, an adjudicatory hearing with an appointed administrative law judge, we were told, would be scheduled. I knew that the judge's findings, presented to the State DEC Commissioner for final decision, might or might not be in our favor and, to me, that unknown was more than a little troubling and scary. An unknown judge, perhaps less than friendly, previously unfamiliar with our case, could decide either way. If we came poorly prepared at that particular time, we could lose in spite of detailed documentation in the DEC files from our years of previous effort.

The uncertainties may have been troubling, as well, to Alfred Eddy, for whom the hearing would also be an added expense. From Ralph Manna's perspective, I surmised, Ray's meeting may have been offered, more than anything, as an occasion for Alfred to more clearly see obstacles in his path, as an opportunity to possibly reconsider his options for the use of his land. Unfortunately, however, Ray's earlier NegDec had certainly encouraged Alfred to proceed. Still, as after PosDecs 1, 2 & 3, this could be another decision point, a time in which an applicant might decide to discontinue pushing his gravel-mining plan.

Boardwalk with ferns

12 DEAL

The first rule of intelligent tinkering
is to save all the pieces.
— Aldo Leopold

T O THE NATURE Conservancy's suggestions that he renew contact with Alfred Eddy concerning the von
Engeln bequest, Attorney Ed King hadn't responded,
apparently for more than four years. Then, David Klein and
Andy Zepp of The Conservancy decided to make contact directly, and to make an offer for Eddy's land. Sometime before
Ray Nolan's DEC meeting of July 13, 1995, they had made
that purchase offer. But, Eddy was intent, still, even after the
DEC meeting, on obtaining approval for his gravel mine.

July 25, 1995. Andy Zepp memo to TNC file:

> I met with Alfred Eddy on Friday [7/21] to revisit
> TNC's purchase offer on his Malloryville tract
> and to discuss the recent meeting between the
> various parties involved in the gravel mining
> proposal.
>
> Up until now, Alfred has been unwilling to
> counter our $700 per acre opening offer. He did
> on Friday: $1 million for 109 acres. He said that
> he was serious and that he had figured that TNC

"didn't have enough money to interest him." He also stated that NYSDEC had underestimated his stubbornness and that he would sue the state if they turn down his latest application. After discussing price for a while, along with his prospects for getting permits to mine, we talked about his various business operations...

Next action: re-contact once NYSDEC issues application decision. AZ

August 1, 1995. DEC's Region 7 had a new Regional Director, Dan Palm. Dan had asked The Nature Conservancy to show him some highly ranked biodiversity sites in Central New York, so David Klein and Andy Zepp invited him to join us at my house. On a warm midsummer day, we hiked through the woodlands, among the wetlands, and over the eskers and kames. As we walked and talked about ecology and natural history, Dan asked about our long opposition to gravel mine proposals. When I expressed my concern about the upcoming adjudicatory hearing, he said, "I will have Ralph Manna call you." On concluding an agreeable, stimulating outing, Dan clearly was pleased with what he had seen and, most importantly, he seemed supportive of our desire to protect the place.

Then, I did receive a phone call from DEC's Ralph Manna. Ralph told me that he was happy with Ray Nolan's meeting, and he said,

> The DEC Regulatory Services Division will be a party to the hearing. We're going to defend our decision to deny the permit, and we're being very careful to prevent that decision from being overturned.

That call, bringing vitally important, wonderfully good news, gave me a great deal of pleasure. Perhaps influenced by Regional Director Dan Palm and an informative walk, Ralph's words were the clearest, strongest, most direct, support from the New York State DEC for Malloryville I had heard in nine years. This time, not a request for more data, more test wells or an impact statement, or yet another meeting looking for concessions, but rather a definitive, firm, "Permit denied." This time the DEC itself, Ralph and his Region 7 Regulatory Services Division, at least, were prepared to defend our wetlands. In effect, they were joining with our coalition, joining our Malloryville team. That conversation, thus, was to stay in my mind as a brilliant highlight marking a crucial point in our environmental journey. Yet, as the weeks passed, we received no word from DEC on scheduling the expected adjudicatory hearing.

Year 10: 1995/96

Because I wanted my Town's presence and support at that hearing, I asked to speak at a monthly Dryden Town Board meeting. And, by then, I had decided I wanted the Town to know of The Nature Conservancy's interest in establishing a preserve at Malloryville. In the years, nearly fifteen, since that Town Board had given unanimous approval of Eddy's last mining operation at the same site over strong objections of neighbors, environmental awareness in the Town government, as elsewhere, had evolved. Now the neighborhood and its wetlands had the support of Zoning Officer Henry Slater, Attorney Mahlon Perkins, Supervisor Jim Schug and a more enlightened, receptive Town Board.

September 5, 1995. A portion of the transcript, slightly edited, of a Dryden Town Board meeting:

> CITIZEN PRIVILEGE OF THE FLOOR: Robert Beck—Regarding Malloryville Bog—would like to invite all officials to visit the bog. I want to thank Atty. Perkins [and Z.O. Henry Slater] for all the letters... written to DEC on this issue. There have been three applications for a gravel mine immediately adjacent to and upslope from the wetlands... The first two applications DEC issued positive declarations requiring a draft environmental impact statement in each case. In both

cases the applicant chose to withdraw... There is now a third application and Mr. Eddy chooses this time to operate the gravel mine himself. In this case DEC issued a negative declaration, which was rescinded upon massive comments from scientists at Cornell and Syracuse Universities, neighbors and others from the town. DEC... [then required] a draft environmental impact statement. That [dEIS] was completed about a year ago and was reviewed [that] summer. Again massive input was put into that and over the following winter DEC reviewed our comments and further comments from the applicant's consultant. In April of 1995 DEC wrote a letter to Alfred Eddy, the applicant, stating they could not issue a permit. This was the official denial [almost] of the permit. Denial based upon our comments, specifically the comments from the scientists concerning the hydrology and the effect of the changes in the hydrology [of] the water source [of] the wetland... [and how it] might impact the quality of the wetland. That led to a meeting in July 1995 which Supv. Schug and Z.O. Slater attended and a lot of issues were covered. The next step is for the applicant. The permit has been denied, but the applicant has the opportunity to pursue it through an adjudicatory hearing, which is to be scheduled. This should be sometime in September or October. To my knowledge it has not been scheduled yet. The adjudicatory hearing would be the last step within the DEC for review of this case. Beyond that if there was further contention it would go to the courts outside of DEC. The adjudicatory hearing would involve an appointed administrative law judge, who is an employee of DEC. That judge would then hold a formal hearing involving sworn testimony and cross-examination. You have to petition to be [a] party at that hearing, in advance. The judge rules as to who gets to have party status. This is a very important step and the judge would write up his review and recommendations. This would then be sent to the Commissioner of DEC in Albany who makes the final decision. This case has gotten a significant amount of statewide attention. The reason is the wetland we are talking about is very special and the best we have in this part of the state. There are ongoing studies with scientists... The wetlands are very complex... There are numerous different kinds of wetlands and are all in close proximity to each other. Several of those wetlands are very fragile. They are unusual and sensitive to the surroundings and exact conditions. That is why we are so concerned because the water from the gravel mine provides the water to the wetland... There are numerous springs along the west side of the wetland immediately adjacent to the proposed gravel mine.

Supv. Schug—wanted to know when the town needed to apply as a concerned party.

Robert Beck—it would be after the hearing is scheduled. I was told we should have received [that notice] by now. All of [us] should receive this information at which point the judge will spell out the rules as to when we need to apply for [party] status. There is a new regional director for DEC who covers our 9-county territory from Lake Ontario to Pennsylvania. He asked to be taken on a tour of the two most significant biodiversity sites in central New York. One that was suggested was the Malloryville Bog, which he visited. He was... impressed with the wetland. Ralph Manna, in [DEC's] Regulatory Services Division, called me and was very encouraging. Ralph told me that Regulatory Services... would be a party to the hearing and present its case as to why they cannot issue a permit... An active participation by the Town of Dryden is [an] important part in this case... The Nature Conservancy has a... definite interest in putting together a permanent nature preserve at the site. They only go after the best, and this is one of the best. They have offered Alfred Eddy money for the gravel mine property and so far the answer is no from him. We are hoping in time he would like to do business with The Nature Conservancy. This is the first step and is critical because the long-term protection of the wetland depends on what happens to that 110-acre gravel mine property. The Conservancy would like to create a 300-acre permanent [preserve]. My 38-acre property is already being used for scientific research and is being used by school groups, individuals, and environmental groups. The Nature Conservancy has regular tours there. It is being used for educational, recreational, and scientific purposes and that will continue. I view this as a wonderful thing for the Town of Dryden. I am asking if it is possible for the town to take a position to be an active participant at the hearing and to state clearly what the town's position is in terms of zoning, condition of the roads, concerns for the neighborhood and concerns of the wetlands... the value to the town of a preserve there that can be enjoyed by all of us. If we don't continue to take a strong stand and do everything we can we could very easily lose the case. The Commissioner himself can overrule the judge so we have to have a good case.

Supv. Schug—from the town's standpoint in going to the hearing is to make sure that they understand if DEC does issue a mining permit, the mining permit is subject to a zoning variance by the Zoning Board of Appeals. Z.O. Slater would speak for us to make sure everything is clear if a permit is issued.

Robert Beck—the neighbors are against it because of truck traffic, dust, noise, and change of character of the neighborhood. The truck traffic [could] go from one truck every hour to one truck every 5 minutes. 100 per day so that is a big change in the neighborhood on these narrow roads.

Supv. Schug—the Town of Dryden will be a party to this when the hearing is scheduled.

Robert Beck—there have been cases where the state has issued permits and the town has not. The applicant started mining and continued mining. The town would then have to sue to try and stop them. This is scary if a person has a state permit and mines and claims the town cannot stop them because it should be grandfathered or whatever. There is an existing mine there [at Malloryville], which has long been abandoned. I think it is important we don't allow it to get to that point. The state should not issue the permit.

Councilman T. Hatfield—if the state issues the permit it should be subject to all local zoning board approval. We should make that part of the record right up front that it is subject to all zoning regulations.

Robert Beck—wanted to know if it would be important for Atty. Perkins to be at this hearing and if so he would like him to attend. (Supv. Schug—Atty. Perkins will attend)

October 3, 1995. Attorney Dan Hoffman, in preparation for the hearing, which still had not been scheduled, wrote to Ray Nolan:

Dear Mr. Nolan: The purpose of this letter is to inform the Department officially that I represent the Friends of Malloryville, an association of citizens from the Malloryville area who are concerned about the potential impact of a mining operation proposed by Alfred Eddy on the neighborhood and on the natural resources in the vicinity.

The Friends of Malloryville will most likely wish to receive party status, and I therefore request that you send me copies of all pertinent notices and correspondence regarding the requested permit. Could you also send a copy of the summary of the informal meeting conducted on July 13, 1995?

...Thank you for your cooperation.

Sincerely yours, Daniel L. Hoffman

Again, as we had experienced before in DEC's SEQR proceedings, months would pass without news, this time no word was forthcoming on the adjudicatory hearing, but changes were occurring in my household and at The Nature Conservancy. Five years and a day after our son Nathan was born, Gwen and I happily welcomed our second child, another boy, Gordon Paul. And Andy Zepp, after valiant effort on behalf of Malloryville, was leaving the Conservancy for a job with the Land Trust Alliance in Washington D.C. (but eight years later, he would be back in Ithaca, hired as Executive Director of the Finger Lakes Land Trust, the very organization he, with our 17 or so founding board members, had started fifteen years earlier). While wishing him well, I was sorry to see Andy go and was concerned about possible loss of Conservancy momentum for our cause. But David Klein hired field biologist Kris Agard (later Kris West) who, joining the staff in a science position, toured the site with me and quickly took a keen and personal interest in the ecology and wellbeing of the diverse and sensitive wetlands, and in encouraging careful research here by college and university scientists.

In Earth's annual revolution around the Sun, its 23 1/2-degree tilted axis being the "reason for seasons," autumn on our portion of the planet had again turned to winter's cold, and winter then to warming and welcome spring, when another important newcomer joined the Conservancy staff. Jim Howe had returned to upstate New York, from his work at the Sonoran Institute in Tucson, Arizona, to fill the Chapter position of Director of Conservation Programs. At his first Central & Western NY Chapter board meeting, as Jim tells me (I was recently off the board after my eight-year stint with the group), the central topic of discussion, encouraged by Director David Klein, was how to proceed on establishing a preserve, specifically, the need to protect the esker and wetlands by striking a deal with Alfred Eddy for his gravel tract.

June 3, 1996, 11:00 a.m. Within days of that board meeting, David and Jim came to my house after they had met, earlier that morning, with Ed King in Ithaca. We talked extensively and walked the properties, enjoying the spring air, the fresh leaves, the loose-banjo-string calls of Green Frogs at the pond, songs of Red-eyed Vireos and Scarlet Tanagers in the woods, and Moccasin Flowers, a lady's slipper orchid, in exquisite pink bloom. I liked Jim Howe right away, and was happy to continue my five-year association and valued friendship with David Klein. We talked strategy and I was gratified that they and the board were committed to finding a way to move the preserve idea forward, and the timing to do that seemed right. At more than ten months since the DEC meeting of July 13, 1995, a hearing had not been scheduled but I believed Ralph Manna and Dan Palm remained on our side. Jim's arrival at TNC, as it would turn out, marked the beginning of a year filled with ambitious renewal of contacts with von Engeln attorney Ed King and landowner Alfred Eddy, a year of strategy and determined negotiation, a year of memos and letters documenting persistent efforts towards a monumental land deal.

June 7, 1996. David Klein and Jim Howe together wrote a memo to their TNC file:

> On June 3, DK and JH visited Ithaca attorney Edward King, one of two trustees of the von

Engeln bequest. King said the bequest now totals $175,000. He would be willing to use it to purchase the esker on the Eddy property as long as he gains assurance that: 1) the esker is protected, and 2) public access is provided for geologists. We agreed to contact Eddy and, if Eddy seems agreeable to selling, to secure an appraisal.

We followed up with a visit and tour of the Malloryville fen with Bob Beck, former CWNY board member and owner of much of the fen [i.e., more generally, the Malloryville Bog complex of swamp, bog and fens]. Beck believes any level of mining could destroy the fen. He believes the DEC will not approve mining on the site and is concerned that a TNC-brokered deal that allows some mining to go forward will result in the DEC permitting a mine that otherwise wouldn't have been approved.

The Eddy property has been mined in the past, apparently without damage to the fen. Several gravel pits can be found on the property. A shallow pit, now reclaimed, also was used as a treatment area for solid waste from septic systems. According to Beck, at least two truckloads of septic wastes were illegally discharged directly into a [wetland near a] stream that runs through the fen.

A few possible strategies:

1) Take a chance that [Eddy's] appeal of the DEC rejection will be denied, then purchase property from Eddy at FMV [Fair Market Value]. Risks are: a) he still will not sell to us because of anger at our role—through association with Beck—in being denied the right to mine, or b) mining will be approved.

2) Step in now and offer Eddy a deal where we buy most of the parcel from him, including all mineral rights, but give him above FMV due to

recognition of deposits and costs invested. Eddy could retain some portion of his property for residential development.

3) Try to broker a deal where some mining can occur.

Info needs

Is Eddy appealing the decision?

When does the statute of limitations expire for appeal?

What is value of gravel deposit?

What is value of raw land without gravel—need appraisal.

Will mining damage fen?

Given value of deposit, how much profit could Eddy make?

What are Eddy's expenses to date?

Will local universities—Cornell, Syracuse, Ithaca College—contribute to purchase of site?

June 7, 1996. Jim Howe, another memo to TNC file:

A minerals specialist in DEC Region 8 told me gravel deposits in the ground, or "in place," are worth between $0.50 to $1.50 a cubic yard. Actual value depends on the quality of the deposit, distance from markets, and degree of difficulty involved in reaching the deposit.

If we accept Eddy's estimate of 980,000 cubic yards on his property, the deposit could be worth between $490,000 and $1.47 million. Bob Beck says a geologist told him the gravel is of poor quality [for making concrete], so a deposit of the size Eddy claims may rank on the lower end of that scale. For an exact estimate of the deposit's size and value, we would have to contact a geological consultant.

June 27, 1996. Jim Howe memo to file:

I spoke today with Steve Eddy, Alfred Eddy's son.

Steve's first question was whether we have found any money to purchase the property and how much we had to spend. I said we may have found some funds, but did not reveal the source or amount. Given his question, my sense is that they may be willing to sell the property.

Steve stressed that his father has invested a lot of time and money in the property and is not willing to see it squandered. He said that everyone seems to be trying to stop them from mining. He also commented that, even though the initial application has been rejected, the decision is not final yet.

I suggested that he and his father give me a tour of the property, and left him our phone number.

July 11, 1996. Jim Howe memo to file:

Alfred Eddy called me today from Pennsylvania. I told him we were still interested in his property and that we should get together on site. He was pleased to hear that I wanted to visit the property. I think he feels that no one can oppose the mine after they see that gravel extraction has already occurred without damage to the fen.

Eddy may still want to mine the property, but I sensed that he is beginning to think he may never get a permit. He asked if there was any way he could mine the deposit on the north end. He doesn't seem to think it's a problem as long as mining activities take place above groundwater. He continually stressed that we should try to "work something out."

Thinking about the hassles he's gone through, however, clearly makes him mad. "I'm gonna fight this thing till I win or lose," he said at one point. He also mentioned that he's sunk a lot of money into the project.

Eddy and I are scheduled to meet on Wednesday, July 17, at 10:00 a.m. at his fruit stand in Ithaca.

July 18, 1996. Jim Howe memo to file:

On July 17, I traveled to Ithaca for a visit with Alfred Eddy and bequest attorney Edward King. Eddy and I walked his property in Malloryville. Eddy is a cagey businessman and a difficult man to interpret. He can begin a sentence sounding reasonable, and end it with a call to arms. He is angry at being portrayed as the "bad guy." He says he bought an existing gravel mine and is now being prohibited from mining it.

Eddy maintains his property has 800,000 cubic yards of high-quality gravel worth $1.00 a cubic yard. We ventured briefly into the wetland complex, which he agreed is unique: "I've been all over the state and never seen anything like it." Still, he contends that mining will not damage the fen, citing the work of his geologist, Brayton Foster. Eddy does not believe Siegel's conclusion that mining will both flood the fen and remove materials that provide minerals to groundwater as it percolates through the substrate. He says he has spent $7,000 on wells that prove otherwise and that his information will prevail before the ALJ [Administrative Law Judge] hearing. He thinks DEC is delaying the hearing until TNC can broker something.

Eddy also showed me some of his land in Ithaca. He owns several agricultural fields, and a few subdivisions that he said aren't selling. I also met his son Steve, to whom Eddy introduced me as "Nature Boy." We ended the day with a tour of his produce business, where we talked turkey.

Eddy would agree to abandon his mining project and sell us the eskers and kames on his property if:

1) We give him a high enough price. Despite many efforts, I could not get Eddy to give me a figure. He does not want us to do an appraisal if it looks only at surface value.

2) He retains lots he can develop for homes. This includes two lots on W. Malloryville Road and several lots west of the property's existing access road. He would be willing to specify the number of lots to be built and where they would be. He is aware that lots next to a preserve would command a higher price.

3) We agree to never mine the property. "I don't want to see you guys mining it," he said. He also would reclaim mined areas.

Later I explained this proposal to Edward King, who asked us to put together a sales pitch for it and run it by him. I agreed that the three of us would come up with an offer for Eddy; we might want an appraisal first. King said the bequest is now $150-160,000 and that he would be willing to spend $120-130,000 total. He said he doesn't care much about the north end of the property, only where the Malloryville esker is. He seemed agreeable to setting up an endowment to manage the property.

Year 11: 1996/97

Gwen and I were beginning our eleventh year in our woodland and wetland home. The immediate threat of a gravel mine next door had lessened, our two young boys were bringing new excitement into our home and we still were reveling in our good fortune to be living in our chosen spot surrounded by idyllic nature.

September 5, 1996. Ed King wrote a letter to Jim Howe:

Dear Jim: As a follow-up of our telephone conversation on Tuesday, September 3rd, in which I asked that you prepare a commitment letter/proposal by the Nature Conservancy to detail how the proposed project will promote the intent of the late Prof. von Engeln as expressed in his Will, I enclose a synopsis-quotation of the pertinent Residuary Trust Directives from that Will.

Be sure to discuss the entire area to be included in the project, and show how a purchase of part of the Eddy property will aid the project.

Hopefully you will be able to sell the von Engeln Trustees a well-presented plan for the development and maintenance of this proposed project. It will also have to pass muster with Vic Schmidt, of course, as a designated advisor.

Sincerely, Edward W. King

Ed King had never really acknowledged Wayne Klockner's excellent preserve proposal of seven years earlier in November 1989, a proposal and concept enthusiastically endorsed by Victor Schmidt, a proposal which I thought was still on the table, never withdrawn by the Conservancy. But Ed seemed not to understand the importance of the Eddy property in safeguarding the wetlands or the value of the wetlands in a preserve in addition to the esker. Prof. von Engeln and Vic Schmidt easily envisioned the complete picture, an integrated story of natural history told by geology and biology together, but Ed King seemed focused, still, on the esker alone, and unwilling to grant the Conservancy a degree of discretion in their potential use of the von Engeln funds. Now David Klein would respond to Ed's request for a new proposal.

October 1, 1996. David Klein's proposal to Edward King:

Dear Mr. King: As per your request, please accept this proposal from The Nature Conservancy to apply the bequest of Dr. O.D. Von Engeln toward the permanent protection of the Malloryville esker and its associated kames, bogs, and wetlands.

As you may know, the mission of The Nature Conservancy is to safeguard the diversity of life on earth—plants, animals, and natural communities—by protecting critical lands and waters. The Conservancy's objective at Malloryville would be to ensure the perpetual protection and wise stewardship of an entire complex of natural and geological features.

With assistance from the von Engeln bequest, The Nature Conservancy proposes to protect by acquisition or conservation easement several key tracts. We would work with cooperating landowners to manage the entire preserve as a natural area available for scientific study and public enjoyment. Such a preserve would protect not only the Malloryville esker, but the associated bog and kame complex downslope of the esker. Because the geology and biology are closely intertwined at this site, a protection strategy must include both elements.

The Alfred Eddy Property

The key property in the Malloryville esker complex is a 109-acre tract owned by Mr. Alfred Eddy of Ithaca. Not only does the Eddy parcel contain a significant portion of the esker, its location immediately adjacent to and upslope from the bog and wetlands makes it critical to their protection.

It also is the most threatened. ...Mr. Eddy applied for a permit to mine 800,000 cubic yards of gravel at the site. In 1987, the New York State Department of Environmental Conservation (DEC) rejected [PosDec(1)] that application due to concerns about noise, truck traffic on local roads, and the hydrology of the Malloryville wetland complex. DEC later approved [NegDec] a scaled-back mine at the site, but reversed the decision in 1993 in the face of staunch opposition from neighbors concerned about noise and truck traffic and from several organizations that feared the mine would disrupt the hydrology of the unique wetland community just east of the mine site.

Organizations expressing concern included the Tompkins County Environmental Management Council, Cornell Plantations, Tompkins County Department of Planning, and U.S. Fish and Wildlife Service. Concerns also were voiced by the academic community, including the Cornell University Department of Natural Resources, SUNY College of Environmental Science and Forestry Department of Environmental and Forest Biology, Syracuse University Department of Earth Sciences, and Cornell University Department of Plant Sciences.

The Threat

Mr. Eddy has appealed DEC's decision to deny him a mining permit. The next step is for his permit application to go before an administrative law judge. Much is at stake. For geologists, mining of the esker and kame will permanently remove a prominent geologic feature from the landscape. In his book The Finger Lakes Region: Its Origin and Nature, Dr. von Engeln described the Malloryville esker as "perhaps the best example of this phenomenon in the Finger Lakes Region." Mining of the esker clearly would be a significant loss to the geologic community, especially given the esker's close proximity to a number of academic institutions.

Biologists also are concerned that mining of the esker will alter the hydrology of the Malloryville wetland complex, an important feature in its own right. The Malloryville bog and associated wetlands are significant largely because of their mineral-rich source of water. The Malloryville wetlands are fed almost entirely by upwelling groundwater; the cold, constant, mineral-laden water nurtures a number of rare plants and natural communities.

Removal of such a large amount of substrate from the watershed would impact the wetlands in two ways. First, precipitation currently trickles through the gravel deposits slowly; removal of the esker would increase the speed at which precipitation enters the aquifer, resulting in flooding of the wetlands. Second, the gravel substrate through which precipitation currently percolates provides minerals crucial to the flora of the wetland community. Without the esker, the groundwater will no longer carry minerals necessary to Malloryville's natural systems.

A New Solution

Previous attempts to acquire Mr. Eddy's property have failed because of his high financial expectations for the land. Mr. Eddy maintains his property contains 800,000 cubic yards of gravel. According to geologists at DEC, gravel deposits "in the ground" are worth between $0.50 and $1.50 per cubic yard, depending upon quality and accessibility. That puts the mineral value of Mr. Eddy's property at between $400,000 and $1.2 million, a figure that places the property out of reach of both the bequest and The Nature Conservancy.

In July 1996, however, Mr. Eddy and a staff member from The Nature Conservancy reached general agreement on a proposal that would protect the Malloryville esker, yet allow Mr. Eddy to receive a financial return from the property in a way that does not involve mining of the esker. Under this proposal, The Nature Conservancy would acquire the mineral rights to the gravel deposits on the property and the surface rights to most of the property. Mr. Eddy would retain 15-25 acres along the southern and southwestern boundaries of the property. (See Attachment One for a rough sketch of these boundaries.)

Land retained by Mr. Eddy would be sold as residential lots or developed for homes. Because the lots would be adjacent to a pristine nature preserve, they would command a high price. Having homeowners in the area also would deter the extensive trespass incidents—off-road motorcycle and ATV use, illegal gravel mining by trespassers, and target practice—currently occurring on the Eddy property.

The specifics of the proposal—including the price for the mineral and surface rights, the number of acres to be retained by Mr. Eddy, and the number of homes to be developed—remain to be negotiated. To begin the process, The Nature Conservancy is currently having the Eddy property appraised. If the trustees of the von Engeln bequest agree to this proposal, The Nature Conservancy stands ready to negotiate details with Mr. Eddy.

Additional Land Acquisition

The Malloryville esker and bog complex is more than just the Eddy property. To ensure the complete protection of the entire system, The Nature Conservancy intends to acquire interests in other lands in the area. We are fully prepared to negotiate the protection of all the tracts within the boundaries of the Malloryville esker and bog complex. (See Attachment Two for a sketch of these boundaries.)

Already, staff members have had fruitful discussions with Ronald Beck and Robert Beck, the owners of two of the largest and most significant tracts in the complex. Ronald Beck owns a 76-acre tract that includes a major portion of the Malloryville esker along Fall Creek, numerous kames, and several kettle depressions. His brother Robert owns a 38-acre parcel that includes significant stretches of the Malloryville esker and a number of fens and bogs. (Attachment Three is a map of the Robert Beck tract.) The Michaels family owns a 24-acre tract south of Malloryville Road that also merits protection. Several other tracts would be pursued after these key parcels are protected. In order of importance, the tracts to be protected are:

Owner & Acreage
  Eddy: 109
  Beck, Robert: 38
  Beck, Ronald: 76
  Michaels: 20
Total acreage: 243

A Preserve Dedicated to Conservation, Education, and Research

The Nature Conservancy would actively maintain the preserve in a way that enhances the research and public education opportunities available at the site. Many of our existing preserves serve as research centers for scientific projects. For example, our Chaumont Barrens Preserve in the towns of Lyme and Clayton is a site of hydrological studies by the University of Georgia, climatology research by SUNY College at Geneseo, and invertebrate inventories and invasive species research by SUNY College of Environmental Science and Forestry. Ownership by The Nature Conservancy would ensure that the research and academic communities continue to enjoy access to Malloryville.

The preserve also would be open to public use and environmental education. At our El Dorado Beach Preserve in the Town of Ellisburg, the Conservancy has erected a bird blind, educational displays describing the dune barrier system along Lake Ontario, and a kiosk welcoming visitors to the site. At Malloryville, The Nature Conservancy would seek to construct similar interpretive displays to highlight the unique wetlands and geologic features present. The enclosed brochure guiding visitors to our Chaumont Barrens Preserve represents the type of literature that could be produced.

The Nature Conservancy also would maintain a field presence at the site. In addition to regular visits by staff, the Conservancy would recruit a local individual or individuals to monitor the preserve. Robert Beck, a former trustee of the Central and Western New York Chapter, has already expressed an interest in this "site monitor" position. Homeowners who purchase lots at the south end of the Eddy property also could be engaged. Moreover, The Nature Conservancy's extensive network of members and volunteers would be tapped for on-the-ground stewardship projects.

We estimate the budget for this preserve as follows:

Land acquisition: $190,000

Administrative costs: $12,000

(Surveys, appraisals, legal fees, title insurance)

Education and interpretation: $8,000

(trails, kiosk, brochure)

Stewardship endowment: $40,000

Total budget: $250,000

These funds would be raised in part by the Central and Western New York Chapter of The Nature Conservancy. Like other chapters of the Conservancy, the Central and Western New York Chapter is self-supporting, raising all its program and capital funds from local sources.

Conclusion

By combining the von Engeln bequest with The Nature Conservancy's own resources and expertise in land acquisition, conservation, and stewardship, the trustees of the von Engeln bequest have a chance to forever protect a geologically and ecologically significant area. The proposal outlined above represents a win-win solution to a proposed gravel mine that could threaten the integrity of the Malloryville esker and its associated wetlands.

In exchange for the support of the von Engeln bequest, The Nature Conservancy is prepared to assume the responsibility of negotiating for, acquiring, and owning and managing the preserve. The Conservancy also is prepared to dedicate its own funding and resources to acquire and manage lands within the Malloryville esker and wetland complex. Moreover, in recognition of the critical role played by Dr. von Engeln, The Nature Conservancy would name the preserve in his honor.

I encourage the trustees to dedicate the resources of the von Engeln bequest to this important project. Thank you again for the opportunity to present this proposal to the trustees of the bequest.

Sincerely, David Klein, Executive Director, Central & Western New York Chapter, The Nature Conservancy

December 6, 1996. Jim Howe memo to TNC file:

On December 2, I met with Alfred Eddy and his attorney Jim Miller to discuss our concept for Malloryville. Miller is a real estate attorney who has done work for the Finger Lakes Land Trust. He had lots of questions: How many homes can be built? How much land do you need? Will you share your appraisal with us? Who did the appraisal? Who has the final say on the project?

Miller said he would call Ed King to find out

how soon our proposal might be approved by the von Engeln trustees. Miller also pretended he knew the size of the bequest; King says he has spoken with Miller, but never about the size of the bequest.

My sense is that Eddy is still interested in working something out. He said he recently spoke to a DEC official who told him they've postponed an ALJ hearing because TNC asked DEC to wait until we had time to work out a compromise. I told him that we don't operate that way.

The three of us visited the site and discussed possible locations for homes. From TNC's perspective, it would be okay to allow several homes west of the access road and perhaps a single home on W. Malloryville Road. Bob Beck says Don Siegel is okay with this. We did not discuss a specific number, but it's clear that the area we're talking about cannot accommodate a lot of homes due to its steep topography. Eddy would like to squeeze in as many lots as possible. "How about 100?" he quipped.

I also told Eddy TNC would help him get his subdivision and zoning approval from the Town of Dryden. Not only does this help sell him on the project, it also keeps us involved in the design process. In other issues, we discussed building a visitor parking lot just east of the [access] road and having Eddy grade some of the abandoned mining areas.

Here are some issues that need to be resolved:
1) How much land do we need, and how much will Eddy retain?
2) How many homes can be built and where will they be?
3) Should we seek restrictions on the land Eddy retains?

4) Can we help Eddy gain subdivision approval?
5) Should there be a house on W. Malloryville Road near the esker? (Beck says no.)
6) Who should we involve in decisions about the number of lots and their location?
7) What is the current zoning?
8) How much do we offer Eddy and when will we know if we can use the bequest?
Next Steps

We should resolve these questions so that if our proposal is approved by the trustees, we are ready to negotiate with Eddy.

December 23, 1996. Jim Howe letter to Alfred Eddy:

Dear Mr. Eddy: As promised, this letter is a formal offer for a portion of your 109-acre property on West Malloryville Road in the Town of Dryden (tax map numbers 24-1-14.2 and 24-1-20.12). As you know, this offer is contingent upon the trustees of the O.D. von Engeln estate accepting The Nature Conservancy's recent proposal to them.

The Nature Conservancy hereby offers you $82,000 for that portion of your property east of the access road, as depicted on the attached sketch map. By our estimate, this parcel is approximately 80 acres. Under the terms of this offer, The Nature Conservancy would acquire all rights to the property, including surface and mineral rights. As you requested, we would agree never to mine the property.

As we have discussed, the approximately 30-acre tract that you would retain is suitable for no more than four residential building lots. Should you seek to develop these lots, The Nature Conservancy would help you obtain subdivision approval from the Town of Dryden by testifying before the local planning or zoning board, provided that any subdivision plan has been shown to The Nature Conservancy in advance and that any issues are resolved in a manner amenable to both you and the Conservancy. We also would be willing to assist your marketing efforts by publicizing the lots in our newsletter. Finally, we would ask that mining never occur on this portion of the property.

As part of this offer we also would require that you reclaim three of the four mined areas on the property to be acquired by The Nature Conservancy. Reclamation would consist of grading the steep slopes on the three northern-most pits.

By accepting this offer, you will realize:
•Cash at Closing—Unlike most other commercial parties, The Nature Conservancy is a cash buyer.
•Timeliness—We are prepared to move quickly in acquiring your property.
•No Broker's Fees or Survey Costs—Selling to The Nature Conservancy allows you to avoid paying commission to a real estate broker. Moreover, we are willing to pay for the survey costs associated with the transaction.

I would be happy to discuss any of the elements of this proposal in greater detail. Best wishes for the holidays, and I look forward to talking with you soon.

Sincerely, Jim Howe, Director of Conservation Programs

Cc: Mr. Jonathan Kaledin, Regional Counsel, NY Regional Office, The Nature Conservancy; Mr. Edward King; Mr. Jim Miller

January 7, 1997. Attorney Jim Miller letter to Jim Howe:

Dear Jim: I was quite surprised to receive your letter of December 23, 1996. Following our meeting and telephone conversation, I was under the impression that you understood that my client is not interested in retaining any of the land on West Malloryville Road. He is prepared to sell all of it or none of it.

He will accept a legitimate purchase offer for all of the land for the sum of $200,000 which Mr. Eddy believes more accurately represents the value of the land. He has no objection to a purchase offer being contingent upon approval of the Trustees of the O.D. von Engeln Estate, provided such contingency is removed within 90 days.

In the absence of a purchase offer from you in accordance with the terms of this letter, we will notify the DEC to immediately schedule a hearing so that my client can proceed with his plans to conduct mining on this property.

Very truly yours, R. James Miller
cc: Alfred C. Eddy; Edward King, Esq.

In the meantime, on February 7, 1997, David Klein talked with Attorney John Murphy of Fleet Bank, Providence RI, the co-trustee of the von Engeln bequest. Murphy seemed agreeable to the Conservancy's use of von Engeln funds, and David wrote: "He [Murphy] has reviewed the file thoroughly now, and seems to be bemused at the length of time that has passed."

But Jim Howe was gathering information on Fair Market Values of gravel properties and didn't rush to respond to Alfred Eddy's attorney, Jim Miller. He found that another chapter of the Conservancy had hired Lakewood Appraisal of Fishkill, New York to determine the market value of a gravel tract in Orange County. That tract, 3.5 times the size of Eddy's, was valued at $430,000. On February 21, Jim spoke on the phone for 45 minutes with Miller discussing gravel values and offered that TNC would "contract with the same firm, Lakewood Appraisal, for an appraisal of the Eddy tract, with the understanding that we [he and Miller] agree to abide by the finding."

Jim was confident that it wouldn't come out higher than Miller and Eddy's price of $200,000 given the $430,000 value of the much larger Orange County tract. And Jim continued, in his memo to the TNC file: "This could be an expensive appraisal, and I recommend we seek reimbursement by the bequest."

February 26, 1997. Attorney Jim Miller wrote to Jim Howe:

> Dear Jim: Thank you for taking the time to talk with me last Friday afternoon... This letter will confirm that you will be sending to me the valuation that was done on the Orange County Gravel Mine showing a valuation $400,000-$430,000...
>
> In any event, it is clear that we could support a value, at a minimum, of $400,000.
>
> As we both know, all of this assumes that Mr. Eddy will obtain a mining permit. While you and I both recognize the difficulties Mr. Eddy faces in obtaining a permit, I need not remind you that he has obtained a permit in the past for this location and, indeed, this location has been mined for gravel in the past.
>
> Mr. Eddy is prepared to invest the necessary time and legal costs to obtain his permit if a satisfactory sale cannot be consummated. In the event a permit were issued, The Nature Conservancy would not be able to obtain this land, and more importantly would not be able to take advantage of the bequest of Professor von Engeln.
>
> On the other hand, Mr. Eddy is prepared to accept the price of $200,000 now, effectively giving up an additional $200,000 of value given the present value calculations that I have included. If the parties come to an agreement at $200,000, the land is protected and you receive a bequest far in excess of $200,000, the excess of which could be used as a stewardship fund. To use your phrase, it seems to me that this is a "win-

win" situation. This seems to me to be a golden opportunity to satisfy all parties: Mr. Eddy, The Nature Conservancy, the von Engeln Trust, and all of the neighbors and various entities that are interested in preserving the Malloryville esker and bog.

Assuming that you are prepared to go forward with this transaction, I have enclosed a proposed Purchase Offer for your review and consideration. If it is acceptable, kindly have it executed and return to me, following of which I will have Mr. Eddy sign it.

If you are not prepared to quickly resolve this matter, I will so inform the von Engeln Trustees. In that event, I am authorized to enter into negotiations with the Finger Lakes Land Trust for a limited period of time before actively pursuing a mining permit.

Very truly yours, R. James Miller

cc: Mr. Alfred C Eddy; Betsy Darlington

March 4, 1997. Jim Howe, however, not willing to be pushed around by Miller's divide-and-conquer tactic, called the Land Trust office in Ithaca and typed a note for his file:

I spoke to Gay Nicholson [Executive Director] and Betsy Darlington of the Finger Lakes Land Trust regarding the Eddy project. They both said that FLLT would never knowingly undercut The Nature Conservancy on a project where we've been negotiating. They were surprised that Jim Miller had sent them a copy of his letter to us and recognized what he's trying to do...

March 18, 1997. Ed King had communicated with Jim Howe and then wrote this letter to Jon Kaledin, the Conservancy's Regional Counsel in the Albany, NY Regional Office (the bold emphasis is King's original):

Dear Mr. Kaledin: Although the Trustees have approved the expenditure of the approximately $3000.00 estimated for the new mineral and surface appraisal of the Eddy land, and have approved the concept of using the bulk of the Trust fund **to acquire the Eddy tract as part of the proposed 240± acre preserve (which is to be named in honor of Prof. von Engeln)** it must be agreed via **at least a written Memorandum of Understanding** between the Conservancy and the Trustees of this Trust [and also acknowledged, to the extent it may be appropriate, within your proposed PURCHASE AND SALE AGREEMENT with Alfred C. Eddy] that the **ultimate price** to be paid for the 109± acres of Eddy land must be **acceptable to the Trustees**.

It should also be understood and acknowledged by the Conservancy that the Trustees are **not fully** committed **to devoting the entire Trust fund** to the purchase of the Eddy land—which, after all, contains only **a relatively small portion** of the esker itself. (Much more of the esker is located on the adjacent properties of Ronald Beck and that of his brother Robert, so the one-of-several options which the "Malloryville esker" represents under the Will of Dr. von Engeln, **might well be accomplished without acquiring any of the Eddy property**; so we would be entitled to have second thoughts about and explore other alternatives if it appears that the Eddy land acquisition would devour the trust assets and leave nothing for any other project and a reasonable endowment for this one.

I think the term "bulk of" may reasonably be interpreted as not less than 85% of the net value of the trust remaining after all administrative expenses (including an application to the Court for approval of this expenditure, on Notice to the Attorney General).

So although the Trustees have expressed their willingness to devote the bulk of the Trust Fund to this project as it was described and formally proposed to us in the 5-page... **letter of October 1, 1996 from David Klein** (Executive Director of the Central and Western New York Chapter of The Nature Conservancy) they do not want to see most of that (or an unreasonable amount of it) devoted solely to the purchase of the Eddy land. The $200,000 figure which has recently been inserted in ¶ 4 of the draft Agreement does not seem reasonable to me: does the project really need **any** of that Eddy land to make it a sound and viable undertaking?

Since **other lands** and assets must be acquired and maintained as an integral part of the project if it is to be doable and viable and to ultimately receive the approval of both the Attorney General and the Court, the Trustees should also receive assurances that there are in place firm and enforceable commitments to provide the Conservancy with those other essential lands and/or rights therein before the Trustees sign a check to acquire any of the Eddy land.

So it must be clearly spelled out and understood that by their endorsing the concept of the project and some substantial funding for it, the Trustees are not agreeing to pay $200,000 for the Eddy land if they do not ultimately think that to be reasonable; nor are they agreeing to pay "acquisition costs" of the Eddy land no matter the total amount and the reasonableness of the items thereof. In other words, carte blanche is not to be presumed.

The rewording of ¶ 4 of the proposed agreement to include a $200,000 price **appears to conditionally bind the Conservancy to that price**, so it is important that the Conservancy understand and agree that the Trustees are not similarly bound to or by that figure—and ¶ 5 of the proposed agreement dealing with funding by the Trust is to be so interpreted. No estoppel is to be deemed to arise against the Trustees or the Trust by reason of our knowledge of your proposed Agreement with Eddy, if in the discretion of the Trustees or by decision of the Court the purchase of his land with funds from this Trust is not ultimately approved.

And since the David Klein letter of October 1, 1996 (addressed to me) constitutes a material inducement to the Trustees to endorse the project and expenditure to the extent they have, it should also be explicitly agreed between The Nature Conservancy and the Trustees that both Trustees must be promptly notified in writing by the Conservancy of **every and all significant changes and likelihood of change** being made in the project in deviation from the Klein letter statement of the project.

And by the same token, ¶ 23 of the proposed Agreement should be augmented to provide that **all NOTICES** from either party to the ultimate Conservancy-Eddy Agreement, shall also be simultaneously delivered to the two Trustees, at their respective addresses...

Semi-Finally, the Agreement or Memorandum of Agreement between the Conservancy and the Trustees should make it clear that if the Eddy land is so ultimately acquired by the Conservancy with these Trust funds, and if the project does not thereafter come to fruition, it shall not be deemed that the Trust, by its funding, has made an irrevocable gift to the Conservancy of the purchase price; but rather, that the Trust shall be entitled to recoup so much of its expenditure as the assets acquired thereby are reasonably worth or subsequently produce.

And finally, I have not had an opportunity to

present this letter to Fleet for its reaction and input: so to a degree this must be considered tentative and subject to further input from Fleet and its concurrence on these points.

I am taking off today and will not be available for discussion of all this until Monday, March 31st. But if you are amenable to drafting a more formal Agreement or Memorandum along these lines, and submitting a copy to Fleet (John Murphy, Esq.) and me, that would be quite helpful to our moving this along.

Sincerely Edward W. King

cc: Fleet Investment Services, Attn: John Murphy, Esq.; David Klein & Jim Howe

April 1, 1997. Jon Kaledin writes to Ed King:

Dear Mr. King: I am in receipt of your letter of March 18th, and wanted to respond briefly to it as well as send to you and John Murphy at Fleet Investment Services the fully executed Purchase and Sale Agreement (the "Agreement") for the above-referenced transaction.

In reference to the Agreement, please note that you and Mr. Murphy have been added as notice recipients in paragraph 23. There were a few other small changes made to the Agreement from the last draft that you received, and I would be glad to discuss any aspect of the Agreement with either you or Mr. Murphy at your convenience.

Your letter of March 18th raises many thoughtful concerns about our potential transaction with Mr. Eddy, and I both thank you for raising them and look forward to discussing them with you and others in the near future. First and foremost, the Conservancy is of course willing to enter into a Memorandum of Understanding ("MOU") with the Trustees of the von

Engeln Trust, and I hope to get a draft of it to you by the end of this week.

I also understand and accept your position about the purchase price and acquisition costs for the Eddy property ultimately having to be acceptable to the trustees; as to the latter, the Conservancy is only looking for assurance that coverage of reasonable direct costs of acquiring the property—appraisal and surveying costs, for example—would be acceptable to the trustees, and as for the purchase price, the Conservancy's concerns are similar to those expressed in your letter, which is why we have made our acquisition of the property contingent upon an independent appraisal that substantiates the asserted property value advanced by Mr. Eddy and his attorney.

Please call to discuss this letter if you desire. Otherwise, I will be getting you and Mr. Murphy the draft MOU in the near future.

Sincerely, Jonathan C. Kaledin, Regional Counsel

cc: John Murphy, Esq., Fleet Investment Services; Carol Ash, David Klein, Jim Howe, Shyama Khanna

May 30, 1997, 10:00. Jim Howe brought Jon Kaledin (from TNC's Albany office) with Jon's son, 4 1/2-year-old Clayton, for an outing with me on a beautiful spring day. A full year earlier on a similar day, just after Jim had started at TNC, David Klein, Jim and I had walked and talked strategy concerning Alfred Eddy and Ed King. Now, with patience, Attorney Jon Kaledin was dealing with the latest of Ed's tiresome requests and Jim was diligently maneuvering with Alfred and Jim Miller.

The complex and detailed Lakewood Appraisal Jim had contracted for the Eddy land, gave three market value estimates for the 109-acre tract: Scenario #1, where mining is not allowed, gave a value of $60,000. Scenario #2, assuming that mining will occur, produced a value of $180,000. And the third, "...assuming a weight situation where there is a 70% probability of scenario #1 occurring and a 30% probability of scenario #2 occurring..." gave a value of $96,000.

The appraisal gave its reasoning as follows:

> Since the regulatory status of the property is uncertain the probability of each case occurring has been estimated. While this probability determination is subjective in nature, it reflects the unknown quality of the regulatory outcome.
>
> Since regulatory agencies responsible for authorizing mining have neglected for several years to make determinations regarding sand and gravel mining on the site, this appraisal examines the property under two scenarios. The first scenario assumes a non-mining use, the second assumes that mining will occur. While the reported value range is based on the subjective probability of each case occurring, the actual most probable value estimate will depend on such future determinations.
>
> Non-mining is allocated a probability of 70% based on conversation with parties involved in the process such as the owner and members of the State Environmental Conservation Department.

June 20, 1997. Jim Howe letter to Attorney Jim Miller concerning the appraisal:

> Dear Jim: enclosed is a copy of the revised appraisal we had done on Alfred Eddy's property in Malloryville. As before, this appraisal was sent to you in escrow with the understanding that its contents are confidential and may not be disclosed to any third party other than your client without our express written consent.

I discussed with the appraiser the concerns you mentioned to me. The appraiser has subsequently modified the appraisal to address them...

I would appreciate the chance to sit down with you and your client and discuss this appraisal in person. The Nature Conservancy would be happy to make you and your client an offer at that time. Thanks for your patience with this process.

Sincerely, Jim Howe, Director of Conservation Programs

June 28, 1997. On a Saturday afternoon in the new house of my sister-in-law (Gwen's identical twin, Gail) and her family in Westford, Massachusetts, I was on a stepladder installing an upper shelf in the kitchen pantry, when the phone rang. Jim Howe was calling to share his news: "We've got an agreement for the Eddy tract." In a just completed meeting and lunch in Ithaca, Jim, Alfred Eddy and Attorney Miller, had verbally agreed on a price for the Conservancy's purchase of Eddy's entire 109-acre property. I hadn't seen the recent trail of letters and memos, didn't know the latest status in protracted dealings concerning either the von Engeln bequest or the Eddy land, and didn't realize either were that close to fruition. Jim's call was a huge surprise. The news was simply fantastic! I was totally elated, buoyant, as though a weight had been lifted, an eleven-year burden relieved, suddenly gone.

Jim's call, thus, would be added to my short list of truly memorable, pivotal moments, landmarks in our story of conservation. Eleven years, shy two months, had passed since Gwen and I, anticipating the move into our new home, first learned of gravel mine plans next door. Throughout three gravel-mine applications, three challenging SEQR proceedings—the third extending nearly five years—and a long-sought, ever-elusive land deal, tenacious teamwork had prevailed. Our long struggle, at last, was over, our defense of Malloryville Bog a sublime and glorious success.

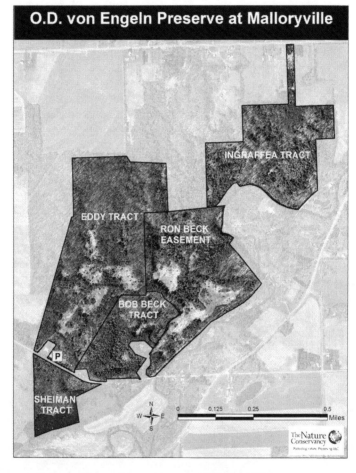

Map of Preserve; established 1997
(Map prepared by Mathew Levine, The Nature Conservancy)

13 CELEBRATION

I did not wish to take a cabin passage, but rather
to go before the mast and on the deck of the world,
for there I could best see the moonlight amid the mountains.
I do not wish to go below now.
— Henry David Thoreau

THE EDDY AGREEMENT alone was monumental, and it was pivotal in our effort, yet Jim Howe was on a roll. Soon he would prove the Eddy tract to be just the ice-breaker, the springboard that would enable serious talks with several more owners of neighboring land, amicable meetings leading to the astonishing, quick addition of three more land deals.

Still, I needed to know more about how he had arrived at the Eddy purchase agreement. Jim was happy to relate events to me. And later I would read his informative, descriptive notes in his TNC memos.

July 1, 1997. Jim Howe memo to TNC file:

> On June 28, I met with Alfred Eddy and Jim Miller at Miller's office in Ithaca. We spent an hour in the office, then went out to lunch for another hour. Miller was in good spirits. He says he

works seven days a week; on the weekdays he goes home for dinner, puts his kids to bed, then returns to the office until midnight. He liked that TNC was willing to meet with him on Saturday. Miller and his family leave on July 4 for a four-week vacation to Wyoming and South Dakota.

By contrast, Eddy was clearly angry with a $96,000 value in the appraisal and couldn't seem to understand why we won't pay him $200,000. Eddy also is busy—he's on the road five days a week now, buying produce at auctions and trucking it to restaurants, prisons, supermarkets, and other buyers.

As we agreed, I offered to combine the land value from the Peatfield appraisal with the mineral value in the Lakewood appraisal. That brought our offer to $123,400, or $125,000. Eddy found that too low. "That's where we were a year ago," he said. "I've been waiting for you people for eight years." He maintains that he's got $200,000 in gravel on the property. I reminded him that: (1) he needs a permit to mine it, and (2) there is a great deal of opposition to the mine. I reviewed all the parties who oppose the mine.

I also stressed that TNC cannot pay above appraised value. Not surprisingly, Miller and Eddy then went after the appraisal. Miller's criticism is directed toward the probability analysis. He contends that probabilities are totally subjective and that the appraisal doesn't discuss how the 70-30 split was arrived at. He noted that if we change the probability analysis to 50-50 we'd be at $147,000. I pointed out that DEC's Ray Nolan and Randy Vaas, two normally staid bureaucrats, told our appraiser that they "feel," based on the work of Syracuse U. geologist Don Siegel, that the mine would have an "irreversible" impact on the wetland...

Miller then reiterated his belief that the von

Engeln money will go away if we don't strike a deal with his client. I told him of our need to stretch the dollars so that we'll have stewardship funds. I also told him we're looking at other properties.

I stressed the tax advantages if Eddy uses the mineral appraisal of $206,000. Eddy didn't see them, but Miller convinced him the money would find its way to his pocket. Eddy's basis is roughly $80,000: $55,000 in land and the balance in expenses involved in seeking a mining permit. Eddy then said he could accept $150,000, which Miller thinks is a great deal for TNC.

We left it at that: (1) Miller would discuss the tax advantages with Eddy's accountant..., and (2) TNC would reconsider how high we can go. We need to reiterate that we can secure the cash quickly. I also would like to try to appeal to Eddy's altruistic genes—he's admitted that he's never seen anything else in the state that resembles the wetlands on Beck's property.

Next Steps

Miller and I are supposed to talk on July 2.

July 16, 1997. Jim Howe memo to TNC file:

Here are a few items that we need to take note of as we write up the purchase and sale agreement for Alfred Eddy's property:

The purchase price is $140,000.

Jim Miller will be on vacation until August 11. He promised Eddy that the deal would be signed before Miller comes back. I don't see a problem there. Miller told TNC to deal with John Hinchcliff, another attorney in his office.

Eddy has agreed to reclaim the existing pits on the property in accordance with DEC reclamation standards. TNC should have to approve the reclamation work before closing can occur and Eddy should be required to discuss his reclamation plan with us before he begins.

Miller has requested that TNC remove the contingency language in the earlier purchase and sale agreement that made our purchase subject to funding from the bequest.

Eddy needs to remove the beehives from the property and haul out an abandoned car—a 1980s-era Ford Fairmont, if you're interested.

In order to complete a survey and EHA [environmental hazard assessment], we should not close on the property before the end of the year. [But events would, in fact, move much faster than that.]

Miller asked TNC to try to get DEC to waive a $900 mining fee. I made no promises, but will make a call to Ralph Manna in DEC's Region 7 office.

So, Jim's skill and hard work had gotten the price down to $140,000 from Eddy's years-long million-dollar holdout, and the formal purchase agreement would be signed on August 19th, closing to be scheduled later. The DEC's adjudicatory hearing was never scheduled, wasn't necessary, and we heard no more about it. Meanwhile, as commitment of the von Engeln bequest remained unresolved, David Klein and Jim had arranged to borrow essential funds from TNC's national coffers, to be repaid later, and were moving forward on other land transactions for the emerging new preserve.

In July on a canoe/camping trip in New York's Adirondack Park with my friend Jere' Fletcher, once a student of mine at Sarah Lawrence College and now an attorney near Rochester, we had set up camp in the motorboat-prohibited, near-wilderness Lake Lila Primitive Area, and had gone out before dinner for a quiet paddle around the peaceful lake, no other human presence evident. Returning to our campsite, we are surprised to see a couple setting up their tent 75 feet from ours. And busy pulling my canoe onto shore, I recognize a familiar voice from the bank above me. "That you, Bob?" "Andy!" I say, with surprise and pleasure, looking up at my friend Andy Zepp whom I hadn't seen for a year or more. In this small world, Andy had driven hundreds of miles with his lady friend-future wife, from his Land Trust Alliance job in Washington D.C. to canoe and camp, as Jere' and I had from our homes, to fortuitously meet at the same primitive, facilities-less campsite where none of us had been before, miles of creek-paddling from the road, in the wilderness. That evening, in pleasant conversation, reminiscing about our mutual experiences with the Finger Lakes Land Trust and The Nature Conservancy, Andy shared with us a bottle of wine and I shared with him the exciting, still-fresh news of the Eddy tract purchase agreement.

Year 12: 1997/98

Making use of property ownership and tax map information I had provided to Wayne Klockner eight years earlier, in October of 1989, for use in his preserve proposal to Ed King, Jim Howe began contacting landowners and arranging meetings. Neighboring owners knew of our long opposition to gravel mining, and Jim broke the news of the Eddy agreement, marking the starting point of a new nature preserve. And, in short order, he had secured agreements for three additional tracts.

First, he worked out with my brother Ron and his wife Carol a conservation easement on their 75-acre punchbowl tract, east and northeast of my property, and containing a long stretch of the Malloryville Esker along Fall Creek. At a price well below market value, the Conservancy purchased the development and timber rights, permanently prohibiting gravel mining, the harvesting of trees in the mature woodlands, and construction of houses or other buildings. And the agreement provided the understanding that the tract remained private without general access to the public, and that Ron retained hunting rights.

Graceful and beautiful as they are to watch, White-tailed Deer, because of their over-browsing and killing of hardwood tree saplings, as well as our native shrubs and wildflowers, are simply too plentiful for the long-term health of the upland forests. Thus, Deer hunting by humans and Coyotes seems to be necessary to retain reasonable ecological balance.

Next, Jim negotiated the outright, fee-simple, purchase of the fen, south across the road from my mine and the Eddy tract, a 21-acre portion of the property belonging to Rich Sheiman who had recently purchased the home and land from Tom and Jennifer Michaels, husband and wife engineering-physics team, when they moved their high-tech small business to Boston.

And lastly, from Cornell engineering professor Tony Ingraffea of Ithaca, Jim arranged the purchase of a stunning 68-acre, undeveloped tract of eskers, kettles and wetlands encompassing the northeast end of the Malloryville Esker, lying beyond the punchbowl and adjacent to a wide-sweeping bend in Fall Creek.

As a result, in a breathtaking whirlwind of activity in less than a few short months, Jim Howe had secured the lasting protection of four properties totaling 273 acres, properties which encompassed two of Malloryville's three Tompkins County-designated Unique Natural Areas (North Malloryville and Malloryville Fen) and the critical Eddy tract.

Before closing, each property had to be surveyed by a licensed land surveyor, and each had to be inspected carefully for hazardous wastes, spills, dumps, barrels and containers, or any other evidence of contamination, an Environmental Hazards Assessment, to avoid risk of future liability and major expense. After each purchase agreement was signed, TNC's Gerry Smith and I spent hours together in the field, walking the tract's boundaries and interior to be certain it was clean. As expected, we found little of consequence on any of the tracts except old fencing and some minor trash, two decades-old well-concentrated smallish piles of empty household bottles and cans and, on Eddy, an old car, some old rusted farm machinery and, of course, the buried septage lagoon. As always, on outings with Gerry, as in our earlier work with our Conservancy chapter's Stewardship Committee, we thoroughly enjoyed our time together and our long conversations. And after each tract's closing, we were out again, together, with hammers, nails and TNC signs to post the boundaries of the new preserve.

Malloryville Bog, the third of the three local Unique Natural Areas, the tract belonging to my wife and myself, with its central location and its exceptionally diverse concentration of wetlands and glacial features, would logically be the highlight of the new preserve. An unspoken understanding, a comfortable trust from the beginning, was shared between the Conservancy staff and myself. We shared the same goals. Except for one question to which I answered, "Yes, I would be willing to do a conservation easement," I had never been asked about my intentions for future ownership of my land. In my letter to Wayne Klockner 8 1/2 years earlier, dated January 13, 1989—before PosDec(2)—urging the Conservancy to establish a Malloryville preserve, I had written only, "While we choose not to sell or donate our property in the near future, we would like to explore other possibilities with you, if this is of interest to TNC." But now, the gravel-mine danger, the external menace threatening to relegate my land to "lost-cause" status, had been eliminated, and a Conservancy-owned nature preserve was in the making. In my thoughts, foreboding dark overcast had given way to cottony-white clouds, weightless in a bright sky of blue.

For Gwen and myself, the decision, now, was easy. I called Jim Howe to say, "We want to donate our land." And, jokingly, I said, "You'd better say 'yes' before I change my mind." Jim said he was thrilled with our offer, and with his consent I would start the process of marking a new boundary to separate our house and driveway from the majority of our land, and would hire a surveyor to map it out.

While flagging trees with red tape in the woods, creating a

new property line part way down the kame from my house—
toward the wetlands in front and to the west, and toward the
pond in back—I found myself pondering the present and the
unknown future. My urge to retain more land for ourselves
meant more land also for future unknown homeowners, possibly less-caring, with more trees and land to degrade adjacent to
the protected preserve. Should I mark further down the slope,
or higher up toward the house? Should we keep more land or
less? With vinyl flagging tape in hand, opting toward less
seemed not so bad, as both we and conscientious future owners could still enjoy Conservancy-protected nature across an
inconspicuous boundary among the maples, oaks, pines and
hemlocks. We ended keeping about 3 acres and donating 35.
The Conservancy paid for the survey and, with Conservancy
Attorney Jon Kaledin, we worked out wording in the deed, for
our boys, Nathan and Gordon, and for us, providing lifetime,
nondestructive enjoyment of the donated land. And, with an
appraisal, we were entitled to claim modest income-tax deduc-
tions for the charitable donation. A couple of months later, on
December 17, 1997, in Attorney Jim Miller's office in Ithaca,
with David Klein, Jim Howe, Jon Kaledin, Gwen, our two-
year-old son Gordon and me in attendance, closing concluded
with smiles and handshakes all around, and Jon surprising me
with a bottle of champagne.

Friday, October 17, 1997, was the day of an unusually
significant gathering. Together for an invigorating tour of newly acquired and promised preserve properties and a lunch at
Dryden's A1 Restaurant, were seven of us: Ed King and John
Murphy, the von Engeln bequest Co-Trustees; Vic Schmidt,
the von Engeln science advisor; David Klein, Executive Director, Jim Howe, Director of Science Programs and Kris Agard
(West), Stewardship Ecologist, all of The Nature Conservancy;
and myself. To my knowledge, no formal decision or written
agreement yet existed for transfer of von Engeln funds to the
Conservancy. But Ed King, now, had come around. With the
vivid, undeniable evidence of TNC's proactive achievements in

land deals, with Alfred Eddy and Ron Beck tracts completed, Rich Sheiman and Tony Ingraffea in progress, and with Gwen and my promised donation of the centerpiece of it all, bringing the preserve total to 308 acres, Ed King, at last, could see the big picture, wetlands included, and could now believe in our success. Our hike through natural wonders and our lunch together seemed, to me, like a victory lap. Together all, Ed King with us, we were putting together a nature preserve of which Professor von Engeln surely would be proud.

November 9, 1997. Three weeks later Victor Schmidt expressed his thoughts in a wonderful, deeply felt letter to John Murphy, with copy to Ed King:

> Dear Mr. Murphy: Thank you for your letter of October 29, 1997.
>
> It was indeed a pleasure to meet you in Dryden on October 17 and to spend several hours talking with you, Mr. Edward King, and Mr. David Klein and three other members of the staff of The Nature Conservancy [i.e., Jim Howe, Kris Agard, Bob Beck], and also walking with the group over a sizable portion of the proposed Oskar D. von Engeln Natural History Preserve, near Malloryville.
>
> I am tremendously pleased by the plans for this Preserve. The area is one I have known since 1932, and to which I have taken classes many times since. The move to preserve it has my wholehearted support, and the assurance that it will be protected gives me a great deal of satisfaction.
>
> My association with Prof. von Engeln dates back to 1932, to my first college course in geology at Cornell. Later, I chose him to be my major advisor for the Ph.D. in geology, which I received in 1947. Thereafter, I maintained close contact with him, and our friendship continued until his

death. During all those years we became well acquainted with each other's philosophy, interests, and aspirations. With this background, I can say without reservation that Dr. von would heartily approve of the current plans for the Preserve.

In his will, Dr. von expressed the wish that his estate be devoted to the establishment of a Natural History Preserve. As his first choice, he named Hendershot Gulf, the so-called "Lost Gorge", which he studied and wrote about. His second choice was the Malloryville esker and associated bogs. He also requested that I act as the scientific consultant for this project.

When I assumed this responsibility, I soon became aware that Hendershot Gulf already was largely owned by the State of New York as part of the Connecticut Hill Wildlife Management Area. It was my advice, therefore, that the Trustees of the von Engeln Estate endeavor, instead, to locate the Preserve at the Malloryville site. Further, it was my suggestion that, rather than establishing a corporation to acquire and manage the Preserve, they work with The Nature Conservancy toward this end. The Nature Conservancy is a highly regarded international organization of which I have long been a member, and whose philosophy, methods, and accomplishments I admire.

In working with The Nature Conservancy we are helping to save an outstanding natural area, with unusual glacial features, considerable wildlife, and a number of particularly rare and endangered species of plants. Besides protecting these aspects of Nature (capitalized, as was Dr. von's custom), the Preserve will greatly increase opportunities for education and scientific research, in association with colleges and universities, including Cornell, and schools in the area.

In summary, it is my conviction, based on

everything I know about Dr. von Engeln, the Malloryville site, The Nature Conservancy, education, and scientific research, that the establishment of this Preserve is an important step in the right direction.

There is one additional matter which Mr. King and I think should be considered. This relates to Dr. von Engeln's wish for Hendershot Gulf. In recent years the New York State Department of Environmental Conservation has indicated its desire to make the Gulf more accessible to the public. At present I do not know what its specific plans are in this regard. Several natural history organizations in the Ithaca area, however, have expressed interest in working with the State towards enhancing the educational value of the Gulf, and it may be that The Nature Conservancy, also, has an interest in doing this. In any case, Mr. King and I think that the way should be left open to explore the possibility that, by supporting such interest, Dr. von Engeln's wishes for both the Malloryville site and Hendershot Gulf can be fulfilled. Toward this end, we suggest that a relatively small amount of money from the von Engeln Trust be retained for the purpose of sparking action by one of the interested organizations.

In conclusion, let me express my hope that the von Engeln Preserve will shortly become a reality, and also my gratitude for your assistance in bringing this about.

Sincerely yours, Victor E. Schmidt

cc: Mr. Edward W. King

Year 13: 1998/99

In September, 1998, eleven months after our "victory lap" walk and lunch, Ed King mailed copies of his thick, detailed Petition and Exhibits for the von Engeln Trust to Vic Schmidt, Jon Kaledin, David Klein and me—unexpectedly receiving it, I was surprised and pleased—requesting our comments and any corrections before he would file it with the court. And six and a half months later, on March 31, 1999, it together with his Settlement of Accounts of Trustees were formally filed with the Tompkins County Surrogate Court Clerk's Office. In them, Ed thoroughly presented his view of events during the lengthy years leading to and through the land transactions including, now, his wholehearted endorsement of the new Preserve under Nature Conservancy ownership and management. With the attached exhibits of many documents, letters and maps, Ed included my letter and map of the esker and wetlands I had mailed to him and Vic Schmidt early in our story (on October 12, 1989), a letter in which I had described Malloryville's uniqueness, my interest here, and urged its permanent protection, a letter which, until then, he had not acknowledged. For his recognition of my role I was thankful, as I felt Ed had come to understand and trust my sincerity and my motives in our long journey.

By the time of writing his Settlement of Accounts, Ed and Victor had decided to not withhold any portion of the funds for other projects and, some time thereafter, the balance of the von Engeln bequest was transferred to the O.D. von Engeln Preserve account of The Nature Conservancy's Central & Western NY Chapter.

September 19, 1998. At the annual membership meeting of our Conservancy chapter—in addition to highlighting the year's accomplishments, hearing a featured speaker, electing Trustees and providing a selection of guided field trips—a tradition has been presentation of the Chapter's "Friend of the Land" recognition. Jim Howe, at the meeting held that year on the Cornell campus in Ithaca, presented the award to me with these thoughtful and generous words:

> How many of you visited TNC's new Malloryville Preserve this morning? How many of you will be going there this afternoon?

Malloryville is The Nature Conservancy's newest preserve. It's a landscape dotted with eskers, kames, and other geological wonders left behind by the last ice age.

At the foot of these glacial landmarks, groundwater bubbles up to support a number of rare plants and natural communities. What supports these plants is the cold, constant and mineral-rich water percolating through the soil here.

Bob Beck has served as the champion of Malloryville for almost his entire life. He grew up here, and his family has owned land here... Bob moved back to Malloryville... and he and his wife, Gwen, bought a house next to the swamp....

We're very fortunate that Bob has been such a strong advocate for this place, because the glacial features that make Malloryville so ecologically valuable also make it economically valuable: The sand and gravel in an esker or kame can be worth hundreds of thousands of dollars.

Not too long ago, the future of Malloryville was not so bright. One of the state's largest mining companies submitted an application to create a 73-acre gravel mine adjacent to the wetlands that make Malloryville so special.

If the gravel deposits adjacent to the wetland were removed, the groundwater chemistry would change and, eventually, so would the wetlands. No longer would we have seen the rare orchids and plants that inhabit the fens and swamps of Malloryville.

Now I think all of us recognize that we need gravel for our roads and buildings. But there are places where gravel mining is appropriate and there are places where it is not.

Bob Beck has long recognized that Malloryville is a place where gravel mining is not appropriate.

When Bob heard about the mine proposal, he quickly assembled a coalition of neighbors, scientists, and conservation organizations to monitor the permit application and ensure that the public interest was honored.

Ultimately, the... mine application was rejected. But two other applications were filed soon after. Thanks to Bob, both applications were closely scrutinized by public agencies.

Bob's perseverance in seeing that the mine received the oversight it needed eventually persuaded the owner of the property to sell to The Nature Conservancy.

And that's a win-win situation for everyone: the owner gets his financial return and the wetlands get protected.

The Nature Conservancy purchased the proposed mine site last fall, and a few months later we acquired four other properties. Today, our Malloryville preserve stands at more than 300 acres of protected lands.

Make no mistake: none of this would have happened without Bob Beck's efforts.

Bob also has made the ultimate contribution to Malloryville, one that goes beyond his time. Last year Bob and his wife, Gwen, added another chapter to their legacy here by donating 35 acres of their 38-acre property at Malloryville to The Nature Conservancy.

Bob, Gwen, and their two sons Nathan and Gordon will continue to live next door. We hope to have them as neighbors for a long, long time.

The Nature Conservancy is honored to present the Friend of the Land Award to Bob Beck.

Word was out of a new nature preserve featuring unusual wetlands and intriguing glacier-created landforms. Requests increased for slide talks and preserve tours from groups including garden, bird and hobby clubs, Kiwanis, the Dryden Historical Society, the Finger Lakes Native Plant Society, the Finger Lakes Land Trust, school groups and college classes (Ithaca College, Cornell University, SUNY Cortland, SUNY-ESF, Syracuse University), as well as Conservancy-organized hikes for members and benefactors. Nearly always, I welcomed opportunities to share my familiarity and experiences with the Preserve's natural history and its protection and, universally, I felt great satisfaction in witnessing enthusiasm in others for learning about, enjoying and saving places of wild nature.

With Conservancy ownership of the Eddy tract, ample parking was newly available there, and organized walks could start near the west side of the wetlands, rather than as always before, at my house or at the old railroad bed, the small space by the road near the end of my driveway where, years before, the train had stopped for Professor von Engeln and his students. At the Eddy entrance, my brother Ron donated and installed a chain-lockable, double steel gate replacing the single cable there, and field trip guests in cars could drive in to assemble at the first of the old gravel pits. From there it was an easy walk on a path into the woods and down the slope to the wetlands. And from the date of the Eddy purchase until a new preserve entrance was created, that would be our main access point. Yet, visitors, as before, still risked trampling wetland vegetation and getting wet feet in traversing sections of swamp, in getting to the acid bog, and in crossing streams balancing on a log or a single-plank bridge, as the boardwalks and two of three footbridges wouldn't exist until nearly four years after the Conservancy's land deals, until time drew close to the formal preserve dedication and public opening.

August 29, 1999. On one summer walk, which I was leading for members of the Dryden Historical Society, a few ladies dropped behind to rest as we continued around the South and East Swamps. Then word came that they had encountered and stirred up some ground-nesting wasps, maybe Yellowjackets, which were angrily flying about close to my plank bridge that we would need to cross to complete our loop. Disappointed, but not wanting our group to risk painful stings of wasps, they agreeing, I decided that we would need to abort the second half of our tour through the preserve and return to our parked cars by walking a quarter mile on the less-interesting West Malloryville Road. But that was a thoroughly unexpected difficulty and, in my experience, has not recurred since.

Meanwhile, stewardship of a preserve, often requiring efforts to control invasive species, environmentalist and Conservancy supporter, George Spak, was enlisted to selectively treat with herbicide the especially noxious Black Swallowwort, beginning its invasion mostly on the 21-acre Sheiman tract south of the road, and some control work was begun against Garlic Mustard and Japanese Honeysuckle north of the road.

Occasional windfall trees and tangles across footpaths were cleared with my chainsaw and sometimes with the good volunteer help of my friend Peter Peroulakis. And concerns had grown about a potential threat to the Preserve's mineral-rich, nutrient-poor fens by nutrient loading from an outside source. Stewardship Ecologist Kris West (formerly Kris Agard, now married to Jim West) had encouraged continuing research by Don Siegel and Barbara Bedford and now, perplexingly, data indicated that groundwater entering the fens contained higher levels of nutrients—nitrates and phosphates—than ought to be the case, the source perhaps being Paolangeli's buried septage lagoon on the Eddy tract or possibly agricultural runoff from farther upslope. Remaining unresolved, that issue requires further study and possible remediation.

Year 14: 1999/2000

Bill Patterson joined the Central & Western NY Conservancy staff as Field Representative, fresh from his time with the Peace Corps, and the Malloryville Preserve quickly became the focus of his work. The Conservancy and I had been asking the question: "Rather than continuing the policy of limiting visitation to invited guests only, how can the Preserve be opened to the general public, encouraging visitation for enjoyment and education, while still protecting the site's fragile resources?" Bill Patterson, with professional competence, personal commitment and quiet good sense, like Jim Howe in land acquisitions, took charge of the next steps in making important things happen.

On numerous hikes, many of us—Gerry Smith, Jim Howe, David Klein, Kris West, George Spak and I, and now Bill Patterson—had been thinking about parking lot location and trail loop designs, with boardwalks and footbridges where necessary. Bill had my map with penciled in suggestions, and he took it from there, picking a choice spot, adjacent to the road at the edge of the Eddy tract, for a new gravel parking lot, kiosk and trailhead, the trail to lead immediately up and over a relatively low spot on the main esker and down to the wetlands. Then, the marked trail, nearly all on my former property, would consist primarily of two loops, the Esker Trail and the Bog Loop Trail, forming roughly a figure-eight totaling about 1 3/4 miles in length.

The trail loops, though mostly on existing paths on dry ground, would each require a section of boardwalk through swamp, the longer stretch through the mineral-poor swamp to the east, passing close by the acid bog. And two new footbridges, plus the one existing, would be necessary, crossing over streams. Knowing that pressure-treated lumber with toxic material to leach into the wetlands ought not be used, and that untreated lumber would eventually rot, I thought that decay-proof, nontoxic composite decking made of recycled plastic grocery bags and wood fibers melted together might be a good choice. I called the Trex Company headquarters on August 14, 2000, and was put in touch with Rick Kapres, their sales representative for the northeastern states, in Pittsburg. After a most promising phone conversation, I notified Bill Patterson who followed through by obtaining from Mr. Kapres the very generous donation and free delivery of several thousand dollars worth of Trex decking, enough for the entire boardwalk and bridge project.

For the technical design and construction management of bridges, boardwalks and a kiosk at the entrance, as well as creation of artwork for kiosk panels and a trail-guide brochure, the

Conservancy contracted with Bob McNamara, a highly skilled and competent landscape architect, naturalist and wildlife artist/author of *Tug Hill : A Four Season Guide to the Natural Side*. At Bob's request, unwanted invasive Black Locust trees, making for highly rot-resistant lumber and posts, from another Conservancy preserve were harvested and milled, to his specifications, for strong structural support under the Trex decking on top.

Year 15: 2000/01

September 28, 2000. Arriving on a flatbed truck, the pallets of Trex were unloaded using a tractor with a pallet-fork loader borrowed from Beck Farms. Bill Patterson had obtained DEC approval for work in the wetlands while continuing also to write descriptive text for the Preserve brochure, getting input from Conservancy staff and me. Then, through fabulous teamwork, volunteer labor with professional guidance, on many, many workdays through an autumn, a spring and an early summer, more than 75 generous workers built the Preserve's new boardwalks, bridges and kiosk. Bob McNamara cut and assembled locust understructure. Busy volunteers operating my miter saw powered by a gasoline generator, cut from piles of twelve-foot Trex boards a thousand three-foot deck pieces to be hauled in countless wheelbarrow loads by more volunteers down winding woodland paths, delivering to still more eager workers nailing decking into place.

In a planning memo, Bill Patterson had written:

> No trees will be cut or removed during construction of the boardwalk as it will be designed to snake among existing trees with minimal disturbance to existing vegetation.

Still, I felt deep misgivings, initially, as I watched construction work begin in familiar, undisturbed, pristine wetlands. But soon I was cheered by the extreme care with which workers were avoiding any damage outside the three-foot width of the boardwalk, by the quality, esthetically-pleasing construction, and by the knowledge that the place could be shared and enjoyed by many future visitors without being trampled and degraded.

In late winter, the summer date of July 21, 2001 had been set for the public Preserve dedication. Conservancy staff in membership and development began preparing lists for guest and speaker invitations and for media coverage, and soon, with spring thaw, boardwalk construction would begin again in earnest. Included in the work crews were eight volunteers from IBM's Endicott Design Center, over a dozen from King & King Architects in Manlius, and a group of summer interns from New York City's High School for Environmental Studies. And, on May 7, 2001, a TNC All-Staff-Work-Day added to the camaraderie and hastened the work along.

Bob McNamara had designed a spur boardwalk leading into the edge of the bog, featuring a twelve-by-twelve-foot viewing platform with railings all around and a railed opening in the center to showcase natural bog vegetation. Except that Bob and David Klein developed a poison-ivy-like rash by contacting Poison Sumac where there wasn't supposed to be any, construction went smoothly and the platform design worked exceptionally well.

Meanwhile, Jim D'Alterio led youth conservation corps workers in leveling up woodland paths, installing wooden steps on steeper slopes and replacing my one, old footbridge. Bill Patterson installed sturdy Locust posts for trail signs at path junctions, and set sixty inscribed pavers, purchased with donations by Conservancy members and friends, in place at the new kiosk. A volunteer tacked small, diamond-shaped, yellow and green Conservancy trail markers to trees, and workers built a split-rail fence next to the parking lot and installed a large, attractive sign near the road displaying The Nature Conservancy's distinctive White Oak-leaf, green logo and identifying the "O.D. von Engeln Preserve at Malloryville." Then Bob McNamara handed me a one-page plan for making a wooden brochure box with a hinged top, three compartments, and a

Plexiglas front.

July 20, 2001. From a few scraps of cedar siding at my house, two salvaged cabinet hinges and a bit of Plexiglas, I built the brochure box and, in the evening, managed to install it at the kiosk as darkness fell. At last light, call notes of a Wood Thrush signaled day's end. Save for attaching a few trail signs in the morning, the Preserve was ready, just in time, for its next-day scheduled celebration.

Then, in evening quiet, in calm air and darkness, I paused for a moment's reflection. For me, tomorrow's event would be a capstone to a fifteen-year effort, and feeling satisfied, I relaxed, as though safely home from an extended journey. With countless memories of events along the path spilling through my mind, two seemed to stand out brightest: a telephone call at the beginning, from my wife saying, "The Malloryville place is for sale," and, after eleven years, the radiant landmark of Jim Howe's welcome words, "We've got an agreement for the Eddy tract." And four years later, tomorrow's occasion would be added as a luminescent beacon in my store of memories. But that event, my thoughts were telling me, held uncommon significance beyond the opening dedication of a new nature preserve and the grateful acknowledgement of Professor von Engeln's vision and generosity. That event would also mark the awesome culmination of fifteen years of cooperation and teamwork, the truly indispensible force that made success possible.

Through my thoughts, that quiet evening, ran images and names of the many, many people, individuals contributing to our success, many of whom were members of our informal, unrecorded coalition of organizations, prominent among them, Cornell University including Cornell Plantations, Syracuse University's Department of Earth Sciences, SUNY-College of Environmental Science & Forestry, Ithaca College, the U.S. Fish and Wildlife Service, New York State's Natural Heritage Program, the Finger Lakes Land

Trust, Tompkins County's Planning Department and Environmental Management Council, the Town of Dryden, local neighbors, at times, the NYS Department of Environmental Conservation, and of course, The Nature Conservancy's Central & Western NY Chapter staff, board of trustees, members and volunteers. In my mind, with deep gratitude, tomorrow's event would be a celebration of extraordinary people working together.

July 21, 2001. After breakfast, earlier having attached my temporary, cedar-board, hand-lettered trail signs to their posts, I walked the paths through woods, swamp and over the esker to join the crowd gathering at the Preserve entrance for the dedication and public opening of The Nature Conservancy's newest preserve.

Under an open-sided white tent, David Klein welcomed the 230 guests, many seated in rows of folding chairs, and announced that a ribbon cutting at the kiosk, catered refreshments and guided walks would follow the invited speakers' comments. "The O.D. von Engeln Preserve is a terrific place to experience the glacial heritage of the Finger Lakes Region," he said. "We've worked hard with community volunteers and dedicated corporate groups to prepare this fascinating and beautiful natural area for people to visit." After recounting briefly the natural history of the Preserve, its eskers, kames, kettles and wetlands, and acknowledging Professor von Engeln's generous and farsighted bequest, David next introduced, in turn, the several speakers, each for their few minutes of comments.

I was first up, but most memorable were Victor Schmidt who delightfully recalled Cornell geology field trips to the Malloryville Esker and experiences as a student and friend of a straight-laced, impeccably-dressed, but good-humored Professor von Engeln; then Bill Patterson who described the careful planning, construction and volunteer support in putting together the new preserve features; and New York State Assemblyman Marty Luster who had prepared thoughtful words to share with the group, words about humanity's need for connection to places of wild nature. Marty said,

> We have places like this to remind us that we are not the sole possessors of the earth.
>
> We have places like this to help us preserve, not only what is natural, beautiful and interesting, but to help us preserve our humanity, our dignity, and our understanding of our place in the world and in the universe.
>
> We have places like this to teach us both gratitude and humility.
>
> We have places like this because we know that once the connection between humankind and wilderness is severed, it cannot be repaired and that without that connection our lives are incomplete and our self-centered drive toward an existence with little meaning, accelerates.
>
> We have places like this because, deep down, we understand that despite all that is happening in our world, it is indeed true, as Thoreau taught us, "In wildness is the preservation of the world."
>
> Finally, we have places like this because of people like you, because of The Nature Conservancy, because of people like Bob Beck whose generosity and commitment has helped make this possible, people like Dr. von Engeln whose life was dedicated to understanding not only the nature of this place, but our connection to it, and people like each of you who have given up part of your everyday life to make certain that the connection never fails.
>
> On behalf of a grateful community, I thank you all.

When David introduced and thanked me, my words to

the group were an expression of my deep gratitude to the many, many players, over many years, who had made that day's happy event possible, farsighted, generous individuals, without whom we would not have found success. I tried to express my sense of awe and my thankfulness for their resolve through eleven years opposing gravel mine applications, for their persistence leading to extraordinary Nature Conservancy land acquisitions, for their excellence in Preserve planning and construction, for their never-failing inspiration and encouragement.

From the summer of 1986 to that day in July of 2001, a decade-and-a-half had passed since Gwen and I had purchased and moved to our property, an unforgettable fifteen years working with dedicated colleagues and friends, defending land and nature. We had travelled a challenging, sometimes uncertain path, confronting obstacles, suffering setbacks and welcoming successes, arriving at length at a thoroughly satisfying destination: a quiet neighborhood and a place of magnificent, unique wild nature, protected. And to me, in a broader sense, our success seemed to stand as a living example of hope, perseverance and limitless possibility when people, undeterred wherever they are, strive together for a greater cause, whether for a neighborhood, an ecosystem, or a rare and beautiful planet.

In conversation and in unspoken sentiment, that day, tangible goodwill flourished. Caring people thinking long term had come together, valuing stewardship and sustainability over careless exploitation, prizing the public good over unwarranted claims of property rights, and treasuring Earth's biodiversity over a diminished planet; people choosing to honor the land ethic, while celebrating a journey at Malloryville Bog.

Kiosk at Preserve entrance

POSTSCRIPT

OX TRACKS IN the fresh powdery snow intersect, then follow the Preserve trail before me. Then they veer off between the trees to my left and continue out of sight into the white-blanketed, frozen swamp. Perhaps, I thought, the tracks were those of the same Gray Fox, in elegant coat of chestnut and gray, that Gwen and I had seen this morning loping effortlessly across the snow in our garden clearing and disappearing into the old punchbowl pastureland.

In the invigorating winter air, I continue my walk, turning onto the boardwalk leading to the bog opening. At the bog-viewing platform, I pause to brush snow off the plaque mounted atop the railing, and I read its inscription:

FLORENCE G. BECK
BOARDWALK & BOG OVERLOOK
"If I live to be 100, I will have breathed
the air of three centuries."
In Loving Memory of "Aunt Floss"
1899–2001
From her Nieces, Nephews and their Families

Only months before the Preserve dedication, the life of Dad's sister, Florence, ended at age 101. As a young teenager, she had written—in a school essay—her farsighted words of

325

living in three centuries. And later in life, she had intently followed our years of effort in protecting our woodlands and wetlands, habitat for her deeply appreciated wildflowers and songbirds, and she was pleased with our success. Aunt Floss had been witness to 100 years of increasing environmental awareness.

The writing of Florence's essay coincided nearly, in 1914, with the death of a visionary pioneer and determined spokesman for wilderness protection. Thinking of John Muir while I stand at the boardwalk railing, I am grateful for his influence and for the natural setting of the bog, with tall trees of swamp and forest around me. Some of Muir's words come to mind:

> The battle we have fought, and are still fighting for the forests is a part of the eternal conflict between right and wrong, and we cannot expect to see the end of it... So we must count on watching and striving for these trees, and should always be glad to find anything so surely good and noble to strive for.

Muir was right, of course, that the conflict would long continue and it does so today. He had experienced, at the end of his life, the bitter loss of Hetch Hetchy Valley in Yosemite National Park, to be dammed and flooded to provide water and power to San Francisco. But culture evolves and attitudes change. Knowing that lasting answers depend upon fundamental change in human thought, Aldo Leopold, a few decades later, put to paper words of wisdom that inspired the environmental movement:

> We abuse land because we regard it as a commodity belonging to us. When we see land as a community to which we belong, we may begin to use it with love and respect.

And he wrote:

> A land ethic changes the role of *Homo sapiens*
> from conqueror of the land-community to plain
> member and citizen of it.

Leopold's words continue now helping thoughtful people comprehend the deep ecological truths of humankind's relationship to our planet. Those words and the writings of many others, eloquent, courageous and controversial—I think of Rachel Carson's *Silent Spring*—surely have shaped society's sense of responsibility toward the environment and surely, even against powerful opposition, are making for a better world.

In my local county and town, I have watched the growing concern for protecting open space and natural areas, and I've participated in developing useful means to help ensure their preservation. Tompkins County's Inventory of Unique Natural Areas prepared by the Environmental Management Council—our detailed descriptive database of some 192 sites encompassing over 15,000 acres, now being updated for the third edition—is used extensively by landowners, developers and local governments in guiding land use in ways that minimize impacts on nature.

The Town of Dryden now employs a professional environmental planner who oversees a highly-qualified staff in the Town's Planning Department. After serving for 25 years, Henry Slater was honored at a grand retirement party, and Mahlon Perkins continues his quality work as the Town Attorney. And I am privileged to serve with excellent colleagues on the Town's Conservation Board.

New York State's SEQR program and the many similar mini-NEPAs around the United States are, for the most part, functioning as intended in "considering environmental impacts equally with social and economic factors." Yet, as we have learned, effective environmental protection may not be routinely assured. Favorable outcomes often depend upon informed citizens and citizen scientists choosing to participate, providing a needed, strong voice for nature.

The Finger Lakes Land Trust, in passing its 20th year, has

achieved phenomenal success in working with landowners, protecting "more than 13,000 acres of the region's wetlands, forests, farmland, grassland, and gorges" in twenty-plus preserves and many more conservation easements. Andy Zepp, who returned to the organization he initiated, continues as its dynamic Executive Director, overseeing a professional staff of ten. And, across the country, more than 1,700 land trusts championed by the Land Trust Alliance have become a major force in land protection.

The Nature Conservancy has celebrated its 60th year while protecting "more than 119 million acres of land and thousands of miles of rivers worldwide"—operating in all 50 states and more than 30 countries globally. Wayne Klockner is State Director of The Conservancy in Massachusetts. And Jim Howe is Executive Director of our Central & Western NY Chapter.

Barbara Bedford and Robert Wesley continue bringing their students to the von Engeln Preserve, its natural diversity serving as a "living classroom" in wetlands ecology. And Donald Siegel is considering retiring, to "start a second career as a jazz guitarist."

As I continue my quiet walk on the wintry Preserve trail, keenly aware of the world's ills, I prefer to see reasons for hope; optimism that our efforts in the fight for good are not in vain. I leave the boardwalk and follow the woodland path. Then, while thinking again of John Muir, I climb the slope of a kame, returning to my sunlit, south-facing house on a tree-covered hill above the wetlands—a hill deposited there long ago by meltwater from an ice-age glacier. Though Malloryville's hilly kames and eskers are small and far from Muir's beloved western mountains, my spirit is ever refreshed by his immortal words:

> Climb the mountains and get their good tidings. Nature's peace will flow into you as sunshine flows into trees. The winds will blow their own freshness into you, and the storms their energy, while cares will drop off like autumn leaves.

TIMELINE

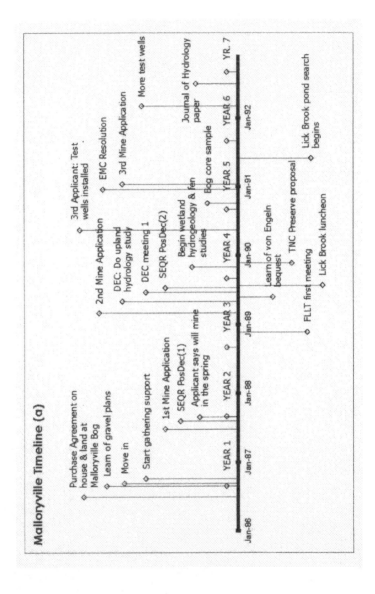

Malloryville Timeline (a)

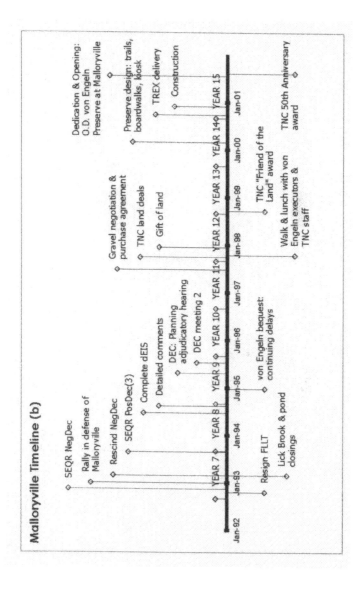

Malloryville Timeline (b)

ABOUT THE AUTHOR

Bob Beck was raised on a dairy farm in Upstate New York, earned a Bachelor of Science degree from Cornell University with a focus on evolutionary biology, and completed all but his dissertation towards the Ph.D. at Cornell. He has been a teacher of biology, animal behavior, natural history, and general science, having taught at Cornell, Ithaca College and Sarah Lawrence College, as well as for docents' training at the Bronx Zoo and for middle-school students at a Montessori school in Ithaca, New York. Bob was a curator at the Cornell Lab of Ornithology's Library of Natural Sounds, and he was a founding board member and the first executive director of the Finger Lakes Land Trust. For his efforts in organizing and leading the defense of Malloryville Bog, he was honored with The Nature Conservancy's "Friend of the Land" award and a 50th Anniversary "Hero" award. Adjacent to his home, he volunteers as preserve monitor and leads frequent interpretive field trips at The Nature Conservancy's 308-acre O.D. von Engeln Preserve at Malloryville. In addition, he has served, for many years, on his county and town environmental advisory boards. And for something completely different, Bob is the founder, owner and operator of a small business devoted to designing and installing custom closet and storage solutions for homeowners.

INDEX

Index

Index

Made in the USA
Middletown, DE
11 November 2020